– The –

GREAT
DERANGEMENT

★ ★ ★ ★ ★ ★ ★ ★ ★ ★ ★ ★ ★ ★ ★ ★ ★ ★

A TERRIFYING TRUE STORY OF
WAR, POLITICS, AND RELIGION

Matt Taibbi

SPIEGEL & GRAU

New York

2009

PUBLISHED BY SPIEGEL & GRAU

Published in the United States by Spiegel & Grau, an imprint of
The Doubleday Broadway Publishing Group, a division of
Random House, Inc., New York.
www.spiegelandgrau.com

A hardcover edition of this book was originally
published in 2008 by Spiegel & Grau.

SPIEGEL & GRAU is a trademark of Random House, Inc.

Book design by Amanda Dewey

Library of Congress Cataloging-in-Publication Data
Taibbi, Matt.
The great derangement : a terrifying true story of war, politics, and religion /
Matt Taibbi.—1st pbk. ed.
p. cm.
1. United States—Politics and government—2001– 2. United States—
Description and travel. 3. Political culture—United States. 4. Taibbi, Matt—
Travel. 5. United States. Congress—Decision making. 6. Iraq War, 2003—
Personal narratives American. 7. Left-wing extremists—United States.
8. September 11 Terrorist Attacks, 2001—Causes. 9. Big churches—Texas—San
Antonio. 10. End of the world—Social aspects—Texas—San Antonio. I. Title.
E902.T345 2009
973.93—dc22
2008032429

ISBN 978-0-385-52062-1

PRINTED IN THE UNITED STATES OF AMERICA

1 3 5 7 9 10 8 6 4 2

First Paperback Edition

CONTENTS

★ ★ ★ ★ ★ ★ ★ ★ ★ ★ ★ ★

— The —

GREAT
DERANGEMENT

INTRODUCTION

★ ★ ★ ★ ★ ★ ★ ★ ★ ★ ★

THIS BOOK came into being by means of a ridiculously long and tortuous series of editor-writer discussions, grotesque literary failures, nervous collapses, abrupt about-faces, cop-outs, lies, and other types of grossly unprofessional behavior. And what's most funny about it is that it ended more or less where it started—as a long examination of where the American public's head is in advance of the 2008 elections, forged in a crucible of flailing, masturbatory nihilism.

I was originally contacted shortly after the release of my last book, *Spanking the Donkey*, not by Spiegel and Grau (which didn't exist at the time), but by Crown, another Random House imprint, in the person of editor Chris Jackson. If I remember correctly, what he wanted was some sort of taxonomic survey of the worst people in American politics and culture—a rogues' gallery, put together in handy reference form, which would be full of various insults and vituperation. At the time I was a little depressed about the number of requests I was getting from editors to whale on people in print and was somewhat afraid that

I was going to be buttonholed, professionally, into a role as a kind of lefty/alternative hatchet man—a liberal Ann Coulter. It didn't help that I was secretly afraid that this very thing was my only salable skill in the American media market.

So I wormed my way out of that idea and somehow sold the good people at Crown on a new, more "serious" subject, one more befitting my status as a "serious" political commentator. This would be an essay of monstrous import about the fake left/right, blue-state/red-state conflict that, I'd hoped to argue, was a fraud being consciously perpetrated on the public by a cultural conspiracy with the outrageously pretentious name "The Thinkophancy." I made it about eleven thousand words into that effort before realizing that even I had no idea what the fuck I was talking about. I vividly remember my last read-through of that text; I literally squirmed in shame. I knew that if I were to finish such a book and actually see it published, I'd be covering Inuit volleyball in Alaska before the release of the 2007 spring list.

So I junked that idea and did yet another about-face, this time selling Chris on a year-long diary of Congress in action. By then I'd done a long piece about Congress for *Rolling Stone* and had been somewhat shocked to see how our government really operates. Having lived outside of the United States for most of my adult life, I was really a neophyte when it came to understanding the mechanics of American power. But after spending a great deal of time on the Hill, I began to develop a theory about American politics as a kind of closed loop of inside players, an oligarchy of commercial interests who ran Washington in conjunction with their hired hands in Congress as a closed shop.

The lawmaking process had evolved over time in such a way that almost all of the important decisions could be made behind closed doors by a few key players in both houses, without debate or discussion and certainly without any real input from the voting public. I was amazed to see that Congress spent most of its daylight hours naming post offices and passing resolutions to honor sports teams, while the important stuff it did—like gut the Clean Air Act as an "emergency" response to Hurricane Katrina—it did in late-night meetings of mostly anonymous committees, out of the (at least potentially) prying eye of the press and the public.

A key point I took home from my examination of Congress was that both parties, Democratic and Republican, were equally guilty in what really was a conspiracy to run the government without outside interference. The only way the public could protest all the handouts and earmarks and fast-tracked tax breaks and other monstrosities was to vote for the other party—and the other party, it turned out, was inevitably whoring for the same monied masters.

Excepting a few rogue, quixotic members who eschewed the usual campaign donors, Congress was mostly a highly advanced, finely tuned mechanism for turning favors into campaign donations and vice versa. It was a system of formalized political tribute not at all unlike that of the old Supreme Soviet, where the daylight hours were occupied with "political debates" about how the USSR could best aid socialist friends in Mozambique or confront American racism in the South, while behind closed doors fat bloated party functionaries conducted the real business of divvying up military contracts and highway concessions.

I was all set to spend a full year covering this business, in particular following the appropriations season, but my day job at *Rolling Stone* unfortunately forced me to travel away from Washington far too much to do that work effectively. I remember trying to fake my way through the project by following a C-SPAN Webcast of an appropriations hearing from a hotel in Islamabad, where I'd been sent to cover an earthquake. Even so I was managing to keep up, but then a few days later in Kashmir

I ate some kind of fruit and nut salad my fixer had prepared for the Eid holiday and contracted a horrible bacterial illness. I was on the way home on an El Al flight, writing a section about Congressman Joe Barton, when I suddenly spiked a fever of about 105 and fell over face-first into my keyboard. Convalescing a few weeks later, a doctor's note in hand, I broke the bad news to Chris that I might have to bail on this project as well. I started to hoard my money in an expectation of giving back my advance.

But then a funny thing happened: while on the road for my magazine in the subsequent months, traveling all across America, I began to notice what I quickly realized was a phenomenon directly related to the mess in Washington. There was a consequence, a flip side to the oligarchical rigged game of Washington politics: apparently recognizing that they'd been abandoned by their putative champions in Washington, the public was now, rightly it seemed, tuning out of the political mainstream.

But they weren't tuning out in order to protest their powerlessness more effectively; they were tuning in to competing versions of purely escapist lunacy. On both the left and the right, huge chunks of the population were effecting nearly identical retreats into conspiratorial weirdness and Internet-fueled mysticism.

As the national affairs correspondent for *Rolling Stone* I had been given a general mandate to seek out and describe the nature of George Bush's America in the post-9/11 era, and as the years went by I began to see the outlines of the grotesque black comedy that had taken root in this country since that singular day six years ago. It all came together for me one day when I tried to imagine the whole thing from the point of view of Osama bin Laden. Here he had gone through all the trouble of attacking New York City, and how did the victim nation respond?

Well, its government responded by counterattacking the

wrong country and passing a whole host of insane laws that had nothing whatsoever to do with terrorism; its president responded by encouraging its citizens to buy Chevys and go on vacations. Then, when it came time to ask why the attack had happened, the president announced that it had happened because the terrorists, well, those folks hated our freedom. Examining this rationale, the mainstream press did not denounce Bush's reasoning as the preposterous horseshit it was, but instead tripped over themselves en masse in a desperate attempt to find new ways to compare their leader to Winston Churchill. Months later, bin Laden himself had been forgotten, and the country moved on to denouncing the real enemy, culminating in the banning of French fries from the congressional cafeteria.

The people, of course, soon recognized that they had been egregiously lied to by their executive and by their supposed allies in the Fourth Estate and began to seek out the *real* explanation for what had happened.

On the right, huge masses of Christians began to understand that New York had been attacked as divine retribution for America's acquiescence in the effort to allow homosexuals to marry.

On the left, they had a different explanation. According to the more educated, sophisticated set of Americans, the Americans who knew how to appreciate *The Wire* or a good Coen brothers film and who in their informed secular worldview felt smugly superior to those half-baked mystical crackpots on the religious right, Islamic terrorism was actually a clever cover story. The actual culprit in 9/11 was none other than our own president, George W. Bush, who had effected a brilliant diversion in bombing Manhattan using Saudi patsies with links to Sunni Islamic radicals, in order to start a war against the nonreligious Iraqi state of Saddam Hussein. Naturally.

From bin Laden's point of view, the whole situation had to be immensely frustrating. He pulls off the crime of the century, of the millennium perhaps, and the victim America turns out to be so wrapped up in its own intramural bullshit that it can't even give him credit for it. America turned out to be, in a way, psychologically immune to attack; its government was too corrupt to fight back, and its people were too crazy to comprehend their position in the world. We were a nation gone completely mad, blind to everything outside our borders, with our effective institutions co-opted by crooks and thieves and our citizens piddling away the last days of their influence reading sacred tracts and spinning absurd theories about the grassy knoll, WTC 7, and the international Masonic conspiracy.

In all of this it seemed to me that what we were living through was the last stage of the American empire. Historians consistently describe similar phenomena in past centuries of human experience. When the Bolsheviks finally broke through the gates of the Winter Palace, they discovered tsarists inside obsessed with tarot cards; when the barbarians finally stormed Rome in its last days, they found the upper class paralyzed by lethargy and inaction and addicted to the ramblings of fortune-tellers. This, too, seemed to be the fate of America, viciously attacked by a serious enemy but unable to grasp the significance of this attack, instead fleeing for consolation to the various corners of its own vast media landscape, in particular seeking solace in the Internet, an escapist paradise for the informationally overwhelmed.

Trained for decades to be little more than good consumers, we had become a nation of reality shoppers, mixing and matching news items to fit our own self-created identities, rejoicing in the idea that reality was not an absolute but a *choice*, something we select to fit our own conception not of the world but of ourselves. We are Christians, therefore all world events have a Christian explanation; we hate George Bush, therefore Bush is the cause of it all.

And directly feeding into this madness was the actual, real

failure of our own governmental system, reflected in a chilling new electoral trend. After two consecutive bitterly negative presidential elections and many years of what was turning into a highly deflating military adventure in Iraq, the American public had reached new levels of disgust with the very concept of elections. People no longer voted for candidates they liked or were excited by; they voted *against* candidates they hated. At protests and marches, the ruling emotions were disgust and rage; the lack of idealism, and especially the lack of any sense of brotherhood or common purpose with the other side (i.e., liberals and conservatives unable to imagine a productive future with each other, or even to see themselves as citizens of the same country), was striking. Politicians, with their automated speeches and canned blather about "hope" and "change" and "taking the country back" were now not only not believed by most ordinary people, but actively despised.

A parallel phenomenon was a growing lack of faith in the mainstream media on both sides of the spectrum. Conservatives and liberals alike accepted unquestioningly the proposition that the stories put out by network news broadcasts and major daily newspapers amounted to little more than a stream of untrammeled, insidious deceptions.

In the 2006 senatorial primary contest between the Jimmy Stewart–esque do-gooder millionaire Ned Lamont and the archetypal Washington whore Joe Lieberman, the fault lines were outlined with crystal clarity: the "People" boosted Lamont with blogs and YouTube broadcasts, while the entrenched political mainstream circled the wagons around Lieberman, with the major news mags and dailies blasting the blogger phenomenon and the likes of asshole *New York Times* columnist David Brooks ascribing the antimedia bias to "moral manias" and a "Liberal Inquisition."

On the right, similar fault lines were appearing. Whereas before conservative anger toward the "liberal media" had been usefully directed against the Democratic Party by Republican strategists, the failure of the Iraq war and also growing disillusionment on the part of Christians who had supported George W. Bush led more and more of those voters to seek out their own enthusiasms. For the first time I started to see and hear people at Republican events who sounded very much like the dissidents on the fringes of American liberalism. The Ron Paul supporters who began to collect around the rallies of assembly-line establishment-blowhard candidates like Mitt Romney were almost indistinguishable from the followers of liberal candidates like Dennis Kucinich; they were similarly against the war, similarly against the conspiracy of business interests that dominated Washington, similarly fed up with standard-issue campaign stumpery. At these events I heard some of the same theories about "peak oil" and the nefarious influence of institutions like the Council on Foreign Relations and the Trilateral Commission that dominated 9/11 Truth rallies. But they weren't liberals. They were ex-Dittoheads and dropouts from the Republican revolution.

The Ron Paul candidacy was an extreme example of outsider politics on the left and right merging; for the most part, the period covered in this book describes left and right retreats from the mainstream that traveled in opposite directions but were parallel in substance. Specifically, I spent time down in Texas with a group of churchgoers who were loyal to an apocalyptic theory of world events, one in which 9/11 and the invasion of Iraq were part of an ongoing march toward a final battle between the forces of Satan and an army of God. At the same time, I found myself involved, at times involuntarily, with the 9/11 Truth Movement.

The similarities between both of these groups were striking and should be clear to anyone who reads this book. Both groups were and are defined primarily by an unshakable belief in the inhumanity of their enemies on the other side; the Christians seldom distinguished between Islamic terrorism and, say, Al Gore–style environmentalism, while the Truthers easily believed that reporters for the *Washington Post*, the president, and the front-line operators of NORAD were equally capable of murdering masses of ordinary New York financial-sector employees. Abandoned by the political center, both groups ascribed unblinkingly to a militant, us-against-them worldview, where only their own could be trusted. What made them distinctly American was that, while actually the victims of an obvious, unhidden conspiracy of corrupt political power, they chose to battle bugbears that were completely idiotic, fanciful, and imaginary. At a time when the country desperately needed its citizens to man up and seize control of their common destiny, they instead crawled into alleys and feverishly jacked themselves off in frenzies of panicked narcissism. Time and again during the research for this book, I encountered people who acted not like engaged citizens looking for solutions to real problems, but like frightened adolescents, unaccustomed to the burdens of political power, who saw in the vacuum of governmental competence an opportunity not to take control of their lives, but to step in and replace the buffoons above with buffoon acts of their own. They made elaborate speeches to no one in particular as though cameras were on them, they dressed in Washington and Jefferson costumes, they primped and preened like they were revolutionaries, modern-day Patrick Henrys and Thomas Paines. And they got nothing done.

I was struck particularly by a meeting of 9/11 Truthers in Austin, Texas, in which a "discussion" of what to do about the conspiracy in Washington devolved into a speech-making session. A group of twenty-five to thirty Truthers filed into a little church on the outskirts of town and, led by a breezy, est-counselorish moderator who enforced tolerance for the viewpoints of all, each participant got up and offered his or her own individual angry theory about the nature of the conspiracy.

Some blamed the royals, others the bankers, others the Trilateral Commission, all blamed decades of Bush family iniquity, and one woman even talked about a conspiracy to hide the discovery of alien technologies at Area 51; everyone made his or her speech, and then the meeting was over with nothing accomplished except a decision to have another meeting.

Having seen all this, what I ended up trying to do in this book was describe the whole outline of the problem. Much of the book focuses on the insider game in Washington, from the corrupt response to Hurricane Katrina to both parties' absurdly transparent attempts to deflect popular opposition to the Iraq war. At the same time I tried to describe the response to this nonfunctioning government across the country, on both the right and the left. What I hope comes through is that the corruption of the system certainly has had consequences in the population, inspiring a nearly appropriate amount of popular disgust and rage, with voters keenly understanding on some level anyway the depth of their betrayal. But the form of the public response turns out to be a grotesquerie.

It turns out that we've been split up and atomized for so long that real grassroots politics isn't really possible; we don't respond to problems as communities but as demographics. In the same way that we shop for cars and choose television programs, we pick our means of political protest. We scan the media landscape for the thing that appeals to us and we buy into it. That it is the same media landscape these new dissidents often reject as a false and misleading tableau dominated by corrupt interests turns out not to be problematic for many. In some cases, like that of those Christians I spent time with in San Antonio, the trusted new figure, a preacher named John Hagee, turns out to be every bit the establishment Washington insider these would-be religious revolutionaries think they're fleeing from. In other cases, like that of the 9/11 Truthers, the radical canonical revolutionary tracts end up including thoroughly commerical mainstream entertainments like *V for Vendetta* and *The Matrix* (at different times I would hear *both* radical conservatives and liberals describe their political awakenings using the phrase "taking the red pill").

In short, what sounds on the surface like radical politics turns out to be just another fracturing of the media picture, one that ultimately will result in new groups of captive audiences that, if experience is any guide, will ultimately be assimilated and electorally coddled by a political mainstream in reality bent on ignoring both sides. For now, however, the situation going into the 2008 election looks something like this: we have a population more disgusted than ever with our political system, one inclined to distrust the result no matter who wins the White House—and should the national election end up being a contest between a pair of full-of-shit establishment conservatives like Hillary Clinton and Rudy Giuliani, it will only confirm the worst fears of both sides and result in an even further bonkerization of the population.

Gone will be the good old days of neat blue-state/red-state hatred—a nicely symmetrical storyline that has always appealed to the *Crossfire/American Gladiators* sports-coverage mentality of the commercial media. In its place, at least temporarily, will be a chaos of lunatic enthusiasms and dead-end political movements to nowhere, with calls for invasions of Babylon and, on the other side, congressional investigations into nonexistent conspiracies. Meanwhile, Boeing, General Motors, and Ford will officially become Chinese companies, and OPEC will begin trading in the euro after American garrisons in Baghdad and Kabul fall to invaders armed with nineteenth-century weapons.

That's one possible future, anyway, suggested by the lunatic present. Of course, the thing about America is that you never know. We have a history of rising to the occasion, but the theory of this book is that history eventually stops repeating itself, and what better time for that to happen than after a massive, nationally televised attack that most of an *entire country* apparently missed the point of? When a people can no longer agree even on the basic objective facts of their political existence, the equation changes; real decisions, even in the approximate direction of righteousness, eventually become impossible.

The Great Derangement is about a stage of our history where politics has seemingly stopped being about ideology and has instead turned into a problem of information. Are the right messages reaching our collective brain? Are the halves of that brain even connected? Do we know who we are anymore? Are we sane? It's a hell of a problem for a nuclear power.

THERE IS ONE SCENE in this book that is a little different from all the rest. One morning in Baghdad, a group of earnest, positive, patriotic young soldiers prepares for a day at work. Enjoying the presence of a reporter, they put on a cheerful, *Up with People*–esque show for the cameras, with each grunt wittily introducing himself, giving his nickname and characterizing his place in the group. There's a scene like this in every American war movie, in fact every group-adventure-type film: one by one you meet the gritty crew of Ripley's ship in *Alien,* or the disparate teenage cast of the latest *Friday the 13th* film: where one's the tough guy, another's the clown, a third is the brooding dissident. "I'm the token African guy," says Jaleel Ibrahim, a black kid from New York, in his turn in front of the mic. "And I'm Sergeant Russell," says the next soldier. "I am soft-spoken and wholesome, but also offended easily."

They're good kids, all of them, despite the self-conscious act. You see, this part, the part where they talk to the war reporter, they have a frame of reference for that. They understand it, they know what it's all about. So they're comfortable and funny in front of the camera, and they even find a way to be civil and friendly to the antiwar reporter, who despite it all is also a character they know.

But a few hours later we're visiting a police station in an unfriendly section of Baghdad, and somewhere nearby there's a huge explosion. None of the Iraqi police are going out to investigate, they're too scared. And these kids, who are supposed to be there directing the Iraqis, are sitting there in the station, with bombs going off nearby, and small-arms fire too, and they have no idea what the fuck is going on. They don't know why they're there and they don't know who it is who's blowing shit up a hundred yards away. They know what they know, and they don't know what they don't know, and what they don't know is turning out to be the important thing.

That moment to me is what this book is about. Inside the bubble we're fine, we make sense. It's what's outside the bubble that we have trouble with.

I would have liked to have gotten more of that, found some better and more forceful ways of describing the amazing weirdness of our almost totally insular existence. But for much of this book I end up playing a traditional and much-loathed role, that of the establishment media spy sent on assignment to denigrate and laugh at the cultural fringes. I was bothered by that problem throughout the project and have no real answer for anyone who wants to throw that charge my way. The only thing I can think to say is that by the end I was no longer sure that what I was dealing with were really fringe movements. The 9/11 Truth Movement in particular I first thought was a small, scattered group of nutcases, but by the end I realized they really were, just as they claim to be, almost everyone you meet. And in Texas, when I hit the pavement to find converts for my crazy church, I expected to be laughed at—but instead found myself embraced and eagerly listened to by almost everybody I approached, an experience I had never had as my actual, secular self.

And that was really the point of one of the last scenes in the book, the one where I crank-call my old church from the safety of my real home, the depraved universe of empty-hearted media creatures, in this case the NFL draft in New York. For as crazy as some of the people in these movements are, they at least believe in something, they have some kind of instinct or urge toward truth or justice or *something*. For the really sad part is that nobody from my neighborhood is offering them shit, apart from a depressing selection of greed fantasies and a kind of slick, smug nihilism with which to pass the time. On that particular day part of me actually missed being in Texas, but the scene eventually finds me back where I started, a bloated smart-ass covered in cookie crumbs enjoying a modern-day slave auction via the one concrete perk of his professional existence, good seats.

If there's a villain in the book, I might offer some of the congressional representatives in the Washington chapters, or John Hagee maybe, but really the best selection might actually be me. And I have no idea exactly what that means, but it's probably not good.

ONE

BORN AGAIN

★ ★ ★ ★ ★ ★ ★ ★ ★ ★ ★ ★

It's a Thursday afternoon in San Antonio and I'm in a rented room—creaky floorboards, peeling wallpaper, month to month, no lease, space heater only, the ultimate temporary lifestyle—and I can't find the right channel on the television. I rented this place, it seems, without making sure that it had ESPN. This realization throws the poverty of the room into relief for the first time.

Shit, it's cold in here, I think, aware of a draft all of a sudden. When I look back at the TV, it's on a gospel channel. A video preacher straight out of central casting is pointing a finger right at the screen—right at me—admonishing me to surrender to God. He's got swept-back white hair, gold wire-rimmed glasses, and a booming hellfire voice that makes the name "A-BRA-HAAM!" come spilling out of his mouth like a brand-new Mustang V-8 turning over for the first time.

"When you give up more than you deserve," he shouts, "God will give you more than you dreamed!" He pauses, letting the words settle in for effect. "I want you to write that down somewhere!"

I shrug and reach for a notebook.

"Write it down: When you give up more than you deserve," the preacher repeats, "God will give you more than you dreamed!"

I nod and write it down in block letters. Why not? I have no idea what the hell it means, but I didn't come to Texas to argue with people. But what exactly do I deserve?

The preacher continues on; his sermon is from Genesis 12, the story about Abraham coming to Egypt and instructing his beautiful wife, Sarah, to say that she's his sister, which in turn allows Abraham not only to avoid being killed but to trade her to Pharaoh in exchange for a mother lode of slaves, asses, and camels. But, as things like this always do in the Old Testament, this unlawful union brings a plague on Pharaoh, and when Pharaoh finds out the reason, he is pissed, screaming to Abraham, "Why saidst thou, 'She is my sister'? . . . Therefore behold thy wife, take her, and go thy way."

At which point Abraham and his people leave, and a few chapters later he gets to go into the tent of his wife's handmaiden Hagar and make a baby with her. This seems like a great deal for Abraham—avoid execution, get a great trade-in deal for your wife, then bang her handmaiden—but I'm not sure I see where the lesson about deserving and dreaming is here. No such problem for Pastor John Hagee.

"You see, it happened to A-BRA-HAAM, it can happen to you!" he shouts. "Nothing is impossible to those who have faith!"

Down at the bottom of the screen there's a notation. "PRAYER LINE: (210) 490–5100." I write that down, too, marking it with a smiley face.

The show ends shortly after that and another, less talented preacher—his Carrot Top–esque shtick is preaching seated at a

desk—comes on and starts babbling about the Christian children in the Sudan being kidnapped at birth and forced to convert to Islam. Here in South Texas everyone for five hundred
miles in every direction is a Christian, but they're constantly
finding ways to think of themselves as a besieged minority. You
hear a lot about our oppressed brothers and sisters in Africa,
India, the Middle East. They're ideal objects of sympathy because they're helpless, they're poor, and it would take them at
least twenty years to reach San Antonio even if they started
swimming today.

Anyway, I hit the mute button, lean back in my chair, look
around at my shitty room, and sigh.

IT'S DECEMBER 2006 and I'm now on hiatus, after spending
the whole fall covering the midterm elections for my depraved
liberal magazine, *Rolling Stone*. I'm here in Texas to work out
the answer to a question that has been germinating in my mind
for some time, and which came to a head after the elections.

Back in the East Coast media world where I come from—an
ugly place where nothing grows but scum, lichens, and Jonathan
Franzen—the sweeping electoral victory by the Democrats was
greeted with a tremendous sigh of relief, as if it were a sign that
our endlessly self-correcting, essentially centrist American polity had finally come to its senses. In that world, there was op-
timism because the people had finally derailed that nutty Bush
revolution, because the country had apparently seen the light
about a pointlessly bloody and outrageously expensive war in
Iraq, and because the cautious yuppieism of the Democratic
Party had been triumphantly rehabilitated, at least temporarily quelling the potentially internationally embarrassing specter
of terminal one-party rule. The pendulum was swinging back,
yin was morphing back into yang. American politics moved in
cycles, and the latest conservative cycle had finally ended.

The election results were being sold, in other words, as a triumph of the American system, of American democracy. Just like the producers for *Monday Night Football*, the counry's political elite likes things best when the teams are evenly matched. As far as the press was concerned, the best thing about the Democratic bounce-back in the midterms was that it set up a great 2008. Even odds, or maybe Dems -1, to reach the White House. American politics had never been in better shape.

I knew better. I had been all around the country in the last year and I knew that the last thing these elections represented was a vote of confidence in the American system. Out There, in states both blue and red, the People were boarding the mothership, preparing to leave this planet for good. The media had long ignored the implications of polls that showed that half the country believed in angels and the inerrancy of the Bible, or of the fact that the Left Behind series of books had sold in the tens of millions. But on the ground the political consequences of magical thinking were becoming clearer. The religious right increasingly saw satanic influences and signs of the upcoming apocalypse. Meanwhile, on the left, a different sort of fantasy was gaining traction, as an increasing number—up to a third of the country according to some polls—saw the "Bush crime family" in league with Al-Qaeda, masterminding 9/11. Media outlets largely ignored poll results that they felt could not possibly be true—like a CBS News survey that showed that only 16 percent believed that the Bush administration was telling the truth about 9/11, with 53 percent believing the government was "hiding something" and another 28 percent believing that it was "mostly lying." Then there was a stunning Zogby poll taken just in advance of the 2004 Republican convention that showed that nearly half of New York City residents—49.3 percent—believed that the government knew in advance that the 9/11 attacks were coming and purposely failed to act.

Not only did voters distrust the government's words and actions; by 2007 they also had very serious doubts about their government's legitimacy. Successive election cycles foundering on voting-machine scandals had left both sides deeply suspicious of election results. A poll in Florida taken in 2004 suggested that some 25 percent of voters worried that their votes were not being counted—a 20 percent jump from the pre-2000 numbers. More damningly, a Zogby poll conducted in 2006 showed that only 45 percent of Americans were "very confident" that George Bush won the 2004 election "fair and square."

The most surprising thing about that last poll was the degree to which the distrust was spread wide across the demographic spectrum. That 71 percent of African Americans distrusted the 2004 results was perhaps not a surprise, given that black voters in America have been victims of organized disenfranchisement throughout this country's history.

But 28 percent of NASCAR fans? Twenty-five percent of born-again Christians? Thirty-two percent of currently serving members of the armed forces? These are astonishing numbers for a country that even in its lowest times—after Watergate, say, or during Reconstruction—never doubted the legitimacy of their leaders to such a degree.

And if distrust of the government was at an all-time high, that was still nothing compared to what the public thought of the national media. Both the left and the right had developed parallel theories about the co-opting of the corporate press, imagining it to be controlled by powerful unseen enemies, and increasingly turned to grassroots Internet sources for news and information. In the BBC/Reuters/Media Center's annual Trust in the Media survey in 2006, the United States was one of just two countries surveyed—Britain being the other—where respondents trusted their government (67 percent) more than they trusted national news reporters (59 percent). A Harris poll that same year showed that some 68 percent of Americans now felt that the news media were "too powerful."

The country, in other words, was losing its shit. Our national politics was doomed because voters were no longer debating one another using a commonly accepted set of facts. There was no commonly accepted set of facts, except in the imagination of a hopelessly daft political and media elite that had long ago lost touch with the general public. What we had instead was a nation of reality shoppers, all shutting the blinds on the loathsome old common landscape to tinker with their own self-tailored and in some cases highly paranoid recipes for salvation and/or revolution. They voted in huge numbers, but they were voting out of loathing, against enemies and against the system in general, not really *for* anybody. The elections had basically become a forum for organizing the hatreds of the population.

And the worst thing was that the political parties at some level were complicit in this and understood what was going on perfectly—which is why together they spent $160 million on negative advertising in this cycle, as opposed to just $17 million on positive ads. There were no longer any viable principles in play. Just hate. And distrust. The system had nothing left to offer the People, so the People were leaving the reservation. But where were they going?

That was what I'd come here to find out. While Washington was still basking in the glow of the Big Win and starting its revolting 2008 party way too early (headline on the *Washington Post* opinion page today: "An Iowan You Should Know," about candidate Tom Vilsack. I should know now? In December of 2006! Are these people insane?), I decided to pick a spot on the map, go there, and get retarded. If the country was going to flip out, I didn't want to be left behind.

THE MUTE BUTTON was still on, but I gathered that the deskbound TV preacher was still blathering about Sudan. They kept alternating close-ups of his face with shots of balloon-headed

Sudanese kids meekly waving the flies out of their eyes. I looked down at my notebook and saw my own handwriting jump back at me: PRAYER LINE (210) 490–5100.

I grabbed my cell phone and dialed the number. Three rings, then a recorded voice answered:

"Thank you for calling John Hagee Ministries. All of our prayer partners are currently busy. You may have called at a peak period. However, your call will be answered in the order it was received . . ."

I frowned and started doodling in my notebook. A year and a half ago I watched a British reporter at the Michael Jackson trial draw a picture of a knife plunging into a dog's head during the cross-examination of Larry King. Since then I can't stop drawing the same thing. I'm now beginning to wonder if the Brit caught the disease from someone else. Perhaps this goes back thousands of years. After a few minutes I heard a click and a young man's voice came on the line:

"Hello, John Hagee Ministries," he said.

"Yeah, hi," I said. "I'd like to make a prayer request."

"Sure," he said. "What are we praying for?"

I paused. When dealing with the kind of people who think Left Behind is really possible and who think Noah really was six hundred years old when the flood came, there is a strong temptation to ham it up, fuck with them a little, offer answers that will at least make them blink once or twice before they swallow them whole. I'll confess to doing this throughout my stay in Texas, and I don't feel a need to apologize for it—I live in this country, too, and sometimes I can't help being angry about how dumb and mean our culture has become, how fast that meanness and dumbness is expanding, and how determined some Jesus-culture merchants are that people like me should not escape it. And so from time to time that anger would come out, in a tall tale or two that would pop out of my mouth in church-going company. But hilariously, the joke would mostly end up cutting both ways. I'd say the craziest, stupidest stuff, trying like hell to get a rise out of people, and not only would I not get one, I'd for the most part be completely ignored—smiled and nodded at, and then just waved on through into my seat in the megachurch. Being a wiseass in a groupthink environment is like throwing an egg at a bulldozer.

That's the way things work in America. You can literally stick a fork into your own eye in public, and so long as your check clears, no one will even bat an eye. There was a lot of this sort of thing in my Texas experience, and it made for a strangely harmonious undertone to my relations with the locals: I kept sticking a fork in my own eye over and over again, and over and over again my new friends would smile like nothing was happening. You can say a lot of very weird shit when you're a Brother in Christ, so long as you don't forget to sing along at the right times.

In that regard, the "prayer request" I ended up making was for a fictional ex-wife who I said had run out on me. I told my prayer line counselor that my betrothed had thrown me over for a Jewish ACLU lawyer named Schatz—that she had jumped in his Saab and run away with him to Paris, to take the Bateau-Mouche ride she said I could never give her. I further told my counselor that I didn't know what "Bateau-Mouche" meant, but I knew it warn't Christian. When I was finished with my story, there was silence on the line for a moment.

"The car was a *Saab*?" the counselor said finally, with appropriate contempt.

I smiled, pleased that he was paying attention to the important details. I added that I didn't like this Schatz fellow at all. That the black curls in his hair looked almost like horns.

"Anyway," I said. "I just want to pray for her, pray that she finds her way back to me, back to Christ."

I held my ear away from the phone, expecting a hangup. In-

stead, the counselor just ate the story whole and plowed ahead
with his computerized compassion spiel.

"What's your name again?" the man said.

"Matt," I said.

"Let's go ahead and pray, Matt," he said.

I bowed my head.

"Father, I ask You," he said, "with Your words, whoever You
put together, no man can separate. Father, I ask You now for
Matt and his wife, Lord Father, for her specifically, Lord, I ask
You that You would bring her back to the right relationship
and the right standing with You, Lord. Father, I pray in the
name of Jesus against every attack and assault of the Enemy on
their marriage, on their relationship. Father, I just ask You right
now to give them freedom, to give them deliverance, Lord God,
from all of the attacks of the Enemy."

I bit my lip. This guy is good, I thought.

"Father, I ask You that as they seek You and put You first,
Lord God, I ask You to provide for them the desires of the heart
and the needs that they seek. I pray, Lord God, that You will
provide them a way that exceeds all that we can imagine, Lord
God. Father, I pray that You would let them be bound again by
the power of Jesus Christ in the middle of their relationship . . ."

The middle?

". . . and that, Lord God, that You will never again allow
them to be in a relationship, Lord God, without putting You
first and foremost in their lives, Lord God. Father, I ask that
You have mercy on them individually, Lord God, and let both
of them come back to their first love, which would be You, Lord
God. In Jesus's name I ask, Lord God, that all of these things be
glorified. In Your name we pray."

"Amen!" I said.

What a performance—totally mechanical, true, but amazing nonetheless.

"Well, alright then," the man said, and hung up.

"Hey," I said, "wait!"

But he was gone.

To be perfectly honest, I knew all about Pastor John Hagee—his Cornerstone Church was one of the reasons I'd come to San Antonio in the first place. Hagee was one of the most influential evangelical preachers in the country—not because his ministry was so very large (although he claimed up to 4.5 million viewers a week for his Sunday sermons), but because of his near-absolute conquest of a very trendy niche in the market: Christian Zionism.

Not exactly a new idea, Christian Zionism in simplest terms describes Christians who believe in supporting, politically or otherwise, the State of Israel. It has risen as a force in international politics primarily because of two factors. The first is a rise in America of belief in dispensationalist Christianity, i.e., End Times prophecies—the belief that Armageddon is coming and that, with it, the True Believers will be whisked up to Heaven by God, while the nonbelievers stay on earth to suck eggs and generally suffer various tortures. The enormous success of the Left Behind books and movies (which depict the earth during Armageddon as a delicious chaos, with airplanes suddenly stripped of their believer pilots, buses flying off highways, blood-soaked atheists realizing their tragic mistake far too late, etc.) helped spread these beliefs, so much so that dispensationalism is now more or less the default doctrine of most Southern Baptists. If you enter a megachurch practically anywhere in America these days, you can expect that much of the congregation will be actively awaiting the end of the world.

But you can't have Armageddon without certain preconditions, and most important among those is a final battle that the Prophet Ezekiel predicted will take place between a satanic army (in most interpretations, a force of Arabs led by Russia) and God's chosen people, Israel. Most End Timers believe the key alliance here will be between Russia and Iran and that only following a savage military confrontation between those states and Israel, probably of a catastrophic nuclear nature, will Christ reappear and begin his glorious second reign.

Thus the whole idea behind Christian Zionism is to align America with the nation of Israel so as to "hurry God up" in his efforts to bring about this key final showdown. Practically speaking, this manifests itself, mainly, in the form of American evangelical Christians endorsing pro-Israel policies, support that Israel itself has been happy to receive (Benjamin Netanyahu has even appeared at Hagee's Cornerstone Church) despite the fact that dispensationalist doctrine also envisions the mass conversion of all Jews to Christianity after the final battle, with dire consequences for those who don't. I wonder exactly how most Israelis would feel about the sudden warmth being shown them by American evangelicals if they knew, for instance, that people like ardent End Timer Hal Lindsey had predicted the "mother of all Holocausts" for those Jews who refused to convert at the Second Coming.

Anyway, Pastor Hagee, that drawling, white-haired, barrel-organ-voiced Texan with the kindly smile who gives such powerful ministry on TV, is one of America's chief pitchmen for Christian Zionism. He founded a group called Christians United for Israel (CUFI), whose mission is to rally Christians to Israel's cause. According to the *Washington Post*, Hagee has regular access to the White House and has many followers among George Bush's staff. Remarkably, when CUFI held a conference in Washington this past summer, no less a personage than Republican National Committee chairman Ken Mehlman gave the keynote address. Also participating as speakers were

Senators Sam Brownback and Rick Santorum, while George
W. Bush and Israeli prime minister Ehud Olmert sent recorded
greetings.

When I first started reading about Hagee and about the
felicitous alliance between the American religious right and the
hard-liners in the Israeli government, my first reaction was to
applaud it as a brilliantly cynical piece of international politics.
Whether it was conceived in the corridors of Mossad head-
quarters or in some dreary archcapitalist think tank funded by
the Smith Richardson Foundation (and I'm guessing it was
probably some combination of both), I had no idea, but it was
unmistakably an ingenious solution to the problem of how to
rally southern conservative Christians a few generations removed from their cross-burning Klan days to the cause of Israel. If it turns out that it was dreamed up by the same guy who
figured out how to get laid-off midwestern factory workers to
whoop for free-trade Republicanism by plastering the airwaves
with French-kissing men, I have to say, that guy deserves some
kind of special medal—a Triple Order of Satan, or something
like that.

But during the election season, I started to wonder if this
kind of thing might eventually backfire on the people who con-
cocted these ideas, if indeed they were dreamed up from on
high. As a temporary electoral gambit designed to garner support for Israel, it's brilliant, but let's not forget that it doesn't
work unless you get tens of millions of people really believing
that the world is about to end. I wonder sometimes if the cynics
in Washington think that they can get away with just bending
the yokels' ears once every four years, cashing in on Election
Day, and then going back to the grimy you-scratch-my-back-
I'll-scratch-yours money politics that dominates everyday life
inside the Beltway.

I think those people forget that after every Election Day,
even after they've been forgotten by Washington, those yokels

are still out there, thinking, waiting, watching. Their minds change. And if their needs are not tended to, they drift away. And if you've gotten used to making political decisions based on the Book of Revelation, you can drift pretty far. I wanted to see how far, exactly—I was going to join the church.

TWO

Congressional Interlude I,

or

Inside the Halls of Derangement

To DIAGNOSE A CANCER, you have to find its source—the organ where the first batches of abnormal cells started breeding and metastasizing. In the body America the most visible symptoms of the national derangement are in the extremities, the huge sections of the population gone far off the farm into distrust and paranoia, the bitter and disgust-ridden electoral contests, the violent rejection of the national media, etc.

Before going to Texas, I went to Washington, D.C., because this is where the disease began. The problem started when our elected leaders started playing a different game from the one the people sent them to play. They corrupted the process, made it sick, and in the end created a new species of government, an organism that functions well to serve its own ends but is nonresponsive to the public need. It's a heart that beats but doesn't pump blood.

This is something different from individual instances of corruption, of a few bad apples taking liberties and stealing a little on the side, here and there. What we have in Washington now is a systemic kind of corruption, a corruption of the whole organism of government. And it's that corruption at the core of the American polity that's radiated into the rest of the population, sending out ripples of madness and discontent.

The nonresponsive government may have sent the people scurrying toward magical or conspiratorial explanations for their betrayal, but when I went to Washington—in the fall of 2005, in the wake of Hurricane Katrina—what I found was a much less exotic, but frankly harder to accept, explanation for why things are falling apart. The best cover our corrupt politicians have for their behavior is the very banality of their crimes; to quote Tolstoy, their corruption is "most ordinary and therefore most horrible." To be robbed and betrayed by a fiendish underground conspiracy, or by the earthly agents of Satan, is at least a romantic sort of plight—it suggests at least a grand Hollywood-ready confrontation between good and evil—but to be coldly ripped off over and over again by a bunch of bloodless, second-rate schmoes, schmoes you *chose*, you *elected*, is not something anyone will take much pleasure in bragging about.

That's why people will think up all sorts of crazy things to explain what's wrong, long before they get around to the actual truth. But it's the simple, unvarnished reality right out in the open that's most frightening.

IT'S 2005, and although no one knows it yet, the beginning of the last Republican Congress of the Bush era, the death spasm of the Contract with America team that had been running the country's lawmaking body for a dozen years. A fall afternoon and I'm entering the Congress, the House, to be exact. On the third-floor corridor snaking around the House gallery a line of tourists waits to squeeze through a metal detector. Lots of families, suckers from the middle of nowhere, here to take a gander at that whole Democracy thing.

A big-assed foursome is at the head of the line. Dad is balding, paunchy, a cop's caterpillar mustache, dense curly black arm hair, wearing a Faded Glory Duo-Stripe polo shirt—I'm guessing a size 9XL, red colored, untucked all around, the Olaf the Tentmaker look. I know the exact brand of shirt because I saw it on sale for seven bucks in a Wal-Mart in Houston a few weeks back and almost bought it, just because it was seven bucks. Mom has messy dirty-blond hair, eyes like a tarantula's, too close together, obstetric hips, and a voice that could break glass. She's wearing a T-shirt that says "ITHACA IS GORGES," but I don't think either of them is from New York State. Two little boys, both pretty young, blank eyes, neither old enough nor guilty enough yet to be villains in the American drama.

Dad leans over to one of the kids:

"Remember what I said," he says. "They can arrest you if you make a joke right up here."

"Is that really true?" the older boy says.

"It sure is, son," Dad says, tapping Junior on the back, speaking with what appears to be pride. They've got great security in this country of ours, really on top of everything. The kid nods, then they all move into the gallery together.

A FEW MINUTES LATER I'm asleep on the other side of the gallery, in the press section. With all the traveling I do, my naps are great black oceans weighing millions of tons; my dreams have no plots and no people, just darkness and wriggling shapes. I love sleeping and do it as much as possible, especially in Congress. I'm awakened, however, by the sound of a falling gavel.

"The chair recognizes the gentleman from Tennessee!"

It's Thursday, October 6, 2005. As is almost always the case, the press section is completely empty. Most of the media sentenced to cover Congress do so from one of Washington's great oases of I-don't-give-a-fuck, the press lounge behind and above me, a lifeless little cave with an oldish Coke machine, three clean toilets, and a lot of milling middle-aged reporter types moving slowly if at all, grazing on paper press releases and the endless drone of C-SPAN on the monitors. In the vast congressional zoo the press lounge is one of the very lamest attractions, the equivalent of a three-goat petting run. And the goats almost never come out from behind their rock, into the actual gallery where they might be seen. They stay in their cave, because most of the time, there's just not a lot for a goat to see in the House gallery.

"Madam Speaker," yawns a voice from below, "I yield myself as much time as I may consume . . ."

The voice belongs to John J. Duncan, Jr., better known as Jimmy Duncan, Republican of Tennessee. Duncan is a conservative's conservative—he was one of the few Republicans to vote against the Iraq war, using the roughly hundred-year-old excuse that it required of us Americans too much involvement in foreign affairs. A classic isolationist and one of many members who occupy an essentially hereditary congressional seat, Duncan assumed his office after the death in 1988 of his father, John Duncan, Sr., who had been elected to office twelve consecutive times. Three hundred years from now, the city of Knoxville's congressman will be a Duncan opposed to the extension of foreign aid to Pluto.

This particular Duncan is easy to spot because he has Newt Gingrich's shock-white Leslie Nielsen haircut. He's also one of many southern congressmen whose glowing white orthodonture is visible from a hundred yards off. From my cozy seat up in the gallery I watch now as these superior teeth begin pleading their case to the Speaker,* who at the moment is not Dennis Hastert but the momlike Illinois Republican Judy Biggert.

---

*These substitute speakers, incidentally, are called Speakers pro tempore, and most every day in Congress begins with the reading of a note from Hastert nominating this or that Republican colleague to act in his stead— one of the first rules of the modern Congress being that the primary actors of the House almost always have something better to do than actually show up on the floor.

One of the great populist myths about Congress is that our elected leaders are lazy bums who do very little work for their money. This is not the case; the vast majority of congressmen and -women actually work surprisingly long hours and have very little free time. One of my earliest experiences in Congress involved following behind Vermont's Bernie Sanders on the way to a committee hearing; when I made a joke about the committee adjourning early to let the members make their tee times, Sanders went ballistic on me. "No way. These guys work hard," he snapped. And as I later saw, he's absolutely right; most members are here late into every weekday evening.

But for all that, the guys who actually run the 109th Congress—Tom DeLay, Hastert, and the rest of the House leadership—are not often visible on the floor or anywhere else.

In any case, Duncan began his remarks:

"Madam Speaker," he said, "I move to suspend the rules and pass the bill (HR 3439) to designate the facility of the United States Postal Service located at 201 North Third Street in Smithfield, North Carolina, as the Ava Gardner Post Office."

Time was taken for the clerk to read this new Ava Gardner bill into the record. The floor was then returned to Duncan, who noted that HR 3439 had been cosigned by all members of the North Carolina delegation. Then Duncan began a lengthy speech on the subject at hand:

"The life of Ava Gardner is a true rags-to-riches story that started on a tobacco farm in the rural South . . ."

I sighed. I had been to enough day sessions of Congress to know how the rest of this drill worked. Across the gallery, I watched with amusement as the ITHACA IS GORGES family gravely considered the great drama unfolding on the floor below them. They probably came here to see, who knows, free trade or military aid or even stem-cell research or something like that debated, and here instead is this too-old starfucking jackass from Tennessee gushing to an almost completely empty hall about what was probably the whack-off sex-symbol icon of his youth, Ava Gardner. Duncan blathered in this vein for some time, then switched gears; the plain-talking southern isolationist suddenly assumed the fruity diction and pointy-headed public persona of a Leonard Maltin or Jeff Lyons:

"In 1946," he said, "she landed her first starring role in the B-grade movie *Whistle Stop*. Later that year, on loan from MGM, Universal Studios cast her in her breakout hit, *The Killers* . . ."

Finally he concluded:

"Ava Gardner, the earthy girl from North Carolina, had beaten the odds to become one of Hollywood's most famous icons."

Jesus Christ, I thought. With all this diva worship, this guy is turning Congress into a West Village revue. Across the way, Husky Fam fidgeted, and Dad frowned; what the fuck was this?

It got worse. When Duncan finished, he was succeeded by a series of colleagues. Danny Davis, the stately black congressman from Chicago, took the podium; his Gardner films of choice were not *Whistle Stop* and *The Killers* but *The Barefoot Contessa*, *The Sun Also Rises*, and *On the Beach*. Davis also noted that Gardner "was married to three legendary Hollywood actors, including Mickey Rooney, Artie Shaw, and Frank Sinatra."

Next in line was Bob Etheridge, the North Carolina Democrat who was the apparent author of the bill. Etheridge reiterated some of the earlier points about Ava Gardner and added that "she was America's sweetheart during Hollywood's golden age" and that she was "the first woman from North Carolina to grace the cover of *Time* magazine."

When everyone was done, Biggert mumbled something about suspending the rules and taking a vote, and a vote was taken of those few members present. When it passed, I heard the blow of a gavel, and the Ava Gardner Post Office officially came into being. Smithfield, strike up the band!

Davis, Etheridge, and Duncan, the trio of Ava Gardner fans, slipped out of the gallery together, chatting on the way, probably comparing pinup-gal memories. The gavel sounded again, and for an uncomfortably long while there were, excepting the Speaker, no representatives on the floor. Literally nothing was happening. The great ship of state slowed, the sails slacked—doldrums again.

The tourists in the visitors' gallery filed out, looking bummed. I went back to sleep.

AN AIDE to a Democratic congressman put it to me this way, over coffee in a basement cafeteria:

"What you see out there is a joke," he said. "What's on the floor on a day-to-day basis—it's theater, not government. It's ten hours a day of naming post offices and congratulating Little League teams. Everyone knows they do all the real business when no one's there. In the middle of the night. Early in the morning, before the sun comes up."

Most anyone who has seen *Mr. Smith Goes to Washington* or is old enough to remember the Schoolhouse Rock jingle imagines Congress to be an august body where a diverse crowd of hundreds of elected officials, representing every remote corner of the country, exhaustively debate all the important issues of the day in electrifying day-long political-philosophical discussions on the House floor.

The reality is that the debate has mostly been removed from the House schedule. In the main chamber, the majority of the House's time is spent on what are called "suspension bills," in which the normal House rules are suspended. In a suspension bill, only forty minutes of debate are allowed, no amendments can be offered, and a two-thirds majority vote is required for passage.

One think tank's report on the use of suspension bills noted that by the 108th Congress—the second Congress of the Bush era—some 79 percent of all bills passed were suspension bills. Until about a dozen years ago, that figure hovered consistently between 40 and 50 percent.

A report by Democrat Louise Slaughter, one of the minority four suffering Democrats on the Rules Committee, put it bluntly:

"House Republicans continued to squeeze out real debate on controversial issues in the House by devoting more and more floor time to suspension bills . . . In the 108th Congress, Republican leaders apparently decided that the House should spend two out of the three days of its already abbreviated legislative week on noncontroversial legislation, such as bills that name post offices and congratulate sports teams."

What these reports don't say in stark-enough terms is that the whole idea behind all of these suspension bills is to make the official business of Congress an endless stream of meaningless, boring, literally unwatchable bullshit. No human being with any self-respect could ever watch more than ten minutes of this stuff per month, and for the leaders of Congress, that's a wonderful thing. Because the real business of Congress happens mostly behind closed doors, in obscure committee meetings, with the most important and weighty of these taking place at preposterous hours and in late-night "emergency" sessions.

No one ever asks why Congress needs to debate massive energy bills, or sweeping, pork-filled highway legislation, or friendlily transparent corporate handouts like the prescription drug benefit bill late at night, when its days are spent naming auditoriums and sending letters to the wives of dead orchestra conductors. Clearly, if the House leaders wanted to, they could take care of all that naming and congratulating in the off-peak hours, or not bother with it at all. This gross scheduling absurdity is much commented upon among congressional staffers, most all of whom interpret this state of affairs the same way.

"The difference between now and before," says Fred Turner, chief of staff of Congressman Alcee Hastings, one of four Democrats on the vital Rules Committee, "is that before, when the Democrats controlled Congress, we held all the key committee hearings at ten a.m. on Tuesday. Now it's three a.m. on Thursday. Everyone knows why they do it: so that the press won't be here to watch, so that everything makes the papers a day late, and so on. They don't want you to watch."

But what happens if you do watch? What will you see?

ON THAT SAME THURSDAY afternoon in October when Duncan, Davis, et al. were rhapsodizing over *Whistle Stop*, the schedule for House activity on the floor had been about par for the course. Frankenstein look-alike and Arkansas Democrat Mike Ross ate a few minutes welcoming his hometown pastor to Congress ("My faith is profoundly important to me, and Reverend Kassos is not only my spiritual adviser, he is my friend and he is my fishing buddy . . .").

Under-investigation Ohio congressman and Jack Abramoff buddy Bob Ney took a moment to honor a soldier who had been shot six times ("Matt Smith represents some of the best America and Ohio have to offer"). Virginia Foxx of North Carolina honored a volunteer firefighter from her district. John Mica of Florida passed a measure renaming a building in the American diplomatic mission in Jamaica after Colin Powell. There were resolutions about National Campus Safety Awareness Month and National Pancreatic Cancer Awareness Month, and the contributions of African American basketball players were recognized.

There was the Ava Gardner Post Office, a statement honoring a Nevada family whose son died in his sleep, a resolution celebrating the career of Simon Wiesenthal, and so on, and so on.

Finally the gavel pounded and the House floor adjourned for

the day. But one floor up, in a cramped room full of puke-green chairs, another wing of the House was just opening for business.

SAINTS HAVE THE VATICAN, Jews the Wailing Wall, warriors the fields of Marathon, Stalingrad, Normandy.

Cynics have the Rules Committee of the U.S. House of Representatives.

The home of Rules is a cramped room with dismal lighting, and on this overcast, unseasonably muggy day, its two-row gallery of vomit-colored chairs is packed with congressional aides and, uncharacteristically, a few reporters.

It's about four thirty in the afternoon, or about a half hour after most of the congressional press called it a day and fled the Hill. The ones who've stayed did so to catch the appearance before the Rules Committee of Congressman Joe Barton (R-TX), the chairman of the House Energy and Commerce Committee, who's here on a semi-important errand.

In the congressional witches' coven of influential blowhard Republican conspirators—a powerful league of villains that at the time included Republican House leaders like Jim Sensenbrenner, Roy Blunt, David Dreier, Dennis Hastert, Mike Oxley, and Tom DeLay, among others—Barton plays the role of the silver-tongued, laid-back, backwoods southern cop, forever knocking out the taillight of Progress.

While other Republican leaders tend to favor a public style of fist-pounding hysterics and outright verbal abuse, Barton will respond to a committee objection to this or that billion-dollar oil company handout by simply leaning back in his chair, smiling, and shrugging. *Shucks, we did the best we could for ya . . . There jes' wasn't anythin' we could do . . . I's real sorry, ma'am, but we just had to kill the shit out of your bill.*

Barton is at the Rules Committee now to shepherd a monstrosity called the Gasoline for America's Security Act—colloquially called the new energy bill, as opposed to the old energy bill, an obscene porkfest passed that summer—through the last stages of the House approval process. With the exception of the initial emergency aid package, the Gasoline for America's Security Act has been, to date, the most important piece of legislation proposed in response to the Hurricane Katrina disaster. It is also the first major piece of Katrina legislation to have made it this far, i.e., to the Rules Committee.

Having taken his seat in the witness chair, Barton now slouches, keeping one elbow propped on the table in front of him and letting one hand dangle to the side. His suit jacket has fallen open and one of his legs stretches forward, poking out from under the table in the general direction of Rules chairman David Dreier.

Barton is loose. He's been cracking jokes ever since he walked in the room, and even when the Democrats on the committee try to ruin the mood by peppering him with nasty questions, he just answers them with a smile. After Barton delivers a baldly full-of-shit summary of the bill at hand, Democrat James McGovern comments that if he had given an answer like that to his constituents at a Massachusetts gas station, they "wouldn't let me leave in one piece."

"Well, what I do at a Texas gas station, when people ask if I'm Congressman Barton," Barton says, smiling, "is this . . . I just tell 'em I'm his driver."

Laughs all around. Even McGovern laughs. A humor non-aggression pact is in force in most of Congress: both parties always laugh at each other's jokes, particularly when they're of the inside-baseball, high-school-yearbook variety Barton has just whipped out at McGovern. A well-timed inside joke is the Get Out of Jail Free card of congressional debate.

Barton is about to say something significantly funnier, but the humor behind the next joke in the pipe is not easy to convey without a little background about the bill, about Barton, about Congress in general. C-SPAN is boring to the average viewer only because no one has time to swallow the backstory. If you follow it from episode 1, it's funnier than Monty Python. Although September, the month of the Katrina disaster, was a little less funny than usual.

So LET'S FREEZE the scene with Barton leaning back in his chair looking eminently pleased with himself, as only a man carrying a full bushel of Hot Steaming Dogshit for the consideration of the U.S. House Committee on Rules can look. The only detectable emotion on the happy halcyon landscape of Barton's good-ole-boy face is a faint air of surprise, as if he were amazed that he was actually about to get away with writing a bill this bad.

For Barton's bill is a new low, even for this Congress. A masterpiece of shameless opportunism and sheer balls, HR 3893 of the 109th Congress, the Gasoline for America's Security Act, was conceived by Barton's office before the bodies in New Orleans had even cooled. The storm hit New Orleans on August 29, and this bill was presented for consideration to the House in what would end up being very close to its final form just over three weeks later, on September 26.

Ostensibly, the problem the bill addresses is the damage caused by the storm to the country's refinery capacity, a problem that came before the public eye via the skyrocketing gas prices that swept the country after the storm. The bill was written in the weepy, hands-over-the-heart, your-pain-is-our-pain language peculiar to corporate handouts disguised as altruistic public relief programs—a literary genre that saw tremendous creative innovation in the period after the historic storm. The relevant passage of HR 3893 read as follows:

(3) Hurricanes Katrina and Rita substantially disrupted petroleum production, refining, and pipeline systems in the Gulf Coast region, affecting energy prices and supply nationwide . . .

(4) It serves the national interest to increase refinery capacity for gasoline, heating oil, diesel fuel, and jet fuel wherever located within the United States, to bring more reliable and economic supply to the American people.

(5) According to economic analysis, households are conservatively estimated to spend an average of $1,948 this year on gasoline, up 45 percent from 3 years ago, and households with incomes under $15,000 (1/5 of all households) this year will spend, on average, more than 1/10 of their income just on gasoline.

The bill, in other words, was written with the aim of sparing less fortunate Americans the pain of spending a tenth of their income on gasoline and helping to avoid even steeper costs.

Barton's plan for achieving this, however, included no new measures whatsoever and did nothing at all about the price of gasoline. Instead, Barton simply used the bill to trot out an ancient, oft-rehashed laundry list of energy industry wet dreams, including the reigning legislative fantasy of the combustible-fuel industry: the repeal of the new source review provision of the Clean Air Act.

The repeal of new source review is one of those things—the opening of the Arctic National Wildlife Refuge (ANWR) for petroleum drilling and the repeal of the capital gains tax being two of the others—that Republican lawmakers ask for whenever any hideous crisis hits the newspapers. The party's gift for this kind of abject political non sequitur has been a defining characteristic for about a dozen years now, but especially in the last five. Terrorists strike New York? We better repeal the estate tax, quick! Asian bird flu on the way? Millions will die—if the Securities Exchange Act of 1934 isn't overturned!

The classic example of this, of course, was Alaska senator Frank Murkowski's heartfelt plea, just two days after 9/11, to open ANWR for oil development, as a means of combating the terrorist threat. Not surprisingly, the Republicans went after ANWR again after Katrina, and also humped another old target—the prohibited offshore drilling zones of the outer continental shelf. Those measures were junked at the last minute in committee, but the gutting of the long-loathed Clean Air Act was the biggest and juiciest prize—and it appeared to have survived in the final version of Barton's gasoline act.

New source review has been a regulatory bee in the bonnet of the energy industry since 1970, when the Clean Air Act Extension first went into effect. Essentially, the measure dictated that pre-1970 plants and refineries could continue to pollute at pre-1970 legal levels, but that new plants and old plants modified with new equipment had to reduce emissions and use state-of-the-art scrubbing technology—an expensive proposition, opponents have long said, for the beleaguered oil industry.

Barton's party had taken several swipes at new source review, all unsuccessful, in the past few years alone. In the spring of 2001, the now-notorious Cheney energy task force issued a report recommending that the attorney general take a look at new source review to see if it was consistent with the law.

The AG never took up that fight, but that might have been because the administration by then had found a new avenue of attack. The hilariously named "Clear Skies" bill of 2002, sent to the Hill by the Bush administration for the consideration of Congress, included a provision that would have exempted all existing plants from new source review requirements.

When that bill was blocked in Congress, the administration went another route, taking aim at the bill via executive branch regulation. In December 2002, the Environmental Protection Agency under Bush came up with a series of loopholes aimed at helping factories and power plants avoid requirements to modernize. The provisions were challenged and mostly defeated in the District of Columbia Circuit Court, but this was no deterrent to the EPA; under a year later, in August 2003, it came out with yet another new rule designed to circumvent new source review, which the court again struck down. New source review, despite repeated attacks, remained a heavy rope around the neck of industry.

Therefore it was with some desperation that Barton decided to apply the non sequitur trick to Hurricane Katrina while bodies still floated in the Ninth Ward. New Orleans is underwater! Quick, repeal those tough air-pollution emissions standards!

Even within the logically discordant parameters of non sequitur politics, this particular piece of legislation was unusually ridiculous and transparent. The ostensible justification for the bill was still about six logical steps removed from the Katrina disaster it was designed to provide an emergency remedy for.

The silliest aspect of the bill was its very status as an "emergency" measure. It would be hard to imagine anything more absurd than the idea of combating a current, immediate national fuel-cost crisis—taking on high fuel and gas prices affecting citizens right now, this week—by passing a deregulation bill that at best provides an oblique and indirect incentive for oil companies to build new refineries years from now at the earliest. Yet the bill was rushed through Congress with all the alacrity of an emergency relief package, as though industry simply could not wait to hurry up and maybe build new plants.

Beyond that, what little logic there was in the bill was based upon the assumption that oil companies even want to build new refineries. As Barton surely knew—he had heard plenty of testimony on the matter in the Energy and Commerce Committee debates over this bill—it had been more than three decades since a major American energy company had evinced any interest at all in building a new oil refinery. In fact, in a thirty-year period dating back to 1975, the federal government had received just one application to build a new refinery.

In truth, the trend in the industry had been exactly the opposite: oil companies had steadily reduced the number of functioning refineries over the years, closing down nearly half of all America's refineries in the course of three decades.

The reason for this was obvious and freely admitted to by industry leaders who met with members of Congress in anticipation of this bill. Fewer refineries meant a reduced supply, which in turn meant higher prices—and higher prices were, for obvious reasons, desirable. The idea of providing subsidies to build new refineries was as absurd as giving away farmland to grow wheat during a grain glut.

Higher prices also meant larger profits for the oil and gas industry. In fact, at the time Barton was writing his relief bill—which was designed, remember, to help struggling oil and gas companies bear the burden of high regulatory costs—the oil and gas multinationals were experiencing record revenues. At the time the bill went to the House floor, ExxonMobil had just come off a quarter with $7.62 billion in profits.

In sum, oil companies had no interest in building new refineries, could easily have afforded to build them even if they wanted to, and were in fact, instead of building or trying to build, closing down existing facilities. For all these reasons, and for many others, the core premise of the Barton bill—that costs associated with new source review were preventing the construction of oil refineries and therefore driving up fuel prices—was clearly absurd on its face. In its own way, even the Bush administration had itself admitted as much years before, when the EPA issued a report flatly denying a link between new source review and refining capacity.

"The NSR has not significantly impeded investment

in . . . refineries," the agency wrote in June 2002, in its "New Source Review: A Report to the President."

Barton's bill almost certainly had nothing to do with refineries at all. Clearly, this was about repealing new source review restrictions on other kinds of Clean Air–governed facilities.

New Orleans was still underwater, gas prices were still soaring, a mean winter for nearly a million displaced persons was just around the corner—and the first emergency response of America's reigning political party is to help the very richest companies in the world get out of paying fines for dumping acid rain on Canada, whether or not they produced gasoline or heating fuel. That's what this bill amounted to. It was an ingenious, inspired piece of cynical insider politics—and Barton was the perfect man for the job.

EVERYONE IN CONGRESS knows what the real job of most House members is: to carry water for their campaign donors. When you get $80,000 from Company X, you're not being paid to vote your conscience. And while companies obviously seek the support of the rank-and-file House members, the giving strategy in this Congress had been honed to an exact science, one that mostly revolves around compensation of the really important members. There's no better proof than the giving habits of certain campaign donors that the congressional apparatus has been manipulated to the point where it can now be controlled by a handful of key players.

To wit, when you're looking at the process by which any bill gets passed into law, on the House side at least there are only a few people who really matter. Those people are the majority leader, the chairman of the relevant "committee of jurisdiction" (i.e., Energy and Commerce for the oil industry, Financial Services for Wall Street firms, etc.), the chairman of the Rules Committee, the chairs of the House-Senate conference committee, the House Speaker, and perhaps a few other members of the conference committee.

These people are important because this small group can essentially ram a bill into law all by themselves. If you control all of these seats, you control every space on the congressional Monopoly board within which the bill can be written or altered unilaterally.

There are four main way stations on the road to a bill's passage. There's the committee of jurisdiction, where the bill, after being introduced, goes through what's called a markup process. In a markup, the committee decides what goes in the bill and what does not. The markup process is supervised by the committee chairman. Theoretically the markup process is put to a general vote by the committee, but in this Congress the reality is that the chairman puts in what he wants and chucks what he doesn't want out the window.

He then sends the bill to the Rules Committee, where other House members from outside the committee—usually freaked-out minority members desperate to stop this or that criminally insane provision cleverly hidden in the committee version—have a chance to submit amendments to the bill. The Rules chairman tries not to laugh, somberly nukes every meaningful amendment request with a pained, regretful expression, and then takes the bill behind closed doors, where it can be rewritten (usually in the middle of the night) to include all the shit the House leadership knew was way too evil to survive public discussion in the original committee of jurisdiction.

Rules then puts the finishing touches on the bill's language and sends it to the floor the very next morning. The version that leaves the Rules Committee is now called not a bill, but a rule. The Rules Committee is supposed to give House members three days to read the rule before it goes to a vote, but the three-day period can be waived in case of emergency. The "emergency" has been in place for five consecutive years now;

virtually every bill that has passed through the House in the Bush era has been voted on just hours after emerging from the hairy womb of the Rules Committee.

After the House passes the rule, which of course no one voting on it has read, the world then waits for the Senate to pass its own hideous version of the legislation. But alas, the bill cannot be sent to the president until the differences between the House and Senate versions—consisting generally of differing sets of campaign donor hand-jobs hidden in the two bills—can be ironed out. This ironing out is done in the conference committee.

The mechanism of conference committee is a special voodoo all unto itself, a monstrously complex bureaucratic maze whose diabolical scheme is known to a select few congressional practitioners. But for the moment, only two facts are important.

The first is that the bill can again be completely rewritten here, rewritten from top to bottom, rewritten even so that it has a completely opposite meaning from the bills that passed the two houses—in a word, rewritten in such fashion as to render the whole process up till now meaningless.

The second is that a majority vote of conference committee members, called "conferees," is not even required for passage. Again, the conference committee chairs are the key players here. Whatever the top dogs from the House and Senate want generally occurs. They redo the bill according to whatever swinish commercial dynamic happens to govern this back-room deal (for the conference hearings are almost always conducted out of the public eye), then send the final version to a vote, again giving the members just a few hours' notice before they make an essentially blind decision on the by-now completely revised legislation.

Somewhere along the line, campaign donors apparently figured out that by a careful stewarding of their contributions, they could—instead of spending gargantuan sums to buy the wide majority of House and Senate members necessary for an open vote on the floor—instead target those members who could simply rewrite the important parts of the bill in secret. God knows when this revelation first hit home, but when they were caught for the first time, one of the key players was none other than Joe Barton.

This landmark nonmoment in congressional history (for although it should have been a huge story, it fizzled to nothing and all the guilty got away with everything, as usual) came in the spring/summer of 2003.

It was the misfortune of Tom DeLay, Joe Barton, Billy Tauzin, and other then-influential House members that a Kansas-based energy company called Westar came under the scrutiny of shareholders for a series of allegedly corrupt practices by its corporate leadership. As part of its internal investigation, the company posted a slew of internal communications on its Web site. A number of those outlined a scheme in which the company leaders, in a series of e-mails traded back and forth, worked out contribution levels for various Republican congressmen in exchange for "a seat at the table" in an upcoming energy bill.

Essentially, Westar paid $56,000 to get an item inserted in the energy bill exempting their company—and their company alone—from a section of the Public Utility Holding Company Act, also known as PUHCA. The only purpose of the amendment was to make possible a split of the company in such a way that Westar CEO David Wittig would get a $15 million payout. These are the kinds of services congressmen perform in reality, putting them morally somewhere on a level between a Rwandan gorilla poacher and a Bushwick Avenue hooker.

Westar's internal memoranda made it clear that they were buying the influence of those members actually important to the passage and/or back-room rewriting of the bill. One memo from Westar VP Doug Lawrence to executive VP Douglas Lake puts it plainly:

> Right now, we are working on getting our grandfather provision on PUHCA repeal into the senate version of the energy bill. It requires working with the Conference committee to achieve. We have a plan for participation to get a seat at the table, which has been approved by David [Wittig.] The total of the package will be $31,500 in hard money (individual) and $25,000 in soft money (corporate). Right now, we have $11,500 in immediate needs for a group of candidates associated with Tom DeLay, Billy Tauzin, Joe Barton and Senator Richard Shelby.

Lawrence then goes on to explain why the influence of each of these members is needed:

> DeLay is the House Majority Leader. His agreement is necessary before the House Conferees can push the language we have in place in the House bill. Shimkus is a close associate of Billy Tauzin and Joe Barton, who are key House Conferees on our legislation . . .

The Westar story looked like clear proof of a number of felonies, and in any case proved in writing what everyone already knew: Congress was for sale. But in the end the only action taken was a nonbinding censure of DeLay by the Ethics Committee.

Significantly, the committee also rebuked Chris Bell, the freshman congressman from Texas who brought the complaint to the Ethics Committee, for the curious offense of using "inflammatory" language in his complaint. The offending language involved, chiefly, Bell's allegation that DeLay had violated federal bribery laws by taking money from Westar in exchange for favors. Bell, incidentally, would have to leave Congress after losing a primary in the wake of DeLay's infamous Texas redistricting plan.

Westar was ultimately fined about $40,000 by the Federal Election Commission, but the case stopped there. As is often the case with corruption investigations involving Congress, the FEC's Westar investigation was ultimately sealed. Most congressional scandals end not when the investigation is concluded, but when it stalls in perpetuity, with the papers sealed to keep the press from fanning the flames any higher.

With the exception of DeLay, most all the members involved in the Westar affair came off clean. Tauzin, the esteemed congressman from the incorruptible state of Louisiana, fared the best of all. He left Congress to take a $2-million-a-year job heading the nation's leading pharmaceutical lobbying firm, PhRMA, seemingly just hours after shepherding the Bush prescription drug benefit bill into law.

Barton, meanwhile, ascended to the chair of the Energy and Commerce Committee, where he continued, by all appearances, to perform exactly the same role he had in the Westar case—the securing of favors for donors at the crucial way stations of the legislative process. Again, this involved stuffing desired bits into bills in the original committee of jurisdiction, keeping undesired parts out, chaperoning the bill through the Rules Committee, coming through in conference, and so on.

Barton performed ably on most all of these counts with the post-Katrina energy bill. The original plan for the bill included virtually the full energy industry wish list, including the opening of ANWR to drilling, the loosening of regulations to allow offshore drilling in the previously restricted outer continental shelf area (also known as OCS, which includes waters off Florida and Georgia, among other states), the repeal of parts of the Marine Mammal Protection Act (allowing the expansion of oil traffic in Puget Sound), and a long list of other horrors.

Eventually the ANWR and OCS provisions were junked, but Barton did manage to put together a bill in the Energy and Commerce Committee markup that included the extension of Clean Air cleanup deadlines for states located upwind of polluting states, the rewriting of judicial procedures to force litigants opposing the construction of a refinery to pay the legal fees of the refinery proponents, and the designation of new classes of federal property for use in private refinery construction. Deregulation and giveaways, all of it—the currency of American congressional politics.

The bill also included a measure against price gouging, which at the time was a hot-button issue, as gas consumers were being hit hard by opportunistic energy suppliers after the storm. But the Barton price-gouging measure affected only retailers and not suppliers, and the only penalty was a one-time $11,000 fine. In other words, Barton's bill punished the owners of small individual mom-and-pop gas stations for price gouging but specifically exempted the large oil companies from the same offense.

The bill also contained no clear definition of what price gouging was. It had no teeth or meaning. High-sounding meaningless bullshit: the currency of congressional public relations.

Michigan Democrat Bart Stupak, a member of Barton's committee, tried to force language into the bill that would have made oil companies subject to price-gouging regulations, but Barton, again doing his job, managed to keep the Stupak language out.

The resulting bill ended up being so completely irrelevant to its alleged emergency function with regard to Hurricane Katrina that even the habitually degraded minority members of Barton's committee permitted themselves a rare spontaneous public outburst, protesting that the leadership had really gone too far this time. Their frustration resulted in a priceless witness-congressman exchange during the markup process, in which the committee all but admitted that the so-called emergency bill had nothing to do with any emergency.

At the end of the markup process, the members of the committee of jurisdiction are allowed to question the committee counsel about the legal implications of the bill. The majority-picked lawyer essentially testifies to what the law means.

Here, California representative Henry Waxman interrogates Tom DiLenge, Barton's squirrelly committee counsel, about the Gasoline for America's Security Act. Specifically, he is asking about the repeal of the new source review provision of the Clean Air Act.

> WAXMAN: Well, let me ask you specifically. Would it
>   apply to chemical plants?
> DiLENGE: It is a stationary source, yes, sir.
> WAXMAN: Would it apply to large manufacturing plants,
>   iron and steel plants?
> DiLENGE: If emitting the pollutants, yes, sir.
> WAXMAN: Okay. Would this apply to large pulp and
>   paper mills?
> DiLENGE: Yes.
> WAXMAN: Coal-fired power plants?
> DiLENGE: Yes.
> WAXMAN: It seems to me that this would apply to every
>   industrial facility with high pollution levels . . .

Waxman asks about the geographic parameters of the bill, then gets around to asking his main question—what does any of this have to do with either gasoline or the hurricane?

WAXMAN: So this would help a pulp or paper mill
in North Carolina to expand and increase its
air pollution without installing modern control
technology. How does that address the harm done by
Katrina? It wouldn't do that.

DILENGE: Well, I'm not sure that I would characterize the
first part of your sentence that way. What it does is—

WAXMAN: No. Does it affect the harm done by Katrina?

DILENGE (*after a long pause, biting lip*): It . . . does not
exclude the harm done by Katrina.

WAXMAN: It doesn't just affect the—it is not related to
the harm done by Katrina?

DILENGE: That is correct.

WAXMAN: Okay. And how would this provision affect
gasoline prices?

DILENGE: I'm not sure I'm qualified to answer that
question.

This exchange took place just days before Barton carried his bill to the Rules Committee. Nothing came of it, of course; there is no technical knockout system in Congress, under which a bill dies if its proponents happen to admit in public to its being bullshit.

WHEN THE MARKUP PROCESS was finished, Barton trotted to the Rules Committee, stopping in the press lounge on the way to give an impromptu presser about the exciting new energy bill. Have to keep the public informed!

I was there: I was curious to see how he'd handle what would doubtless be rigorous questioning. But alas, most of the questions involved asking Barton why it is that the Democrats were so hung up on state-directed solutions to the gas-supply crisis, to which Barton—seated comfortably, with his legs crossed, in an informal posture on the sofa in the middle of the lounge—replied that he just didn't know how it was that the Democrats still didn't understand the realities of market economics.

The crowd of reporters nodded and jotted down Barton's answer in their notebooks. The House press lounge is a very strange place. Normally, any place where large numbers of reporters congregate can be counted on to be a filthy, paper-strewn human barnyard, full of foul language, discarded pizza crusts, and atrocious hygiene. But the House press lounge has a dress code—every man in a necktie, women in business casual at worst—and decorum is fairly rigidly enforced. One of my first experiences in Congress was a chewing out by a female reporter who caught me in the lounge without a tie on and told me to "have some respect."

"For what?" I'd said.

"For democracy," she hissed.

In any case, this unsmiling crew crowded around Barton now and copied down his gospel. The good chairman made it almost all the way through the press conference without answering a really tough question—until, finally, a *New York Times* reporter hit him with an unfriendly one.

"Chairman Barton," he said, "your opponents say you're just exploiting the hurricane to do what you haven't been able to do in years past. What do you say to that?"

Barton smiled, sighed, then shook his head, waited a moment, and raised an index finger dramatically. "Let me tell y'all something," he said finally, after a long pause. "One thing I'm not . . . is an exploiter!"

I thought he was going to go on from there, but he didn't—that was the answer. He leaned back in his chair and folded his arms triumphantly.

A reporter next to me jotted down in her notes:

One thing not = exploiter

The moment past, Barton smiled and took the next question. Soon after that the press left for the day, and Barton grinned, picked up his briefcase, and crossed the hall to confront the Rules Committee.

THESE DAYS they're in charge, masters of their domain, but back then, the four Democratic members of the Rules Committee were some of the very saddest politicians in Washington, victims of some of the most severe ritualistic political abuse Congress has seen in quite some time. Over the years, the role of the minority party in Congress and in particular this committee has decreased steadily, to the point where the year 2005—this year—would become the first time in congressional history in which no "open" rules would be sent to the floor from the Rules chamber. In layman's terms, this meant that the Rules Committee this year would not send a single rule to the floor that would be freely debated, and the number of Democratic amendments would be smaller than ever. With dictatorial Rules chair David Dreier commanding the committee with iron discipline, the roles of the four Democrats on the committee—Louise Slaughter of New York, Doris Matsui of California, Alcee Hastings of Florida, and Jim McGovern of Massachusetts—would be reduced, quite literally, to bitching and moaning as loudly as possible during those few Rules hearings that would be held during daylight hours. That was the only job the Democrats had that year: whine and bitch with maximum pathos, in the vain hope that someone in the audience might notice exactly how disgusting and irrelevant the legislation being sent to the floor actually was.

"It's basically hopeless," said McGovern. "Basically we don't have much room to do anything, but occasionally, if we're really pathetic, we can shame them into cutting back a little."

McGovern is the House standup comedian. Stocky, bespectacled, and bald, he looks like a veteran character actor, the kind who might play a sitcom hardware store owner, or the cuckolded murder suspect in a *Law and Order* episode. The House is full of amateur comics, but McGovern is one of the Hill's few true masters of the one-liner; this makes him ideally suited for this saddest of congressional jobs. For this reason the city of Worcester, Massachusetts, can be proud of McGovern, who has found more ways to say "You've gotta be fucking kidding me" than any other congressman in the Bush years.

On the day the gasoline bill goes to Rules, all four Democrats are in place right from the start and all four are antsy, tapping pencils against their table places on the left-hand side of the room. I slide into the back row, a few minutes before Barton strolls in to take his seat in the witness chair. None of the reporters from the briefing across the hall in the press lounge a few minutes ago have bothered to come in here. There are three rows of chairs in the gallery, and the crowd looks mostly to be made up of aides to the day's witnesses, who include Barton and a few other members of the Energy and Commerce Committee. As usual, the Rules hearing is strictly an insider deal, no C-SPAN cameras, no reporters, nothing. The lone civilians look to be me and a pair of bloggers.

Dreier, the chairman, is, as usual, not chairing the hearing. Like Charlie in *Charlie's Angels,* the well-dressed Dreier (who in 2004 won the prestigious Roy Cohn Award, given by gay activists to the closeted politician most hostile to gay political interests) tends to play up his scary-villain rep by remaining off camera as much as possible. In his place he usually trots out the committee's resident ballcarrier, Lincoln Diaz-Balart of Florida. A nephew of Fidel Castro and a faithful devotee of the cologne-soaked car-salesman look popular among some southern congressmen, Diaz-Balart is one of the House's all-time blowhards, a guy who before the Republicans took control of the House made a career blasting the Democrats for not allowing open-rule bills to reach the House floor. "You know what the closed rule means," he said, back in 1992. "It means no discussion, no amendments. That is profoundly undemocratic."

That was then. Thirteen years later, Diaz-Balart is presiding over a Rules Committee that no longer allows any open rules, but the lack of democracy doesn't seem to bother him now. Not much does. The Floridian seems happy most of the time, and never happier than when he can kick off a Rules hearing with some good old-fashioned ball-washing:

"I just want to commend Mr. Barton for his continuing hard work on very tough issues and hard work in an important way focused on this issue close to recent national disasters, the refineries in this country," he said as Barton slid into his seat. "I was really shocked [he put his hand over his heart] to see that as we quadrupled our gross domestic product we have not built a single refinery. If that is not an ultimate example of sitting on our superpower laurels, I don't think anything is. We have to address these issues if we are to continue to be the strongest and most dominant economy in the world. And I just . . . I want to commend the chairman for his hard work!"

"Thank you," said Barton.

Diaz-Balart opened the floor for questioning. One by one, the Democrats listed all of the reasons this emergency refinery hurricane bill had nothing to do with gas, refineries, or the hurricane. Slaughter, the Democrat from Buffalo, read Barton a quote from the *Washington Post* noting that the United States has not built a refinery since 1976 and that most oil executives feel the number of refineries needed to be reduced, not increased. She also quoted the chief refining director at the American Petroleum Institute, Edward Murphy, who said that there was no shortage of capacity.

"Do you think that passing the bill will change their minds and they will suddenly want to build refineries?" Slaughter asked. "Or are they going to take the less regulations on Clean Air and run and be happy?"

Barton smiled and twirled a pen in front of him. "Well, I want to reemphasize we are not reducing the environmental requirements on a refinery," he said. Then, seeming inspired to add an additional comment, he straightened up in his chair and clasped his hands in a prayerlike posture.

"I think it is a good thing that we have environmental law," he said piously. "And I think that it is a good thing to enforce it."

A few of the Republicans on the panel chuckled. The Democrats all rolled their eyes. Barton's facial expression was deadpan, his mouth a completely level plane. Environmental law is good. That was a hell of a line, under the circumstances.

McGovern started in next. He returned to the theme of the bill having nothing to do with gas prices or emergency relief and noted that oil companies in America had closed thirty refineries in the past three decades. He also raised a question about a provision of the bill that would allow oil companies to receive public land giveaways—closed military bases from the government that could be handed over in order to build, in theory anyway, new refineries. It was my understanding of the bill that the land transfer could be accomplished by means of a simple decree by the governor of the state in question, and McGovern noted that as well, complaining that "closed military bases could be given to oil companies to build refineries without allowing any public input."

"That's not true," retorted Barton.

"What would be the public input, other than the governor?" McGovern asked.

Barton took a deep breath.

"Well," he said, "on the federal land, the president is against a particular piece of federal property, which could be a military base as a particular. Then you go and you have the open meetings and all of that and you put it out for bid. You solicit requests for an RFP. Then again you know the hope is that by expediting the permitting, by not changing the requirements of the permit, just by expediting the decision-making process that you get enough certainty into the process that the people that have the capital will come forward and want to utilize it."

Everybody in the room looked around, wondering what the hell Barton just said.

"But," Barton added, smiling, "we are not short-circuiting any existing regulatory requirements."

The blogger guy next to me leaned over.

"What the fuck did all that mean?" he asked.

"I'm not sure," I said.

Neither, apparently, was McGovern. "Um," he said, "let me move on to my next question . . ."

One by one, the Democrats whaled away at Barton, and the chairman just stayed cool and deadpan the whole time. The ranking Democrat on Barton's Energy and Commerce Committee, the elderly John Dingell of Michigan, showed up and testified basically that the bill was a bunch of bullshit.

"I had the president of one of the major oil companies in my office," he said, glancing over at Barton, who turned his head away. "I said, 'What do you need to make for more oil refinery construction? To encourage it?' He said, 'Well, we don't really need more refinery construction, and the reason is that we lose money on refineries. The refineries are a necessary thing to get rid of the oil that we produce, but not really useful and valuable for a money-making system.' "

Dingell cleared his throat. "Now that doesn't say anything bad about the oil companies," he said. "But it does tell you that this bill ain't much, and it does tell you that this bill is probably a political exercise."

Barton shrugged at all this.

"I mean, you know, reasonable people can disagree," he said. Then, again smiling suddenly, he added, "I don't really have an answer for you other than, I feel your pain."

Again chuckles from the Republican members. Eyebrows all over the room raised. It took serious balls to joke about pain with putrefied, gas-filled bodies still floating in New Orleans and refugees still spilling out of the Superdome by the thousands.

For a short time the committee room was actually quiet, as if a moment of silence needed to be held in honor of this new low.

"Wow," the blogger whispered.

"Awesome," I agreed.

A moment later McGovern jumped back in, noting that Barton's bill contained a maximum fine for price gouging of $11,000 per day, which of course was meaningless to a billion-dollar oil company but significant to an independent service-station owner. All the bill did was force independent operators to keep their prices low, which you had to figure was really more of a favor to the oil companies than to the customer. Beyond that, it did nothing whatsoever to lower gas prices in the wake of the hurricane or to lower heating-oil prices in the northern states, which were staring at a long winter of shortages.

"In New England we are headed for a cold winter, and people need relief now," McGovern said. "Your bill does nothing that I can see now or in the near future, and that is why it puzzles me why this bill had to be rushed here, why there couldn't have been extensive hearings, and why there couldn't have been more input leading up to this."

Barton shrugged at all this. He shrugged more when there were more complaints from Dingell and Slaughter about the Clean Air rollbacks and the failure of the committee to allow Democratic substitutes and the failure of the bill, in general, to do anything that could be classified as a legislative response to a natural disaster. Finally Barton seemed to get fed up with all of this criticism and took a stand. He noted again that people at the pump in Texas were bugging him about gas prices.

"They say, What are you going to do about this? And I say, We're going to start this process," he said. "And they say, What are you going to do this week? I'm paying fifty dollars twice a week. And I understand that. But in a market economy you've got to start somewhere."

He cleared his throat, smiled slightly at the corners of his mouth, and pressed on.

"You know, there was a famous British scientist named Faraday," he said. "And he was once showing Queen Victoria one of the first electric lamps in Great Britain . . ."

"Where's he going with this?" the blogger whispered.

I shrugged. Barton continued:

"And she looked at it and said, Well, that is a novelty, but of what use is it? And he said, Your Highness, of what use is a newborn baby?"

Barton made an emphatic gesture, half throwing up his hands, as if to say, You feel me? And then he abruptly stopped talking.

The room fell silent; a few gasped.

"Wait," the blogger said. "I missed that."

"It's a newborn baby," I whispered.

"What is?" he asked.

"The bill," I said. "It's a useless piece of shit, but so is a newborn baby."

"Oh." He nodded. "Wow."

"Wow," I agreed.

A few minutes later, Barton folded up his stuff and left the room. Not long after, the hearing adjourned. The Dems waddled out the front door, like a bunch of sad baby ducks without a mother. Diaz-Balart disappeared through a back door, the Republicans following him, to hammer out the final product.

THREE

THE LONGEST THREE DAYS
OF MY LIFE

★ ★ ★ ★ ★ ★ ★ ★ ★ ★ ★ ★

Do you seek to live a "more abundant life"? Are you tired
of dealing with emotions and pain that seem to plague
your daily interactions—especially with those you love?
Are you looking for resolutions to relational issues in your
family?

Through the Government of Twelve Encounter
Weekends conducted by the Ministry of Reconciliation
Department you can find answers to these questions.
The wounds of our past will dictate the quality of our life
today.

—CORNERSTONE CHURCH WEB SITE

I pulled into the church parking lot a little after 6:00 p.m., at
more or less the last possible minute. The previous half hour or
so I'd spent dawdling in my car outside a Goodwill department
store off Route 410, clinging to some inane sports talk show
piping over my car radio—anything to hold off my plunge into
Religion.

But there was no turning back now. Besides, where would I go? Back to Washington? The whole purpose of that exercise had been to see exactly how little our national politicians gave a shit about the People, a group whom I presumably felt sympathy for. That shouldn't change now, despite the fact that I was currently feeling like I'd rather gouge my eyes out than go on to spend a long weekend in Hill Country praying to Jesus with my fellow man. I sighed and pulled myself out of my car.

There was an old-fashioned white school bus in front of the church entrance, with a puddle of heavyset people milling around its swinging door. Some of these were carrying blankets and sleeping bags. My heart, already pounding, skipped a few extra beats.

The church circulars had said nothing about bringing bedding. Why did I need bedding? What else had I missed?

"Excuse me," I said, walking up to an in-charge-looking man with a name tag who was standing near the front of the bus. "I see everyone has blankets. I didn't bring any. Is this going to be a problem?"

The man was about five foot one and had glassy eyes. He looked up at me and smiled queerly.

"Name?" he said.

"Collins," I said. "Matthew Collins."

He scanned his clipboard, found my name on the appropriate sheet of paper, and x-ed me out with a highlighter. "Don't worry, Matthew," he said, resting his hand on my shoulder. "A wonderful woman named Martha is going to take care of you at the ranch. You just tell her what you need when you get there."

I nodded, glancing at his hand, which was still on my shoulder. He waved me into the bus.

I had been attending the church for weeks, but this was really my first day of school. No more fleeting conversations in the church alcove. No more furtive handshakes during the "greet your neighbor" portions of Sunday services. I had signed up for three solid days of sleepaway Christian fellowship in the Texas Hill Country, responding to a series of church advertisements hawking an "Encounter Weekend" whose program was described with an ominous vagueness. The church Web site indicated that those who went away on the Encounters would learn the "joy" of "knowing the truth" and "being set free."

That had sounded harmless enough, but now that I was here and surrounded by all of these blanket-bearing people, I was nervous. For a minute I had visions of some charismatic ranchland Jesus, stoned on beer and the *Caligula* director's cut and too drunk late at night to chase after the minor children, hauling me into a barn for an in-the-hay shortcut to truth and freedom. Ridiculous, of course, but I really was afraid, mostly of my own ignorance and prejudices. I had never been to something like this before, and I didn't know how to act. I badly wanted to be invisible.

The bus was nearly full, and mostly quiet. Here and there a few people sitting together or near each other huddled and chatted, but I could see right away that a great many people on the trip had come alone, like me. They were people of all sorts: younger white men in neat middle-class haircuts, a matronly Mexican woman quietly reading a romance novel, a few scattered weatherbeaten black folk in secondhand clothing whom I pegged right away as in-recovery addicts, a couple of ten-alarm soccer moms who would prove the loudest people on the bus by far, a few quiet older men of military bearing.

The one obvious conclusion anyone making a demographic study of the Cornerstone Church population would come to would be that it's a solidly middle-class crowd. These are folks who are comfortable eating off paper plates and drinking out of gallon jugs of Country Time iced tea over noisy dinners with their kids. They're people who grew up in houses with backyards and fences, people with families. This particular journey to God is not a pastime for the idle rich or the urban obnoxious.

I sat down next to a frankly obese Hispanic woman who was carrying what both looked and smelled like a paper bag full of cheeseburgers. She was frantically looking around in all directions, as though wondering if everyone in the surrounding seats was watching her out of the corner of an eye and waiting for her to open the bag and start eating—which, sadly, they were. I felt sorry for her.

"Hi," I said. "I'm Matt."

"Oh, hello!" she said, shaking my hand. "I'm Maria."

"Some weather we're having, with this rain," I said.

"Tell me about it!" she said. "It truly is an act of God that I even made it here today." She told a story about having to drive down from Austin in bad weather. God had helped her four or five steps along the way. Meanwhile, the older Mexican woman in front of me was talking to a man on the other side of the bus.

". . . and just felt like God was telling me that I had to come here, and . . ."

"It just seems like God really wants me to come on this trip," continued Maria. "Otherwise, I would never have made it."

"It looks like God is going to give us a rainstorm all the way to Tarpley," I heard a voice behind me say.

This oddly uniform style of dialogue ringing all around me made me shift in my seat. I felt nervous and unpleasantly certain that I was about to be found out. When Maria asked me why I'd come on the retreat, I bit my lip. When in Rome, I thought.

"Well," I said, "since the New Year, I've just been feeling like God has been telling me that I need to get right spiritually. So here I am."

I paused, wincing inwardly. An outsider coming into this world will feel sure that the moment he coughs up one of those "God told me to put more English on my tee shot" lines, his dark game will be instantly visible to all and he'll be made the target of one of those *Invasion of the Body Snatchers*–style point-and-screech mob scenes. But nothing could be further from the truth. You simply cannot go wrong praising God in this world; overdoing it is literally impossible. I would understand this better by the end of the weekend.

Maria smiled. "I feel the same way. Have you ever been to one of these Encounters?"

"No, I haven't," I said.

"Me neither," she said. "I'm really excited."

"They're wonderful," said the matronly Mexican woman in front of me, turning around. "They really change you forever."

Clipboard Man now stood up at the front of the bus and made a number of announcements, then asked us to gather together and pray before our departure. "Lord God, we ask you to bless this bus, and to bless this journey, Lord God, so that we might arrive at the ranch safely . . ."

We all hung our heads and asked God to bless the bus. When we were done, the driver swung the door shut and we moved out onto the highway.

I SLUNK IN MY SEAT, trying to look inconspicuous. My disguise was modeled on other men I'd seen in church—pane glasses and the very gayest blue-and-white-striped Gap polo shirt I'd been able to find that afternoon. Buried on a clearance rack next to the underwear section in a nearby mall, the Gap shirt was one of those irritating throwbacks to the *Meatballs/*seventies-summer-camp-geek look, but stripped of its sartorial irony it really just screamed Friendless Loser!—so I bought it without hesitation and tried to match it with that sheepish, ashamed-to-have-a-penis look I had seen so many other young men wearing in church. With the glasses and a slouch I hoped

I was at least in the ballpark of what I thought I needed to look like, which was a slow-moving hulk of confused, shipwrecked masculinity, flailing for an Answer.

One of the implicit promises of the church is that following its program will restore to you your vigor, confidence, and assertiveness, effecting, among other things, a marked and obvious physical transformation from crippled lost soul to hearty vessel of God. That's one of the reasons that it's so important for the pastors to look healthy, lusty, and lustrous—they're appearing as the "after" photo in the ongoing advertisement for the church wellness cure.

In these southern churches there are few wizened old sages such as one might find among Catholic bishops or Russian *startsi*. Here your church leader is an athlete, a business dynamo, a champion eater with a bull's belly, outwardly a tireless heterosexual—and if you want to know what a church beginner is supposed to look like, just make it the opposite of that. Show weakness, financial trouble, frustration with the opposite sex, and if you're overweight, be so unhealthily, and in a way that you're ashamed of. The fundamentalist formula is much less a journey from folly to wisdom than it is from weakness to strength. They don't want a near-complete personality that needs fine-tuning—they want a human jellyfish, raw clay they can transform into a vigorous instrument of God.

Trying to be exactly that—the jellyfish, that is—I slumped in my seat and buried my face behind a copy of *Tribulation Force*, the second book in the Left Behind series. For some time I sat there wondering about the names in the book—half of them are either building terms or elements (Steele, Plank, Barnes, Jetty, Stonagal) or derivatives of southern city names (Hattie Durham). Were these books written in a Home Depot in North Carolina?

Across the aisle and a few rows back, a man about my age, also wearing glasses and also slumped in his seat, read from a

book called *They Shall Expel Demons*. Maria, meanwh[...]
etly munched her cheeseburgers, glancing sideways occa[...]
ally, trying not to look self-conscious.

"I WAS VERY, VERY, VERY GOOD—at everything!" shouted our hulking ex-paratrooper pastor, Phillip Fortenberry, into the barely visible mouth mic that curled around his ruddy face. "I was a Green Beret—top of the class. Six foot four, two hundred and twenty-five pounds. A star athlete, basketball player. Starting outside linebacker on the varsity football team . . ."

The crowd cooed as our spiritual leader rattled off his macho credentials. Our supercowboy pastor was the perfect foil for the *Revenge of the Nerds*–style crowd of fatties, addicts, loners, and broken-home survivors populating the warehouse-sized building where we were all destined to spend the next three days together.

Bearing a striking resemblance to ex–Vikings quarterback and notorious ESPN loudmouth Sean Salisbury, Fortenberry had bounded onstage upon our arrival in a plaid western-style shirt and crisp, belt-tightened rancher's blue jeans hiked up to an uncomfortable height on the strapping hard fat of his middle-aged trunk. He did everything but tape-measure his biceps in his introductory speech. His autobiographical tale of an angry overachieving youth who fell into a young adulthood of false pride, only to rebound and be reborn as a turbocharged, army-trained enemy of Satan ("A friend of mine once joked that he saw my picture hung up in a post office in Hell," he quipped) with no fewer than two graduate agronomy degrees from Texas A&M, was to serve as the first chapter of our collective transformation—and to work it had to impress the hell out of us scraggly wannabes.

It did. "I'm going to start tonight by telling y'all two stories," he began.

The first was a story from his army days, about having to take a training flight in the Pacific Northwest as a young man and being trapped in the back of the transport plane when the landing went wrong and the plane ended up crash-bouncing along the runway.

Fortenberry told stories well, but he lingered for quite some time on a loving description of the interior of a C-130, which I thought at first was a rhetorical mistake—until I saw both the men and the women glowing with excitement as he recalled the plane's unusual flush-against-the-fuselage seating arrangement.

"If you've ever been in the back of a C-130, you know what I mean," he said, and I saw nodding heads all through the audience. The pastor subsequently would not miss a single chance to drop the name of a piece of military equipment.

The second story was more personal. It was about being a little boy in a small southern town whose father ran around on his mom with a local barmaid. Dad used to bring little Junior to play golf with him, keeping his arm around the barmaid in the golf cart for the entire eighteen holes; finally Dad left Mom to shack up with the barmaid in a house down the road. Dad was so busy with the barmaid that he never came to see Junior's ball games. But from time to time he would come home to Mom, moving back into Junior's world, turning his life upside down.

"And every time he came back," the pastor said, waving his hand up and down, his voice fairly breaking with tears, "it was like one more bounce along that runway, bouncing in that C-130, tearing my little boy's world apart."

The pastor fell silent, still using his hands to demonstrate that bouncing transport plane of fate, as he surveyed his hushed audience. Fortenberry then stood staring at his audience in full preweep, his eyes wrinkling with incipient tears. The grown macho man unashamedly breaking into boyish tears in public is one of the weirder features of the post–Promise Keeper Christian generation, and Fortenberry—himself a Promise Keeper, incidentally—had it down to a science.

"You never came to my ball games, Dad . . . ," he'd screech, his face wrinkling like a raisin with grief at the words "ball games."

I heard sniffles coming from the audience.

Sensing he had his crowd in an emotionally vulnerable state, the pastor then plunged into a story about how his bitterness at his father's abandonment had pushed him, in high school, to become just about the best basketball player you could imagine. Young Fortenberry, we learned, had scored lots and lots of points in high school and had many great games. How great were those games? Well, he told us, they were really great. Some of the stories wandered irrelevantly into the specific stats of some of those games; he also punctuated his storytelling with oddly vigorous and adept pantomimes of jumpers and hook shots. It was a weird scene, like listening to a married man wax poetic to a mistress in a roadside motel room.

"But after a while I realized that all those thousands of jump shots"—here he mimicked a jump shot—"and all those thousands of moves"—he ducked his head back and forth Tim Hardaway style—"hadn't brought me any closer to Dad."

Fortenberry was a goofball, but the whole setup, I quickly realized, was designed to follow the same mythology as army boot camp. You show up out of shape and with bad hair and your shirt untucked and find yourself mesmerized by a drill sergeant with a Euclidian crewcut and a rock-hard stomach who's older than your dad's dad but can do ten times as many pushups as you can. The front door to a system that transforms the very flesh on your body.

It wasn't just Fortenberry's Green Beret background that brought home that sensation. Upon arrival at the ranch we'd been asked to dump our bags in a barracks up the road from the main building. There were four dormitories—two each for the men and the women, with separate quarters for the guests and the "life coach" volunteers of each gender. The barracks themselves featured two long rows of bunk beds set against a glistening red floor that almost exactly recalled the set of *Full Metal Jacket*.

After dumping our bags we were all quickly herded back into the main building, which had a stage and an ad-hoc place of worship (complete with a dozen or so rows of folding chairs) at one end and a set of cafeteria tables at the other. A nest of life coaches buzzed around the building entrance, flashing beatific smiles, checking lists of names and handing out stick-on name tags to each of the arriving guests. En route to our seats at the "chapel" we Encounterers had also passed a table where another volunteer hawked a strange selection of goods: Snickers bars and other assorted snacks and sodas (flat rate of a buck apiece), copies of that same *They Shall Expel Demons* book, and small vials of Exodus brand anointing oil.

"How much for the anointing oil?" I'd asked, smoothing out the MATTHEW COLLINS name tag on my shirt.

"Six dollars," answered a fortyish man with a too-happy smile.

"I'll take some," I said, pulling out my wallet.

He handed it over. "It's really good anointing oil," he said. "You can read all about it in Acts."

I wondered what separated good anointing oil from bad anointing oil. Then I found myself a folding chair in the "chapel" and opened up the binder full of materials we'd been handed at the building entrance, glancing here and there as Fortenberry went into his speech. The cover of the binder was marked RELATIONSHIP SEQUENCE DIAGRAM and the binder contained a weirdly complex flow chart full of circles and arrows that I gathered offered a kind of road map to spiritual regeneration.

The program revolved around a theory that Fortenberry

quickly introduced us to called "the wound." The wound theory was a piece of schlock biblical Freudianism in which everyone had one traumatic event from their childhood that had left a wound. The wound necessarily had been inflicted by another person, and bitterness toward that person had corrupted our spirits and alienated us from God. Here at the retreat we would identify this wound and learn to confront and forgive our transgressors, a process that would leave us cleansed of bitterness and hatred and free to receive the full benefits of Christ.

In the context of the wound theory, Fortenberry's tale suddenly made more sense. Being taken on that eighteen-hole golf trip with the barmaid, and watching his family ditched by Dad, had been his wound. It was a wound, Fortenberry explained, because his father's abandonment had crushed his "normal."

"And I was wounded," he whispered dramatically. "My dad had ruined my normal!"

The crowd murmured affirmatively, apparently knowing what it was to have a crushed normal.

Fortenberry went on, wantonly spinning psychological metaphors in his rhetorical wake. "You know our soldiers in Iraq—one of them occasionally gets hit by friendly fire," he said. "Say you're one of those soldiers and you get hit in the leg. You look down and you quickly determine that there's no arterial breach and no broken bone."

The crowd murmured again; the phrase "arterial breach" had been a hit.

"It's one of those things where you either keep on going or you lay down and die. So what do you do? You put some gauze on it."

Within a few minutes we had wandered into a world where your "gauze" was some temporary psychological solution you applied to your "wound" after your "normal" was disrupted. Fortenberry took this set of metaphors and ran with them straight for the hyperbolic end zone, talking about situations when you might add more gauze, or change your gauze, or find out that your gauze was infected—I couldn't keep them straight after a while. And I wasn't alone. Within a day a youngish woman during a question-and-answer period raised her hand.

"Yes?" the pastor said. "You in the front."

"I guess my question is," said the girl, "like when you have a wound, and you put some gauze on it, and then years later you take it off, and it's sort of half healed—I mean, what is that? Is that like a scar?"

Fortenberry was absolutely stumped by that question, and I didn't blame him. In any case, after introducing us to the concept of wounds and normals and gauze, Fortenberry told us one last cautionary tale before sending us to our first group session.

It was about a paratrooper who had done a tandem jump with a training dummy for some army exercise or other, only to have the dummy's chute fail to open. The dummy had plunged to the ground, crashing through the trees and landing with a thud in a bush. Fortenberry's army buddy had taken advantage of the situation to have a little joke at the expense of some other exercising soldiers on the ground who weren't privy to the fact that the troopers were jumping with dummies. The army buddy had cried and wailed in asking where the "body" had fallen, leaving the soldiers on the ground to think that someone had just been killed.

"My buddy's not saved. He made a good joke of it," Fortenberry explained. Then he quickly turned serious and explained that the soldiers on the ground had felt guilty because they'd failed to help what they thought was a fallen comrade. Why? Because they'd been afraid to look behind the bush.

"So I'm telling you now, as you go into your groups," the pastor explained, "don't be afraid to look behind the bush."

I wrote in my binder: LOOK BEHIND THE BUSH. Then I waited as my name was called out for group study.

• • •

THE GROUPS WERE SEGREGATED. Men with men, women with women. Each group was led by a life coach, who was actually a recent graduate of the program. At the beginning of the group stage the coaches were all called up to the front of the chapel, and Fortenberry would call out the coach's name first, then the names of his group members. The male coaches almost to a man had bushy mustaches of the state-trooper/Pontiac-dealer genus.

My coach's name was Morgan. Morgan was a big man, ex-military, with curly black hair, a black mustache, and a softening middle. He looked a little like a post-rehab version of Keith Hernandez—soft-spoken, deferential, all nose and mustache. Morgan had originally come on the Encounter Weekend at the behest of his wife, who apparently was a coach long before he was.

There were four other men in our group. Besides myself, there was Jose, a huge Mexican with a sheepish expression and a steam-boiler body; Aaron, a squat and alert Pennsylvanian with a clean-and-jerker's build; and Dennis, a somewhat vacant and medicated-looking man pushing forty with a bald head and stubbly beard. Dennis looked like a distantly menacing version of Homer Simpson after electroshock therapy. Seated just a few feet away from us in our tight circle, he gazed out at us like he could barely make out our faces. I was worried about him from the start.

Once Morgan had us all gathered together, we looked for table space in the cafeteria area of the main building. Ominously, each of the cafeteria tables had a fresh box of Kleenex resting on top of it.

"Well," Morgan said, "I think what we're going to do, to start, is this. I'm going to tell you my story about my wound, and then we're going to go around in a circle and each of us is going to just tell his story. Is that okay?"

Everyone nodded. I noted with displeasure that I was seated first after Morgan in clockwise order. Already I was panicking; what kind of wound could a human cipher like myself possibly confess to?

Morgan told his story. I was so nervous that I could barely listen, but from what I could make out, he was not doing so well with the group. Even a perfunctory look at my fellow group members told me that we had people here with some very serious problems, and yet Morgan's wound was a tale that wouldn't have even ruined a week of my relatively privileged childhood, much less my whole life—something about being yelled at by his dad while he was out playing with remote-controlled airplanes with his friends as a thirteen-year-old. He hammed up his trauma over the incident in classically lachrymose Iron-John-in-touch-with-his-inner-boy fashion (again, there is something very odd about modern Christian men—although fiercely pro-military in their politics and prehistorically macho in their attitudes toward women's roles, on the level of day-to-day behavior they seem constantly ready to break out weeping like menopausal housewives), but his words were bouncing off a wall of unimpressed silence radiating from the group.

"Anyway," he said, "that's my story. Does anyone have any questions?"

Blank stares. This was a tough crowd. To buy time, I asked, "Did you ever talk to your dad about that incident?"

He said he hadn't, then said something about never really making up with his father. Five minutes into our group acquaintance, we were at a full 9.5 out of 10 on the International Uncomfortable Silence scale.

Morgan turned, glanced again at my name tag, and sighed.

"Well, uh, okay, then," he said. "Matthew, do you want to tell your story?"

My heart was pounding. I obviously couldn't use my real past—not only would it threaten my cover, but I was somewhat reluctant to expose anything like my real inner self to this ideologically unsettling process—but neither did I want to be trapped in a story too far from my own experience. What I settled on eventually was something that I thought was metaphorically similar to the truth about myself.

"Hello," I said, taking a deep breath. "My name is Matt. My father was an alcoholic circus clown who used to beat me with his oversized shoes."

The group twittered noticeably. Morgan's eyes opened to tea-saucer size. I closed my own eyes and kept going, immediately realizing what a mistake I'd made. There was no way this story was going to fly. But there was no turning back.

"He'd be sitting there in his costume, sucking down a beer and watching television," I heard myself saying. "And then sometimes, even if I just walked in front of the TV, he'd pull off one of those big shoes and just, you know—whap!"

I looked around the table and saw three flatlined, plainly indifferent psyches plus one mildly unnerved Morgan staring back at me. I could tell that my coach and former soldier had been briefly possessed by the fear that a terrible joke was being played on his group. But then I actually saw him dismissing the thought—after all, who would do such a thing?

This one fleeting error of judgment would leave me shackled to a rank character absurdity for the rest of my stay in Texas. Less than twenty-four hours later I would find myself reading aloud a passage from my "autobiography" describing a period of my father's life when he quit clowning to hand out fliers in a Fudgie the Whale costume outside a Carvel ice cream store:

> I laugh about it now, but once he chased me, drunk, in his
> Fudgie the Whale costume. He chased me into the bath-

room, laid me across the toilet seat, and hit me with his
fins, which underneath were still a man's hands.

Again no reaction from the group, aside from an affirming nod
from Jose at the last part—his eyes said to me, I know what you
mean about those fins.

Anyway, on that first day I eventually tied up my confession with a tale about turning into a drug addict in my mid-
twenties—at least that much was true—and being startled
into sobriety and religion after learning of my estranged clown
father's passing from cirrhosis.

It was a testament to how dysfunctional the group was that
my story flew more or less without comment. Our group completely lacked chemistry. No one person in it had a natural af-
finity for any of the others.

Jose, the big Mexican, was a sensitive guy with a temper
problem and a history of drug use who was trying to make
his marriage work after a rough childhood that involved some
pretty serious parental neglect. Joe, the white suburban son of
a badgering, emotionally unavailable mother—he'd put the
dishes away in one place, and Mom would tell him that he was
supposed to put them somewhere else—was struggling himself
with being emotionally unavailable in his relationships.

Dennis claimed that he had recently been made aware of recovered memories of some truly horrific childhood experiences.
He spoke to us through a whisper, through a haze of psychiatric
meds, and when he was finished with the group work drifted
right back to his deeply concerned-looking wife, who was with
her own group somewhere else in the building.

I got the strong sense that Dennis was panic shopping for
psychological miracle cures and that this had not been his first
stop. He looked like a man who had already reconciled himself

to suicide and was here only as a last favor to someone, probably his wife. Everyone in the group seemed afraid of him.

There was no bringing us together. An ethnic barrier separated Jose from the group; I was a fraud; Aaron didn't really have serious problems and was really too "normal" for the rest; and Dennis was painfully adrift from all humanity, not just us. The group's dysfunctionality was hammered home at the end of our first meeting.

When each person had finished telling his tale, Morgan tried to ask a few perfunctory questions ("So when your father called you names, Matt, how did that make you feel?") and then move on to the next person.

But some of us—Jose and me in particular, at first—tried to get into a little more detail, to show that we were at least listening. For instance, when Dennis told his story, we each asked him about his hospitalization, what kind of therapy he'd been in, what medications he was on. Our coach, meanwhile, seemed to be staring ahead with his eyes glazed over even through Dennis's Dickensian tragedy.

But when Dennis finished and Aaron casually mentioned that he had come to Texas to hunt, Morgan snapped awake.

"Really?" he said. "You hunt?"

"Yes."

"Wow, I love hunting," Morgan said. "What'd you get?"

Aaron shrugged. "Well, I got a coupla black bucks. A ram—"

Morgan nearly jumped out his chair. "Really? A ram? Where did you get a ram?"

They went on like this for a while. Meanwhile, Dennis, minutes removed from his terrible confession, looked directly down at his lap, picking at a scar on his arm. Aaron glanced sideways at him nervously.

• • •

SO IT BEGAN. Our meetings were a prolonged, cyclical course of group-directed confession and healing that began on Friday evening and continued almost without interruption through Sunday afternoon. The basic gist of our group exercises was this: we were each supposed to reveal to one another what our great childhood wounds were, then write a series of essays and letters on the wound theme, taking time after the writing of each to read our work to one another. The written assignments began with an autobiography, then moved on to a letter written to our "offenders" (i.e., those who had caused our wounds), then a letter written to Jesus confessing our failure to forgive our tormentors, and so on.

After each of these grueling exercises we would first have lengthy, fifteen- to twenty-minute sessions singing unbearably atonal Christian hymns. Then we would have teaching/Bible-study sessions led by Fortenberry on the theme of the moment (e.g., "Admitting the Truth About Our Wounds") that lasted an hour or more. Then, after Fortenberry would waste at least half the session giving us the Marlboro Man highlights of his professional résumé ("I was the manager of the second largest ranch in America, eight hundred and twenty-five thousand acres . . .") and bragging about his physical prowess ("If someone was to slug me, I could whip just about anyone here"), we would go back to the group session and confess some more. Then we would sing some more, receive more of Fortenberry's hairy lessons, and then the cycle would start all over again. There were almost no breaks or interruptions; it was a physically exhausting schedule of confession, catharsis, bad music, and relentless muscular instruction. The Saturday program began at 7:45 a.m. and did not end until ten at night; we went around the confess-sing-learn cycle five full times in one day.

• • •

WE WERE ABOUT a third of the way through the process when I began to wonder what the hell was going on. The retreat's Relationship Sequence Diagram redemption strategy and Fortenberry's blowhard-on-crack-act/wound gobbledygook were all suspiciously secular in tone and approach. I had been hearing whispers throughout the first day or so to the effect that there was some kind of incredible supernatural religious ceremony that was going to take place at the end of the retreat ("Tighten your saddle, he's fixin' ta buck" was how "cowboy" Fortenberry put it), when we would experience "Victory and Deliverance." But as far as I could see, in the early going, most of what we were doing was simple pop-psych self-examination using New Agey diagnostic tools of the Deepak Chopra school—identify your problems, face your oppressors, visualize your obstacles. Be your dream job. With a little rhetorical tweaking and much better food, this could easily have been Tony Robbins instructing a bunch of Upper East Side housewives to "find your wounds" ("My husband hid my Saks card!") in a commune in Miami Beach or the Hamptons.

True, I could see some other angles to what was going on as well. Virtually all of the participants of the Encounter identified either one or both of their parents as their "offender," and much of what Fortenberry was talking about in his instructional sessions was how to replace the godless atmosphere of abuse or neglect that the offenders had provided us with God and the church. He was taking broken people and giving them a road map to a new set of parents, a new family—your basic cultist bait-and-switch formula for cutting old emotional ties and redirecting that psychic energy toward the desired new destination. That connection would become more overt later in the weekend, but early on, this ur-father propaganda was the only thing I could see that separated Encounter Weekend from the typical self-help dreck of the secular world.

But then, midway through Saturday, Fortenberry and the coaches started to show us glimpses of the program's end game. The wound, it turned out, was something that was inflicted upon us because of a curse, a curse that perhaps spanned generations in each of our families. Alcoholic parents abused their children, who in turn carried their parents' curse to their adult lives and became alcoholics themselves—only to have children and continue the pattern again. Now, why was that curse there to begin with? Here was where we could get into religious explanations, see the footprint of Satan, etc. We were unhappy because of earthly troubles from our childhoods, but those troubles were the work of a generational curse, inflicted upon us by devils and demons—probably for unbelief, bad behavior, disobedience, worship of the wrong gods, and so on.

This little bit of semantic gymnastics helped transform all of us at the retreat from being merely fucked-up to being accursed carriers of demons. Having ridden an almost entirely secular program to get our biographies out in the open in a group setting, Fortenberry could now switch his focus to the real meat and potatoes of the weekend—Satan and the devils inside us.

He started off slowly, invoking the godly curses of Genesis—the sweat on Adam's brow, the pain of Eve's childbirth, etc.—the punishments for eating of the tree of the knowledge of Good and Evil. "How many of you women out there have had babies?" Fortenberry asked. "Can I see some hands?"

A dozen or so hands were raised.

"Now, did it hurt?" he asked.

Laughter. Of course it hurt.

"Let me ask you a question," he said. "Why do alcoholics give birth to alcoholics? Why do the fatherless give birth to the fatherless?" He paused. "There are some people out there who will tell you it's genetics. It's in our genes, they say. Well, I tell you, it's not genetics. It's a generational curse!"

Fortenberry then started in on a rant against science and

against scientific explanations for cycles of sin. "Take homo-sexuals," he said. "Every single homosexual is a sexual-abuse victim. They are not born. They are created—by pedophiles."

The crowd swallowed that one whole. One thing about this world; once a preacher says it, it's true. No one is going to look up anything the preacher says, cross-check his facts, raise an eyebrow at something that might sound a little off. Some weeks later, I would be at a Sunday service in which Pastor John Ha-gee himself would cite former FBI agent Paul L. Williams in claiming that Al-Qaeda was in possession of nuclear bombs and planning on exploding them in seven American cities in the year 2007. Hagee neglected to mention that Williams orig-inally predicted that those bombs would go off on the precise date of August 6, 2005. When they're away from the cameras, the preachers feel even less obligated to shackle themselves to facts of any kind. That's because they know that their audience doesn't give a shit. So long as you're telling them what they want to hear, there's no danger; your crowd will angrily dismiss any alternative explanations anyway as demonic subversion.

A team of twenty of the world's leading scientists wouldn't be able to convince so much as one person in this crowd that homosexuals are not created by pedophiles.

But what created the original pedophilia? What brought such foul curses down on the houses of us poor Christians? Fortenberry rattled off a list of reasons. They included: denying the word of God, "sexual sins, especially incest," the breaking of convenants, bestiality, violence, failing to reconcile with parents or children, dishonoring parents, etc. Then he started talking about even stranger things—like having pictures of dead people in the house, "witchcraft-type stuff," as he put it.

"You're either blessed because you're obedient or cursed be-cause you're disobedient," he said.

At this, he told a story about a nephew of his who called him up with a problem one night. This nephew had figured into other stories during the weekend—like Fortenberry himself, he was supposedly a physically imposing guy, "three hundred pounds, easy," and a bold preacher of the word of God.

"He's something," the pastor said. "He went to an antiwar rally in Washington, D.C., once and asked them antiwar protesters"—the words fell out of his mouth like dead snails—"he asked them, 'Hey, can anyone speak here?' And they said yes, and he got up with a megaphone and started tellin' them about the gospel."

This story elicited raucous applause. I could feel the crowd's collective blood rising at the mere mention of antiwar protesters. Weirdly, I actually forgot for a moment that I was one and had probably been at that Washington protest.

Anyway, this same nephew had called up Fortenberry one night and told him that he was having trouble with his kids. Apparently they had had some problems with disobedience, and Fortenberry's nephew had been wondering what it was his kids had done to separate themselves from God. But he hadn't taken the step of calling big Phil Fortenberry for help until one terrible day when things took a dramatic turn for the worse.

"Both of his kids had fallen on the ground in respiratory distress, half-conscious, writhing around, gasping for air," Fortenberry said. "And I said to my nephew, I said, it isn't something they've done. It's something you've done."

The crowd murmured in assent.

"I told my nephew to look around the house," Fortenberry continued. "I said, 'Do you have a copy of *Harry Potter*?' And he said yes. And I said, 'That's your problem.' So I told him to go get that copy of that book, tear it in half, and throw it out the window. So he does it, and guess what? Both of those kids stood up completely recovered, just like that."

He snapped his fingers, indicating the speed with which the kids had jumped up in recovery. The crowd cooed and applauded. I frowned, wondering for a minute what life must be like for a person mortally afraid of toothless commercial fairy tales. It struck me that Phil Fortenberry's nephew was probably more afraid of Harry Potter than of Macbeth, which to me said a lot about this religion and about America in general.

During a break in these lessons about curses and demons, a pair of youngish women came and sat at my end of the chapel. One was a heavyset blonde in her late thirties/early forties with a broad smile and a warm, inviting face who looked like she might have been a grand Texas dame in her youth. The other was a thin, somewhat nervous-looking woman in her early thirties with sad eyes and freckles who looked a little like a pale, depressed version of Joan Allen.

"Hi," said the blonde. "Can I ask, did you come here by yourself?"

I smiled. "Yes," I said.

"Oh, good," she said. "So did my friend Janine here. So y'all should get along real good."

She indicated the thin girl, who blushed. It was a very forward setup, and I was momentarily embarrassed, but at the same time I was beginning to despair of making any friends at the retreat and was relieved to meet some friendly people. I smiled, recalling Fortenberry's words: Don't be afraid to look behind the bush. I shook Janine's hand, and we all introduced ourselves. The blonde's name was Laurie.

Laurie was a piece of work. She had a great sense of humor and was absolutely uninhibited. I would later find out that she was a terribly lonely woman who had recently been the victim of some extremely malicious gossip at the hands of other church members. But at the moment she was a real breath of fresh air to me—a genuinely friendly person reaching out to someone sitting quite conspicuously by himself.

"We were looking around the room and wondering if there

were any men here, and then I saw you and I was like, 'Look at that one,'" she said, holding up a hand and making the r-r-r-r purring-cat-claw gesture.

"Um," I said.

"I said to myself, 'He looks like Tom Selleck, he does.'"

I laughed. I couldn't possibly look less like Tom Selleck.

"Who's Tom Selleck?" said Janine.

We all ended up eating together during meals for the rest of the weekend and became fast friends. Laurie was a joke-a-minute entertainer. In our very first meal together, she told a surprisingly bawdy joke about an elderly couple who strip down naked, getting ready to have sex. Just before they jump into bed, the wife stops her husband. "I should warn you," she says. "I have acute angina."

"Thank God for that," the husband says. "Because your tits look like hell."

At this, Janine covered her ears.

"I've got another one," said Laurie. "This guy goes to a doctor—"

"I can't hear this," said Janine, standing up. "I promised myself I would be pure."

"Oh, honey," said Laurie.

"No, I mean it." And Janine walked away.

They asked me about my past. I told them a story that was in the ballpark of the truth, that I'd been married to a Thai woman who'd recently left me (actually I still had a Thai girlfriend). Appropriately enough, we'd just finished hearing a sermon from Fortenberry about King Solomon and how he took foreign wives from among the Perizzites, the Jebusites, the Ammonites, the Moabites, etc. "It's just like that story about King Solomon," I said. "He took foreign wives and they led him away from God. It was the same with me."

"You were unequally yoked," said Janine, who was recently

divorced and still in obvious distress because of it. "I know how that is."

"Wait," said Laurie. "Which story about King Solomon? I missed that."

"Oh, you know, honey," said Janine. "The one with all them ites."

"Oh, right," said Laurie.

"My wife was like that," I said. "I came home one day, and she was wearing a beret and had her bags packed. And she says to me, 'I want to go to Paris! I want to ride the Bateau-Mouche!' Like I'd been stopping her."

"What's the b-b-b . . . ," began Laurie.

"The Bateau-Mouche," I said. "It's some kind of French riverboat. People eat lunch on it and stuff."

"And she thought you were tying her down? Keeping her from that?" asked Laurie.

"Exactly," I said.

"Well, that's awful. She sounds like a confused person," Laurie said supportively.

"That she is," I said. "But I keep telling her, God still loves her."

"The funny thing," Laurie said, "is that you kind of look French."

I nearly spit up my unsweetened iced tea. The curse of John Kerry! The sad thing is, I knew what she meant. Christians have a certain look, and I don't have it. The more "French" you look, the less Christian you probably are.

They started talking about the Victory and Deliverance that was coming up the next day. I was still unclear about what this was, although I understood that it had something to do with casting out demons. Laurie, for one, was very excited about the whole thing.

"I'm really looking forward to it," she said, slapping one of her ample thighs. "I'm hoping to lose about forty pounds' worth of demons."

"Hey, that's true," said a man at our table. "They must weigh something, right?"

"Well, I hope so," said Laurie seriously.

"I think there's something to that," I said. "A new fitness program. Dematrim."

There was an uncomfortable pause at the table; my joke was not completely appropriate. But Laurie came to my rescue.

"Dematrim, I like that," Laurie said coolly. "I could use some."

But by that evening, Laurie was a little bit chastened. "You know all them jokes I been making about myself?" she said, looking troubled as she dropped her heaping tray of public-school-style spaghetti on the cafeteria table.

"Yes?" I asked.

"Well, my life coach tells me that's bad. She says it's like a curse. I'm bringing a curse upon myself with all of that self-defecating humor."

"I think you mean self-deprecating," said one of the other men at the table.

"Oh, goodness, yes," she said. "Self-defecating would be something else, wouldn't it, sweetie pie? Anyway, they say it's bad."

"That's really a shame," I said. "I didn't know that."

"Well, it's true. And I don't want any more curses."

"Me either," I said.

HERE I HAVE a confession to make. It's not something that's easy to explain, but here goes. After two days of nearly constant religious instruction, songs, worship, and praise—two days that for me meant an unending regimen of forced and fake responses—a funny thing started to happen to my head. There is a transformational quality in these external demonstrations of faith and belief. The more you shout out praising the Lord, singing along to those awful acoustic tunes, telling people how blessed you feel, and so on, the more a sort of mechanical Christian skin starts to grow all over your real self. Even if you're a degenerate *Rolling Stone* reporter inwardly chuckling and busting on the whole scene—even if you're intellectually enraged by the ignorance and arrogant prejudice flowing from the mouth of a terminal ambition case like Phil Fortenberry—outwardly you're swaying to the gospel and singing and praising and acting the part, and those outward ministrations assume a kind of sincerity in themselves. And at the same time, that "inner you" begins to get tired of the whole spectacle and sometimes forgets to protest—in my case checking out into baseball reveries and other daydreams while the outer me did the "work" of singing and praising. At any given moment, which one is the real you?

You may think you know the answer, but by my third day I began to notice how effortlessly my soft-spoken Matt-mannequin was going through his robotic motions of praise, and I was shocked. For a brief, fleeting moment I could see how under different circumstances it would be easy enough to bury your "sinful" self far under the skin of your outer Christian and to just travel through life this way. So long as you go through all the motions, no one will care who you really are underneath. And besides, so long as you are going through all the motions, never breaking the facade, who are you really? It was an incomplete thought, but it was a scary one; it was the very first time I worried that the experience of entering this world might prove to be anything more than an unusually tiring assignment. I feared for my normal.

I had these thoughts on the morning of our third day at the retreat. There was a buzz in the air all through the campus. It was the buzz of a Christmas morning, or a Super Bowl Sunday—something big about to happen. I saw Laurie and Janine at breakfast.

"You excited, honey?" Laurie asked.

"You know it," I said. "I'm ready for some healing."

"Oh, me too, sweetie," she said. "It's funny, last night I had a little bit of an upset stomach. I didn't understand what it was, but then my coach was telling me—it was the demons, they don't want to come out. So they were raising trouble."

"I see," I said.

Janine, solemn-faced, nodded, as if to say, It's true, they were.

After breakfast I ran into Aaron. I'd gathered from a few fleeting conversations with him outside the sessions that he had high hopes for this retreat; I think he had struggled with his temper and his relationships at home and he was really hoping to find something that could exorcise the anger and bitterness inside him. And the more he heard in classes, the more he liked. "It's so great," he said. "Some programs and churches, they give you little parts of the Bible, but this is the only one that just gives you the whole thing. It's just so obvious—why wouldn't you want this?"

"I totally agree with you," I'd said.

Now it was the morning of the Deliverance, and Aaron had an expectant look on his face. He looked like a man who had been up late dreaming of some kind of release and who was going to be very disappointed if he did not feel actual demons leaving his body.

"You ready for this?" he asked.

"You bet," I said.

"Yeah, well, I hope it works," he said, and walked off.

Finally we gathered in the chapel for the Deliverance. Fortenberry, dressed in his standard western shirt and hiked-up jeans—his jeans might have been a little tighter this morning—sauntered up to the lectern wearing a solemn and dramatic expression. "Someone told me this morning, 'Phil, you've got your game face on,'" he said, and I agreed with him—although I might have had a different read about what kind of game he was preparing for.

"This is fixing to be the biggest spiritual battle that ninety-nine percent of you will ever face," he said. "But let me tell you something. It's already been won. It was won two thousand years ago."

The crowd cheered. As the applause tailed, he held his hands up Mussolini-fashion, asking for quiet. The crowd complied. It was quite dramatically done, this whole business, whatever we were working toward. And at that moment, I spotted a younger kid who had been at the retreat all weekend working a sound board for the musical parts zipping behind the crowd to some kind of dimmer panel. He turned a switch and the lights dimmed slightly; though it was morning, the light in the building was unnatural, like the light outside during a partial eclipse.

Throughout the whole weekend, Fortenberry had been setting himself up as an athletic conqueror of demons. His usual shtick was to start off a story acting like he was skeptical of such things ("I was one of those people who thought speaking in tongues was silly"), then talk about how he was sucked in to the amazing truth against his reservations. He described one story about demons in particular.

"If you're thinking, 'Maybe I don't believe all that stuff about demons,' you just be there tomorrow morning," he'd said the day before. "I was like that once before myself." And then he told a story about ministering to some man, and how as soon as he touched him with anointing oil, the man recoiled from him. "He shot across the room and looked back at me with eyes that were not his own," he said. "And he says to me, 'I think I have a demon.' And I said to him, 'I think you're right.'"

The crowd laughed. Fortenberry went on.

"I looked at him and I was like, 'Holy-y-y smoke!' Anyway, I musta cast about twelve to fifteen demons outta that man."

At other times the pastor would delve into a strange sort of demonology, explaining the rules of demonic possession. "A Christian has all power over every demon in you," he explained. "If a demon is in you, it's because he has a legal right to be there. What you have to do is concentrate on how he got that legal right."

I assumed that the "legal right" had something to do with having offended God somehow, having committed some iniquity that opened the door for the demon to enter. My Christian friends—both at this retreat and in other places later on in my experience—would talk a great deal about "doors" and "windows," worrying quite a lot about opening doors for demons and laboring quite intensely to "keep those doors closed" once the demons were gone.

Other times Fortenberry would unintentionally be quite prescient. "You just never know with demons, how close they might be," he said. "You might be sitting right next to one, and you'd never know he was even there."

Two old ladies sitting next to me looked my way and winked. I felt a lump in my throat.

Occasionally Fortenberry would cite scripture in explaining his rules about demons, but other times he would seem to just pull stuff out of his ass. In the same way that I was conscious of my own real self becoming fatigued and giving way slightly to the robot Christian on the outside, I could feel that my brain had decided to stop worrying about which of Fortenberry's pronouncements were utter two-bit traveling-circus horseshit and which ones were just confused theology dreamed up with at least some passing reference to the actual Bible. Once you get past a certain point in this process, it really doesn't matter. You take it all in like it's all of equal import, and when he's done talking, you just sing along to the songs again.

Anyway, we were now at that fateful "tomorrow morning," and Fortenberry looked like a quarterback about to take the field before a big game. The life coaches assembled around the edges of the chapel, huddling together like insects. For this particular session the men were on one side of the chapel and the women were on the other; mirroring them, the male coaches huddled at the front of the chapel behind Fortenberry on our side, while the female coaches huddled on the other.

The coaches were carrying anointing oil and bundles of small paper bags.

Fortenberry began to issue instructions. He told us that under no circumstances should we pray during the Deliverance.

"When the word of God is in your mouth," he said, "the demons can't come out of your body. You have to keep a path clear for the demon to come up through your throat. So under no circumstances pray to God. You can't have God in your mouth. You can cough, you might even want to vomit, but don't pray."

The crowd nodded along solemnly. Fortenberry then explained that he was going to read from an extremely long list of demons and cast them out individually. As he did so, we were supposed to breathe out, keep our mouths open, and let the demons out.

And he began.

At first, the whole scene was pure comedy. Fortenberry was standing up at the front of the chapel, reading off a list, and the room was loudly chirping crickets back at him.

"In the name of Jesus, I cast out the demon of incest! In the name of Jesus, I cast out the demon of sexual abuse! In the name of Jesus . . ."

After a few minutes, there was a little twittering here and there. Nothing serious. I was beginning to think the Deliverance was going to be a bust.

But then it started. Wails and cries from the audience. To my left, a young black man started writhing around in his seat. In front of me and to my right, another young black man with Coke-bottle glasses and a shock of nerdly Jheri curl—a dead ringer for a young Wayne Williams—started wailing and clutching his head.

"In the name of Jesus," continued Fortenberry, "I cast out the demon of astrology!"

Coughing and spitting noises. Behind me, a bald white man started to wheeze and gurgle, like he was about to puke. Fortenberry, still reading from his list, pointed at the man. On cue, a pair of life coaches raced over to him and began to minister. One dabbed his forehead with oil and fiercely clutched his cranium; the other held a paper bag in front of his mouth.

"In the name of Jesus Christ," said Fortenberry, more loudly now, "I cast out the demon of lust!"

And the man began power-puking into his paper baggie. I couldn't see if any actual vomitus came out, but he made real hurling and retching noises.

Now the women began to pipe in. On the women's side of the chapel the noises began, and it is not hard to explain what these noises sounded like. If you've ever watched the *Houston 560* or any other gang-bang porn movie, that's what it sounded like, only the sounds were far more intense. It was not difficult to figure out where the energy was coming from on that side of the room. Some of the husbands glanced nervously over in the direction of their wives.

"In the name of Jesus Christ, I cast out the demon of cancer!" said Fortenberry.

"Oooh! Unnh! Unnnnnh!" wailed a woman in the front row.

"Bleeech!" puked the bald man behind me.

Within about a minute after that, the whole chapel erupted in pandemonium. About half the men and three-fourths of the women were writhing around and either play-puking or screaming. Not wanting to be a bad sport, I raised my hand for one of the life coaches to see.

"Need . . . a . . . bag," I said as he came over.

He handed me a bag.

"In the name of Jesus, I cast out the demon of handwriting analysis!" shouted Fortenberry.

Handwriting analysis? I jammed the bag over my mouth and started coughing, then went into a very real convulsion of disbelief as I listened to this astounding list, half laughing and half retching.

"In the name of Jesus Christ our Lord, I cast out the demon of the intellect!" Fortenberry continued. "In the name of Jesus, I cast out the demon of anal fissures!"

Cough, cough!

The minutes raced by. Wayne Williams was now fully prostrate, held up only by a trio of coaches, each of whom took part of his writhing body and propped it up. Another bald man in the front of the chapel was now freaking out in Linda Blair fashion, roaring and making horrific demon noises.

"Rum-balakasha-oom!" shouted Fortenberry in tongues, waving a hand in front of Linda Blair Man. "Cooom-balakasha-froom! In the name of Jesus Christ I cast out the demon of philosophy!"

Philosophy?

Up in front of me and to the right several rows ahead, I saw Aaron looking around sadly. I wondered for a moment if he had seen me "puking" into my bag, and I felt awful suddenly at the possibility that he had—I had deceived him. He looked seriously distressed by the proceedings, which clearly were not working the way he'd wanted.

As for the rest of the crowd, it was obvious that virtually everyone was play-acting to some degree or another. I was reminded of the Tolstoy story *Kreutzer Sonata*, when the male narrator described marriage as being like the bearded-lady tent in a French circus he'd seen. You pay a few francs to go in, and when you come out, and the carnival barker shouts at you, "Was

that not the most amazing thing you've ever seen, monsieur?"—
well, you're too ashamed to admit that you've been had, and so
you nod your head and agree: Oui, monsieur, it was really something! That's how people come to say marriage is a blessing, and
that's how you can get fifty-odd high school graduates puking
demons into three-cent paper bags for a Deliverance.

The whole thing—the demonic expulsions, the trading of
miraculous wives' tales, the crazy End Times theology based on
dire predictions that come and go uneventfully once a year or
so—it's all a con that is done with the consent of the conned.
Which is what gives it strength. If everybody agrees to believe,
it is real.

The hooting and howling went on seemingly forever. It was
nearly an hour and a half before Fortenberry was done. He had
cast out the demons of every ailment, crime, domestic problem,
and intellectual discipline on the face of the earth. He cast out
horoscopes, false gods, witches, intellectual pride, nearsighted-
ness, everything, it seemed to me, except maybe *E. coli* and John
Updike novels. At least four of the men and about six of the
women writhed and screamed and fussed themselves into sheer
physical exhaustion, collapsing in chairs by the time it was over.
Several of the coaches actually had to bring Wayne Williams
and the other young black man behind the chapel to subdue
their demons. By then most of us men were just sitting there
mute, looking around absentmindedly, waiting for it to end. I
was sitting there, clutching my demon vomit bag—perhaps the
single greatest souvenir of my journalistic career—when I made
the mistake of closing my mouth. A coach rushed over to me.

"Matthew!" he snapped. "Keep your mouth open! Let the
demons out!"

"Oh, right!" I said. I straightened up and opened my mouth
in the shape of a letter *O*.

Meanwhile, Fortenberry was tiring.

"I cast out . . . uh . . . In the name of Jesus, I cast out the demon of pornography. I cast out, in the name of Jesus, the demon of disconnect."

Fortenberry shook his head as though trying to revive himself. He had been at this for a long time. His stamina really was astounding, a testament to his military training.

When it was done, I ran up to Aaron.

"How do you feel?" I said.

"I don't know," he said sadly. "I actually don't feel all that different."

"Well, that's okay," I said. "Neither do I."

"No?"

"No."

He frowned and walked away, looking more upset than he had when he'd arrived.

Laurie ran over.

"How'd you do, honey?" she asked.

"I don't know," I said. "I think I only lost about a half-pounder. You?"

"A half-pounder. You're cute. I feel so relaxed, I feel great," she said. "But I have to say, I was watching you, and I felt like—I felt like you were holding back a little."

I gulped hard. "Really? I mean, I coughed into the bag and everything."

"No, you were holding back. Maybe you're not ready for this yet," she said.

"It's not that," I protested.

A frightening thought shot through my head. It occurred to me that over the last decades any number of our prominent political leaders (from Jimmy Carter to Chuck Colson to W himself) had boasted publicly of their born-again experiences, broadcasting to Middle America an understanding of their personal relationships with God. But whereas once these conversions were humble things—Billy Graham whispering and putting his hand on W's shoulder in Kennebunkport, or even (in the case of Tom DeLay) a flash of recognition while watching a televangelist program—the modern version might very easily be this completely batshit holy-vomitus/demon-exorcism deal. The thought that *any* politician could claim this kind of experience and not be immediately disqualified from public service seemed utterly terrifying.

We were called back to chapel, and this time the drill was speaking in tongues. We were asked to come up to the front of the chapel and let a life coach anoint us with oil, hold our heads, and speak to us in tongues. Fortenberry instructed us to "just let it out. Just let it out and it'll come out."

He didn't come right out and say, Just act like you're speaking in tongues. But it was damned close. Once again, Fortenberry greased the process by telling us a story about how he'd once been at a service where folks were speaking in tongues, and he was skeptical, but it had just flown right out of him—and now it just shoots right out of him, almost on command.

I went to the front. One of the coaches grabbed me by the shoulder and sploshed a big puddle of oil on my forehead. Then he began to speak in tongues:

"Gam-bakakasha. Hoo-raaa-balalakasha . . . Come on, Matthew, let it out."

American Christians who speak in tongues basically all try to sound like extras from the underworld set of *Indiana Jones and the Temple of Doom.* If you want to pull it off and sound like a natural, just imagine you're holding a rubber replica of Harrison Ford's heart in your hands: Umm-harakashaka! Loopa-wanneee-rakakakasha, Meester Jones!

But I didn't think of this at the time and just went another route.

"Let it out, Matthew," the coach repeated, clutching my forehead. "Just open your mouth."

I shrugged and rattled off the lyrics to the song "What Is Autumn?" by the Russian rock band DDT:

What is autumn? It's the sky
The crying sky below your feet.
Flying about in puddles are the birds and clouds.
Autumn I've not been with you for so long!

It's actually a beautiful song, but with my eyes rolled back in my head and recited in Russian it sounded demonic enough.

"Hmm, very good," my coach said. "Good job, Matthew."

I kept going, on to the next verse. "What is autumn? It's a stone . . ."

"Okay, that's good," the coach said, annoyed, moving to the next guy.

"Uh," said the next man, a small, bent, elderly fellow who had come here with his much larger, bottle-blond wife.

"Let it out!" the coach barked.

"Phhhhh-shhhhaka . . . ?" the old man pleaded.

"Let it out!"

"Ra-ka-ka-shhhhh . . . Pork-manka!"

"It's important that you practice," said Pastor Fortenberry. "It sounds silly, but when you're at home, when you have a little time, just try to let it out. You'll get used to it, and soon you'll be speaking in tongues like nobody's business!"

He then pronounced us baptized in the Holy Spirit and fully qualified now to cast out demons.

He held up his hands in triumph.

"Hallelujah!" he shouted.

The crowd jumped up, and we all threw up our hands.

"Hallelujah!"

He called out Hallelujah! again. We repeated after him. And we repeated after him again.

Arms in the air. Hallelujah! Hallelujah! Hallelujah!

I felt a twinge of recognition from somewhere as I threw my arms up over and over again.

We had graduated.

• • •

AT THE END of the weekend we were gathered in the chapel
one last time. We were told that they were going to play a very
important recording for us.

The recording, it turned out, was the Voice of God. A female life coach cranked up the volume, and a Don Pardo–style
radio voice, only lower a few octaves and with a tone of terrible
otherwordly conviction, boomed out over a CD player:

"My child," it began. Then it continued:

> You may not know me
> But I know everything about you.
> I know when you sit down and when you rise up.
> I am familiar with all of your ways.
> Even the very hairs on your head are numbered . . .

Christians are fond of repeating this biblical maxim (Matthew 10:29) about God knowing the number of hairs on our
heads. In the crowd now there was much nodding and even a
little bit of weeping as this crudely altered recording boomed
out over the dimmed light of the chapel area—many members
of the flock were clearly very affected by the idea that some
unknown voice actor knew the number of hairs on their heads.
The recording continued:

> I offer you more than your earthly father ever could.
> For I am the perfect Father.
> Every good gift that you receive comes from my hand.
> My thoughts toward you are as countless as the sands on the
>   seashore.

It went on like this for a while. By the time the recording
was over, there was much sniffling and crying. After all this

talk of wounds and this cathartic confession about our parents, hearing this crazy Mr. Clean voice assert himself as our eternal dad was too much for some of the people in the room—particularly when it ended like this:

My question is . . . Will you be my child? I am waiting for
*   you.*
Love, your dad.
Almighty God.

Sometime later, we were dismissed. Back at the barracks, I found Dennis lying in a fetal position on his bunk, eyes shut. I stopped in front of him, thought about waking him, then thought the better of it, grabbed my stuff, and rushed out, not saying good-bye. Jose shook my hand warmly on the way out, then hurried away. Aaron I later saw walking with a blank look on his face back toward the barracks, but I never got a chance to speak with him again.

In the main building I saw big Maria, who had grown progressively cheerier throughout the weekend, laughing joyfully and embracing several women who presumably had been in her group. Earlier in the weekend I'd made it a point to wave to her whenever I passed and sit near her at meals when she was alone, but now she looked enraptured with new friendships and scarcely recognized me when I waved good-bye.

I hitched a ride home with Laurie and Janine, who had driven to the ranch in Janine's car. "Wasn't that recording wonderful?" Laurie said.

"Oh, yes," said Janine. "You never heard that before?"

"No," said Laurie.

"Neither have I," I said.

Janine turned on some Christian tunes; I fell asleep in the backseat, mentally and physically exhausted. At the beginning of the weekend I'd been fairly bursting out of my skin from the stress of having to play this difficult role, plainly freaked out by the whole scene, but that was a distant memory now. I closed my eyes to the gentle acoustic strumming of Janine's CD and slept a deep mannequin sleep.

BY THE END of the weekend I realized how quaint was the mere suggestion that Christians of this type should learn to "be rational" or "set aside your religion" about such things as the Iraq war or other policy matters. Once you've made a journey like this—once you've gone this far—you are beyond suggestible. It's not merely the informational indoctrination, the constant belittling of homosexuals and atheists and Muslims and pacifists, etc., that's the issue. It's that once you've gotten to this place, you've left behind the mental process that a person would need to form an independent opinion about such things. You make this journey precisely to experience the ecstasy of beating to the same big gristly heart with a roomful of like-minded folks. Once you reach that place with them, you're thinking with muscles, not neurons.

By the end of that weekend, Phil Fortenberry could have told us that John Kerry was a demon with clawed feet and not one person would have so much as blinked. Because none of that politics stuff matters anyway, once you've gotten this far. All that matters is being full of the Lord and empty of demons. And since everything that is not of God is demonic, asking these people to be objective about anything else is just absurd. There is no "anything else." All alternative points of view are nonstarters. There is this "our thing," a sort of Cosa Nostra of the soul, and then there are the fires of Hell. And that's all.

FOUR

Baghdad Interlude,

or

The Derangement at War

I'D BEEN IN IRAQ for close to two months, as part of an ongoing assignment for *Rolling Stone*. After a stint with the grunts at the Rustamiyah base, I was with a new unit, the Bloodhounds of the 615th MP, a police transition team with responsibility for a somewhat quiet sector of western Baghdad.

Being embedded, I divided my time along much the same lines as the soldiers' time was divided. I spent the vast majority of my day cozily consuming Baskin-Robbins ice cream sundaes, Whopper Juniors, and full-blast air-conditioning behind the high, high walls of whatever base I happened to be on at the moment. But then a short stretch of most every day I spent out on patrol with this or that MP unit, driving around hot sections of Baghdad or Mosul or Tal Afar or whatever city we happened to be in at the time. We were visiting police stations and ostensibly providing "support" to local cops, although it was abundantly clear to most all the soldiers I spent time with that the real mission was to drive around in circles so as to provide the enemy with a target once daily.

Over time I started to feel in my bones that this weird walled-off archipelago was itself a profound metaphor for American domestic reality. The high walls around the forward operating bases, or FOBs—at places like Camp Liberty they appeared to be upward of twenty or thirty feet tall in parts, lined with knots of barbed wire and gun turrets—were supposedly there to keep insurgents out of the American compounds. But the more I looked at them, the more they reminded me of the freaky-tall bulwarks on *King Kong*'s Skull Island: masterpieces of architectural overkill, the panic visible in each extra foot of protection, walls designed to keep something *in*, not out. In America we live in a bubble and the rest of the world is a dangerous mystery, about which many legends may be spread by those cunning and unscrupulous enough to bother. The outside world has become scary enough that most of our people have decided not even to bother trying to figure it out—which is how you end up with such lunacies like *They hate us for our freedom* and *9/11 was an inside job*. If you're confined to the territory of the bubble in your search for explanations for an event like 9/11, those are the kinds of explanations you'll come up with.

A key aspect of the derangement is this cutting off of the people from outside reality. We are like a person slipping into paranoid psychosis for whom hallucinations and imagined conversations increasingly take the place of real object relations in the outside world. A paranoiac can handle those imaginary conversations just fine—but shake him by the shoulders and force him to focus, and he might very well stare back at you in terror, not knowing who you are or what you want. In that one panicked moment before he can think of some new fantasy that explains what's happening before his eyes, you'll see the whole sorry deal laid bare.

In Iraq, where those occasional clashes with the outside are of the rudest possible variety, I saw those moments over and over again. These Bloodhounds in Baghdad were about to drag me to one more.

THE BLOODHOUNDS are an active-duty unit normally based in Germany—a close-knit, professional, idealistic group of young kids so cheerful and hardworking it was almost off-putting. In my getting-to-know-u first day with the squad—an early-morning meeting in a Camp Liberty parking lot that had been arranged by army press officers—the Bloodhounds had done a zany around-the-campfire-type group introduction (in which each soldier gave a nutty capsule description of himself) that was like something out of *Up with People*.

"My name is Josh Billingsley, and I have an abnormally large head," said one, who really did have a big head. Everyone laughed.

"I'm Jaleel Ibrahim," said the next soldier. "I'm the token African guy."

More laughs.

"And I'm Sergeant Russell," said the third. "I am soft-spoken and wholesome, but also offended easily."

Jesus, I thought. Is this war, or a boy-band audition? At first I'd found the happy-go-lucky attitude of the Bloodhounds horrifying; in the middle of all this twisted violence and un-reasonableness, spending time with this cheery group was like having to look at a happily panting golden retriever in the front seat while handcuffed in the back of some serial killer's car. But over time I came to understand that it wasn't a put-on at all, that these kids really loved and cared for one another. A lot of them came from tough backgrounds, and this unit was the best family they had.

· · ·

THERE IS a lot about the army that's bullshit and a crock—just watch any USO show—but the teamwork and the camaraderie, the way a bunch of lost teenagers are molded into proud men and women, all of that stuff is very real. Watching it in action can be very moving. The army, in some ways anyway, is unquestionably good for young people.

Such ruminations get to the heart of why the embed process is so dangerous and insidious. A journalist who slips into the habit of rooting for a bunch of nice kids like this in a place like Iraq might easily find himself missing the overall point of his assignment. This, certainly, had happened to me. It wasn't until my tour in Iraq was just about over that I realized I'd been conned, that I was spending far too much time watching these kids interact with one another and not nearly enough time wondering what the hell we were all doing here. But that's the story you get when you can't really look behind the wall for twenty-three hours out of every day. And even in that one hour, your insight is limited to turning your head on a swivel in the back seat of a Humvee somewhere, watching for pieces of trash on the road.

ANYWAY, WHEN I joined the 615th that morning, the soldiers were in their usual playful mood. Specialist Pamela Wall, nicknamed "Humboldt" for her not-infrequent spaceouts, did her Asteroids impersonation for the group, an almost completely indescribable spastic side shuffle that I guess was an attempt at imitating a floating spaceship. Squad leader Sergeant Whitman, a straight-as-an-arrow Bill Paxton look-alike, wrestled goofily with Sergeant Daniel Biederman, trying to snare him in a headlock.

I gritted my teeth nervously, looking left and right. I'd been hearing explosions all morning. I couldn't tell whether I just hadn't heard them early on in my trip, whether they were actually getting more frequent, or whether I was just stressing. But it seemed to me now like every one of these early premission briefings was being interrupted by IED blasts right outside the gates. The sense that the violence was increasing seemed to penetrate even the happy-worker-elf vibe of the 615th. The morning briefing continued, with the group's laid-back southerner, Sergeant Conn, relaying the announcements of the day.

"Okay, we have a new acronym," he said, referring to a ubiquitous insurgent weapon that had up till then been known as an explosively formed projectile. "The EFP will from now on be called an AAIED, for anti-armor IED—"

BOOM! The squad shuddered as the sound of a massive explosion rocked the compound. The blast sounded like it came from somewhere just outside the camp exit.

"Fuck!" whispered a soldier named O'Braden, who was standing next to me. He shook his head in frustration.

"Somebody just had a bad day," editorialized Conn.

Conn was about to start up the briefing again when yet another blast rocked the compound. This one was even bigger—or seemed bigger, anyway.

BOOOOOMM!

"Damn!" said Conn.

"Jesus!" said O'Braden.

A hush fell over the squad. Everybody tried to shrug it off, but I could see it had an effect—throughout the squad you could see bugged-out eyes and wringing hands and a few involuntary glances in the direction of the FOB gates. The briefing went on. Owing to a new directive—issued in the wake of a recent incident in which a Humvee driver's leg was severed by an EFP and stuck in place on the truck accelerator—we had to practice a new drill for slowing down the Humvee in case of such an event. We piled into the trucks, and each of the drivers practiced slumping over in his or her seat. In the truck I was in, a soldier named Schumann fell over, resting her face on the steering wheel, and stared blankly out the truck window. Since I was going to be in the car, I had to do the drill, too—so I practiced pushing her limp body out of the way, reaching over the seat, and grabbing the e-brake. After a minute she looked up. "Okay?" she sighed. "Are we done?"

"Yeah," whispered Conn. "We're done."

SOON AFTERWARD the briefing ended and we rolled out of the FOB, headed for yet another police station.

The four-vehicle convoy of the 615th zoomed through western Baghdad, winding through back roads, jumping median strips and driving against traffic on two-lane streets, twisting into dead ends and doubling back again. In the backseat of the second truck I furiously copied down the dialogue between gunner, driver, and truck commander:

Clear low wires!
Yeah, clear low wires, sorry.
Crossing over, flipping a bitch!
Flipping a bitch, crossing over.
Got a box up on the road.
Trash pile on the right!

In my previous embed assignment the lexicon had been a lot different. If the wisecracking grunts of the 158th MP were an X-rated vaudeville show—a gang of guardsmen from Oklahoma who spent most of their time swearing like sea captains and singing songs like "Gay Factory Worker from the South" while they burned up the highways—the 615th was an after-school special. All the classic high-school types were represented. O'Braden, the driver in my truck today, was the reformed Judd Nelson discipline case, a brooding, dark-haired sentimentalist who gushed about the sacrifices soldiers had to make. Bastien, the skinny, hyperactive gunner, was the class fuck-up, the kid who sits in the back row shooting spitballs. Sergeant Biederman, the squad leader today, was . . . well, I don't know who he was in the movie. In this unit he's a quiet leader who always seems a little exasperated, trying to keep it all together but occasionally losing his patience. A slight man at 130 pounds with a cherubic face, he's been struggling today with the seventy-odd pounds of gear he has to carry with his uniform—not with the weight but with the arrangement—and is anxious to get to the station so he can redo some of the straps on his pouches.

Got a green truck on the left!

Got a blown-up piece of shit on the right!

Making a left—correction, right.

Alright, coming out. Train tracks! Gonna be a tight fit.

Hold on, Bastien.

Alright, you're clear of the wire.

We slithered under the low wire of the side street. Biederman looked out the window and sighed. The young sergeant had had shit luck ever since I arrived. The first time we'd made this trip, to the Al Mamoon police station, there'd been a friendly-fire incident on his watch. The IPLO (a civilian American policeman contracted to train Iraqi forces) assigned to us, some cop from Georgia who'd been hired to teach self-defense to Iraqi cops, had been fiddling with his Glock pistol just inside the precinct gates when suddenly the weapon fired.

Biederman had been standing with his back to the IPLO, talking to me, when the shot went off. The look on his face recalled a cartoon character whose hat flies ten feet in the air in surprise. He immediately pushed me behind a car (not that I needed any help to run and hide), pulled out his weapon, and went over to investigate. Nobody was hurt, fortunately, but upon learning that it was gunfire from our own party Biederman sagged visibly, like an animal taking a bullet. The look on his face said it all: This is the last fucking thing I need!

The IPLO was himself a symbol of everything that was fucked up, myopic, and stupid about the war. If you viewed the occupation as a luxury government employment program for American security-industry types—a kind of gold-leaf Tennessee Valley Authority for connected ex–Pentagon execs and retired cops and soldiers, all of whom could come to the Valley and set themselves up with a nice six-figure-or-better job inside the bubble—then you might think this made sense, having some monolingual Georgia cop come all the way to Baghdad at a taxpayer-supported rate of nine grand a month to teach hand-to-hand combat techniques to Iraqi cops who'd be shot or bombed long before they got within a hundred yards of an insurgent. But if you were a Sergeant Biederman and it was your job to transport said Georgian through dangerous enemy territory so that he could collect on this insane version of federal welfare, then it couldn't possibly make less sense. The idea that any of us might actually get killed so that this redneck retiree could buy his wife a new living room set was such complete and utter madness that it simply was not possible to think about it.

But Biederman resisted the urge to complain too much about the obvious, although you could still see in his eyes his frustration at this absurd assignment, which nearly ended in this overpaid civilian shooting someone in the foot right in front of a goddamned reporter.

"Jesus" was all he'd said, shaking his head.

Now we were heading back to the same station. Biederman said nothing, but he looked like a man needing a nap.

We went into the station. Biederman directed some of the guys to take up watch positions on the roof; meanwhile, he and I, along with Schumann and the medic White, repaired to an unlit little room on the first floor of the station designated for use by the Americans. He took off his gear and repacked his pouches so that they fit more snugly. Like most of the soldiers, Biederman had had to pay for a lot of the stuff he carried on his body out of his own pocket. One soldier in the 615th estimated that the average tally for all the special pouches, gloves, and protective gear most soldiers in Iraq wear is about four hundred bucks. There are all kinds of ancillary costs to fighting in Iraq. Soldiers pay for their own Internet access, for their phone calls home, in some cases for their own armor. Looking at Biederman, I remembered suddenly having an aide to Bernie Sanders explain to me how a government that spends more than $600 billion a year can end up short the money needed for body armor and other equipment for soldiers in the field—congressmen tended to raid the operations and maintenance part of the defense budget for their earmark requests, specifically that part of the budget that paid for soldiers' equipment. (They took $9 billion out of the O&M accounts alone in 2005, for instance.) The huge bloated weapons systems they tended to leave alone.

His uniform rearranged successfully, Biederman pulled up a chair and sat down. I took off my ballistic vest and lazily filmed another pair of soldiers who'd come in and taken to filling out a Mad Libs questionnaire.

"Number?" said the first soldier.

"Um," said the second. "Sixty-nine."

"Name?"

He paused. "Powell."

"Noun?"

The second soldier paused. "Vagina," he said.

"Year?"

The second soldier paused at this one. "Nineteen sixty-nine," he said, predictably.

Suddenly there was a huge explosion.

BOOOOOOOOMMMMM!

We all jumped sideways and covered our ears. That was close, really close. From the sound of things, a car bomb not far from the station. We looked out the window; a thin plume of gray smoke wafted up in the distance. Despite the obvious proximity of the explosion, none of the Iraqi Police in the station moved so much as an inch.

"They don't go to check it out?" I asked Biederman.

He shook his head. "We have to make them go," he said.

"They're scared," said Schumann. "Wouldn't you be?"

"Well, yes . . . ," I said.

"They're not really cops, the way we have cops," Schumann added. "They don't, like, enforce traffic laws or anything."

"If one of their guys is involved," added White, "they'll rush out there. But if not . . ."

The IPs sat down, nervously stirring their tea. Out the window, I could have sworn I actually heard the sounds of flames licking the air—that was how close the burning car hulk was.

A few minutes passed. The soldiers finished their Mad Lib and started reading.

"Write down in sixty-nine words or less," giggled the first soldier, "why you think that Powell should be elected vagina of the year."

Biederman said nothing. Somewhere down the hall, the civilian instructor from Georgia, the same one who'd nearly shot us by accident a few days before, was giving an ad-hoc class in a cramped old supply room. The last time I'd checked, he was using the Hacky Sack champ Winslow to demonstrate to the explosion-averse IPs how to get out of a headlock.

"You push on the elbow sharply like this," he said, "and you just slide out like so . . ."

The IPs, standing in a mute semicircle, waited for the translation and nodded. I went back down the hall to the unlit room with the Mad Lib players.

It was almost time to head back out. Explosions in the morning, gunfire on the way, another explosion at lunchtime . . . but at least we got a Mad Lib finished and spent a few hundred taxpayer bucks an hour teaching a couple of lazy-ass Iraqi cops who will never leave their police stations for any meaningful reason to practice self-defense techniques against criminals they will never apprehend. Plus, we had time for an MRE lunch. They sure didn't have packs of Skittles at Bastogne!

Sure, this made sense. This was worth the trouble, this Iraq war.

Biederman sighed, shook his head, and looked up at no one in particular.

"What the fuck are we doing here?" he whispered.

I shrugged. Who knew?

"Jesus Fucking Christ," he muttered.

We got into the trucks and went back home.

Sometime later, when I'd find myself holed up in a similarly isolated retreat in the Texas Hill Country with the ex-military preacher Phil Fortenberry—talking about enemy aircraft and arterial breaches with somewhat older men and women, many of them ex-soldiers moved on to a different but no less confusing stage of life—I wondered if somehow the army, with its same tireless belief in American can-doism and its same sit-in-a-circle get-to-know-u rituals, doesn't prepare some of these kids for future Encounter Weekends. Maybe it was a stretch, but there was something about this weird sojourn through the violence and trauma of Iraq, continued on later through sexual brokenness and loneliness and substance abuse and all the other existential horrors of life in a massive industrial empire like ours—something about going through all that with only a third-rate carnival barker like Phil Fortenberry or some other midlevel officer to make sense of it for you was what made it hard to imagine anything sadder.

FIVE

DISCOVER
THE DIFFERENCE

★ ★ ★ ★ ★ ★ ★ ★ ★ ★ ★ ★ ★

IN ORDER TO BECOME a full-fledged member of the Corner-stone Church you must take a class—another excruciatingly dull seminar led by an admonishing fourth-tier minister with an unresolved power complex. It's actually a two-day course: a two-hour Friday-night jaunt and a six-hour haul the next morning.

I skipped the Friday-night session, spooked by the life coach seminar the night before. At that class, I had been shocked and horrified when a nunlike post-chemotherapy church administrator passed out forms asking for our Social Security numbers for a "routine" background check—a potentially fatal development for my entire satanic enterprise. Note to Christians: demon journalists do not fear the word of the Lord, but they do fear the national credit inquiry system. I left abruptly in the middle of that class, citing an emergency phone call—leaving my increasingly hormone-crazed companion Laurie, who'd cheerily kept my seat warm for me before I showed up, to finish out the gig alone.

"But where are you going?" she asked.

"I'm . . . sorry," I stammered. "I've got to go. I've got a problem."

Concerned, Laurie called me several times the next day, pleading with me to come to the Friday-night membership class. But I was afraid that one, too, would require some kind of incriminating ID, so I cooked up a real tearjerker of a story to get out of the Friday session. Even I was ashamed of laying this one on my Sister in Christ.

"It's my ex," I explained on the phone. "It turns out she wants to get a divorce right away. She's apparently met somebody . . ."

"I'm so sorry," she said. "That's what I was going through recently."

Soon Laurie was rambling about her ex. I blinked off the Internet screen I'd been reading and cracked open a soda. This was going to take a while.

Laurie's phone calls were epic events, although they didn't require much participation on my part. She made one call that lasted long enough for me to watch nearly two entire DVD episodes of *House* on my computer, hitting the pause button only occasionally to offer a "Yeah" or a "Mm-hmm." She occasionally forced me to interrupt. In one call a few days before, for instance, Laurie had revealed to me that her ex-boyfriend, Rick, who'd recently binned her for a younger woman, was some kind of supergenius—a supergenius who drove a really big truck, lived with his mother, and had been unable to fix her skeet launcher.

"He's got a two hundred IQ, honey," she whispered. "I mean, he's brilliant. He's not like you or me."

"Wow," I said.

"We were a good couple in that way, though," she added. "My IQ is one eighty-nine."

"Mm-hmm," I said, reading about the Barry Bonds contract dispute on ESPN.com. "Right."

"I mean, we had this remarkable energy—"

"Wait a minute," I said. "What did you say your IQ was?"

"A hundred and eighty-nine, honey," she said.

I frowned. "Wasn't Einstein's IQ around there some-where?"

She paused. "Well, probably, honey," she said. "I had that test taken when I was a child. Of course, I've lost some of it since then—I just don't read enough."

"Naturally," I said. "Who has the time?"

"Oh, tell me about it, sweet baby," she said. "I just get so tired after work . . ."

The conversation ended an hour later. I could see very clearly that Laurie was suffering; she was terribly lonely and still coping with the death of her husband from the year before. But for some reason her anxiety had gone into overdrive in the past week. She was fidgeting, calling everyone, fussing—she couldn't sit still. Her storytelling was increasingly manic. In this latest call, the Rick story was evolving. Apparently the cad not only owed her money but earlier in the week had given his cell phone to his new younger girlfriend and had the younger girl-friend call up poor Laurie and bitch her out. Much drama en-sued, with Laurie—"just to help her out"—quickly informing the new girl that Rick would never give her a baby, because he hates babies. And also because, Laurie added, he had problems with his libido, problems that were exacerbated by his mother's habit of stealing his Cialis, which she diabolically did to prevent him from getting it on with women. Without Cialis, Laurie in-sisted, "it wadn't happening." By the time I had all this grasped in my head, she had gotten back to the money.

"It's like you said, he used me," she said. "And I don't think I'm ever going to get that money back."

"Mmm, probably not," I said.

"I was even thinking about 1099-ing him," she said.

I had no idea what she meant by that, but I played along. "Good thinking," I said. "Let's see how his two hundred IQ copes with that!"

"Exactly, sweet baby, exactly."

I was starting to get calls like this every day, which was another reason I skipped the Friday class. However, I decided to go to the one the next day. When I arrived, I was shocked to find that Laurie wasn't there. I slumped in a pew and began taking notes as the pastor, Stephen J. Sorensen—a paunchy, impatient-sounding man with a Rumsfeldian voice who looked like he'd just shot a 98 on the links and was scanning the audience for someone to blame for it—explained the vagaries of membership. I arrived during some kind of sermon in which Sorensen was comparing God to alcoholism:

"When you take on too much alcohol," he said, "you as you begin to disappear!"

He pantomimed a drunk's stagger down the street, ending in a collapse.

"It's the same thing with the Holy Spirit," he said. "The more drunk you are with the Holy Spirit, the less in control you are. The more God, the less you. The more God, the less you act like yourself."

There were about a hundred people in the church; all nodded eagerly.

I nodded too, but just as I did, I saw a familiar face in a center pew. It was Laurie, shouting and gesturing for me to come and sit near her.

"Come here, baby!" she said.

I sighed, gathered my shit, and walked over.

Laurie mobbed me as soon as I sat down. When I didn't turn the page of my study binder fast enough, she pointed to the right page and made me turn it faster. If I didn't read along or make a note at the right time, she'd nudge me, sometimes adding something that she thought the pastor missed. Then, while Sorensen was ranting, she started in on me about signing in.

"Did you sign in?" she whispered.

"And so God said that homosexuality is an abomination," Sorensen droned. "He didn't say it was not quite right. He said it was an abomination."

"Uh, no," I said.

"Well, you've gotta sign in!" she whispered, more loudly now. "You're in the tribe of Ephraim! That's our group, honey, that's our group!"

"Right, well, I'll do it after," I whispered, eyes still facing forward.

"But where did you sign in when you came in?" she nudged me.

"On the 'no tribe' sheet," I said firmly. "I'll do it in the right place later."

Sorensen continued about gays: "And so God doesn't change his mind when society changes its mind . . ."

"But the sign-in sheet . . . ," Laurie continued.

Heads started to turn. Meanwhile, Janine showed up and sat down on the other side of Laurie, and soon Laurie was doing the same thing with Janine. Janine and I exchanged glances. Sorensen continued his lecture, and soon Laurie was raising her hand when he mentioned the church elders. Laurie wanted to know how many elders there were. But she totally misunderstood the meeting; there was no place here for questions and answers. This was a we-shut-up-and-listen, they-tell-us-what-we-need-to-know type of deal. But Laurie kept wagging her hand. Sorensen ignored her.

"Laurie, honey, I don't think this is really question-and-answer time," Janine whispered finally. "Just remember your question and ask him later."

"I just want to know how many elders there are," Laurie whispered.

"Okay, well . . ."

We broke for lunch. On our way out of the church, we spotted a couple, Murray and Miriam, whom we'd met at the Encounter Weekend and eaten with there. We all decided to go to the nearby cheap-ass Chinese buffet. There were five of us, and Laurie kept wanting all of us to go in her car. We eventually settled on two cars, but it took a while; Laurie and Miriam disagreed pointlessly about the travel issue, then glared at each other in the parking lot. I smelled a needlessly megacomplicated experience coming.

When we got to the restaurant, I wanted to sit next to Janine, who I thought was a very nice, very sad young woman—I liked her enough, in fact, that I made it a point to stay away from her, not wanting to infect her with my evil journalistic tentacles. But when we got to the round table, Laurie maneuvered in such a way that there was no way for me to sit near Janine; she plopped right between us. We prayed, thanked the Lord for the food, then started eating.

Miriam and Laurie, both heavyset and both older blond women, one conspicuously married and one conspicuously widowed, sat opposite each other, feverishly spooning mounds of shitty Chinese food into their mouths. I sensed some kind of preternatural antagonism between the two and immediately grew nervous.

"The thing about Luther," opined Miriam, "is that what he did back then is different. I'm just saying, modern-day Lutheranism is almost indistinguishable from Catholicism."

"Hmm, right," said Murray, her heavyset, affable, yes-man husband.

"In what way?" said Laurie.

"Well, Lutheranism is different than your basic liturgical faith . . ."

"Aturdical?" said Laurie. "What's that?"

"Liturgical. In a liturgical faith," said Miriam, "you'd have this whole schedule planned out. They'd do a sermon on January first, and then the next January first you'd do the very same sermon."

"Oh, well, we don't do that in our church," said Laurie. "In our church . . ."

Miriam was a quietly triumphant mom who'd laudably made it to a comfortable place in life with a good husband after rougher times in her youth—she told me she'd lived off food stamps in a ratty house with seven people in it when she was younger. She was happy with who she was, and seemed pleased to give her opinions on things and not to care one way or another what anyone else thought about them. And every time she offered one of those confident opinions, it upset Laurie for some reason.

We started talking about the morning's lessons. One of the things Sorensen had cautioned us about was people who come into the church claiming to be prophets and claiming to know the true Word of God. Sorensen said that all such comers to Cornerstone were traditionally told that they would be allowed to preach, so long as they went to "see Steve"—i.e., him—first. "Nobody ever comes," Sorensen said contemptuously. Apparently no itinerant false prophet would be fool enough to try his wares under the withering eye of Pastor Sorensen.

I picked at my food with my chopsticks. In the pointy-headed northeastern America of my experience there were no legends of wandering prophets, no dinner-table discussions about personal salvation. But in the rest of the country you had this weird dichotomy, an advanced industrial economy confidently riding the superconductor and the microchip into the space age while most of its population hurtled backward away from the Enlightenment, living out a *Canterbury Tales*–type quest for revelation in a culture dominated by superstition and mystery.

I had wondered during the lesson just exactly how often

strangers showed up in San Antonio megachurches claiming to be prophets. The group at the Chinese-food place now educated me. While the false-prophet thing did occasionally happen, the bigger problem, they said, was that there were people in Bible-study/cell meetings who would sometimes show up, claiming to "have a word." "People will come and they'll start saying, 'I've got a word' and such," Miriam said. "It happens."

"Course it's different when somebody comes and says, 'God talked to me the other day and said such and such,'" said Murray. "That's different, that's okay."

"It's just different when someone comes in and starts talking about how they've got a word," added Miriam. "People'll always have a word."

At this we entered a danger area when Miriam and Murray mentioned that they were planning on being cell leaders in this church. We congratulated them, in response to which Miriam wondered if she and Murray might not have some of the same problems they'd had as cell leaders in their last church, when certain people talked out of turn and were forever claiming to "have a word," which I guess meant claiming to have some kind of revelation from God. To be honest I didn't know what the fuck they were talking about, and it kind of freaked me out.

"I mean, some people have problems," she said.

"Well, everyone has problems," said Janine, who always tried to offer a generous opinion about people.

"No, I don't mean ordinary everyday problems," Miriam said. "I mean submissiveness problems. Authority problems. And right away"—here she looked at Murray and rolled her eyes—"I know who we're going to have problems with."

Clearly she was talking about some third party I didn't know. Janine and Laurie instantly hushed her up.

"Shhhh!" said Janine.

"Don't say it!" said Laurie. "Curse! Curse!"

"I'm just saying," said Miriam, shaking her head, "that there are certain people . . ."

"Don't!" said Janine. "Don't say it out loud! It'll come true!"

"Shh!" Laurie hushed.

"Yes, that's true, it is a curse if you say it," mumbled Murray agreeably, munching his food. Soy sauce stuck to his mustache.

I leaned back in my chair. What the fuck was going on?

"I don't understand," I said. "She can't say something out loud because that might be a curse?"

"That's right, honey," said Laurie.

"You see, Matthew," said Janine, leaning over, "the Devil can't hear your thoughts. He can only hear what you say out loud."

"Oh, right," I said. "Of course. I forgot."

"Thing is, there's a fine line between saying a curse and telling the truth," Miriam said. "I don't see how we can talk about a problem that might happen if we can't talk about a problem."

"She's got a point there," I said.

"Well, let me tell you how we do it in our group, honey," Laurie said to Miriam archly. "We don't do it that way at all."

A nasty discussion ensued, with Laurie challenging Miriam about her apparent unwillingness to let others speak and to leave her old group behind. Now, Miriam had given no indication that she was living in the past or planning on remaking her old group routine in the new church or anything like that—she was just telling a story about the way things had been in her old church. But Laurie wouldn't leave it be.

"You've got to leave all that behind, honey," she said. "You've got to let go. I have to say, if you're going to be a cell leader, I'm concerned that you're bringing this negative attitude to it."

"I am not," snapped Miriam.

"This is good tea," I whispered to Janine.

"Yes, it is," she whispered back.

"I'm just saying, you can't be bringing that negativity into your group," said Laurie. "Now, let me tell you how it's done in our group . . ."

Eventually Miriam got up in a huff and walked away for a moment, and the table fell silent. Laurie, still pounding a mound of battered crab legs—her fourth plate—was in an advanced state of anxiety. You could almost see the waves of fright emanating from her. She needed desperately to engage somebody about something, but there was no place for her to put all of her energy. The table was deathly silent for a moment except for the sounds of purposeful, joyless munching. I smiled at Laurie, then listened as Murray suddenly mentioned something about not being able to eat any cake, because they only had chocolate cake and he didn't like chocolate.

"Well," I said, "there's flan up there, if you like that."

Laurie exploded in laughter.

"Excuse me?" I said.

"Flan!" she chuckled. "Oh, you're cute, honey, you really are. 'Flan.' It's pronounced flaaahn, sweet thing."

I was pronouncing it "flan," like "fan"—correctly, it seemed to me.

"Actually, no," I said. "It's flan, like fan."

"Oh, sweet baby, I don't mean to step on your toes," she said, "but you're wrong. It's flaaaaahhhn," she said, giving me a long hoity-toity *a*, like the *a* in "wand." "It's from the Spanish."

I bit my lip.

"Actually, it's not Spanish, it's—never mind," I said. "You're right."

I jabbed violently at a piece of phony kung pao chicken.

"You're not offended, are you, honey?" Laurie said.

"No," I whispered. "I'm fine."

Actually, I wasn't fine. I sat there for a moment in silence, trying desperately to get a grip on myself. I was losing control of my cover.

The rest of the lunch followed a similar pattern. There were several more disagreements over minor doctrinal questions. I had begun to understand that the whole business of being this kind of Christian is mainly wrapped up in a tireless study of various dos and don'ts—how to get through the day and interact with other human beings without slipping and inviting a demon into one's home or one's abdomen. That meant you had to know everything there is to know about all of the don'ts; with idol worship, for instance, you had to spend lots of time discussing with your Christian friends what constituted idol worship and how to avoid it. A great many conversations will therefore be held in situations like this about the relative permissibility of things like crucifixes and portraits of the dead and plastic Virgin Mary statues. At this lunch, Murray opined that the Catholics were obviously idol worshippers because of their worship of the Virgin. Laurie chimed in that the rosary, too, was a kind of idol worship. A range of idol candidates was then discussed in succession.

After a while you begin to realize that there is no such thing as traveling through life quickly in this world. With demons lurking in even the most harmless-seeming transactions, every outing ends up getting bogged down in these anxious procedural discussions. It can get pretty bleak.

Finally the check came. We calculated that each person owed exactly ten dollars, not including the tip. The couple Miriam and Murray gave exactly twenty-one dollars. Laurie kept trying to say that the tip had been added to the bill automatically, even though, as an examining Janine pointed out, there was clearly no tip indicated on the bill. Minutes passed . . . meanwhile, the small bespectacled Chinese waiter, who was about to get stiffed on his tip, quietly dropped five fortune cookies on the table.

Laurie, Miriam, and Murray all reached for the cookies and started to unwrap them. Janine gathered hers in and tried to hide it under her plate. I caught sight of the waiter glancing miserably at the empty center of the table and was suddenly annoyed.

"Fortune cookies," I snapped, "are a curse."

The three cookie eaters instantly dropped their cookies.

"Oh, I know," said Laurie. "That's why I don't believe in them."

"But you're eating it," said Janine.

"Oh, well, I guess I am," Laurie said.

"They're witchcraft!" I said. "Just like horoscopes."

Everyone hung their heads. Murray sighed.

"I guess you're right," he said. "They are just like horoscopes."

"Yeah," said Miriam. "They're about tellin' the future. That's not right."

Everyone glumly tossed their cookies back into the center of the table. I kept mine, however, sliding it into my overcoat pocket. Quietly, we went out of the place, leaving a 10 percent tip. The waiter glared.

WE WENT BACK TO CHURCH for the tail end of our membership orientation. The whole tone of Pastor Sorensen's presentation shifted from a morning of religious banalities into an afternoon of political paranoia, dire warnings to the flock about what might happen to all of us should the forces of secular humanism seize control of America. This was sort of typical of the church, sticking your political content at the end of your meat-and-potatoes personal revelation stuff. Much of what he talked about concerned the church structure, specifically the "Government of Twelve" cell-group network, a hierarchy of "tribes" under which various individual Bible-study groups would meet. The groups were led by cell leaders, who were usually a married couple with a home big enough to accommodate large meetings.

According to Sorensen, one primary reason for creating the cell network was to preserve the church in case . . . well, in case something happened to the church.

"I'll tell you one thing," Sorensen said. "If Hillary Clinton should ever become president, God forbid . . ."

The crowd hissed and booed. Sorensen raised his hands.

"If, God forbid, something like that were ever to happen, one of the first things they'd try to do is tax the churches. You can count on that," he said.

The crowd gasped at the audacity of the suggestion. I found it ironic that by singling out Hillary specifically, Sorensen had just done the one thing that made the church no longer deserve tax-free status. But he wasn't finished:

"But another thing we have to worry about is that, if there were ever to be a terrorist attack here in America," he said, "this church is one of the first places they'd attack. Because they know that Pastor Hagee is one of their biggest enemies."

Jesus Christ, I thought, inwardly groaning. Laurie elbowed me and nodded gravely; I nodded back, then made sure to clap.

It went on like that for a while. The whole sermon was one unending fusillade against the perils of self and of the outside world. The only proper course of action, he continually hammered home, was to submit oneself entirely to the church— everything else was deadly and Hell-inducing.

"How many of you have subverted your natures for Christ?" he asked.

Hands flew up.

"That's good. We all have natures and we all have to forcibly subdue them . . ."

He went on, asking the crowd what it thought of fanatics. "My definition of a fanatic is someone who loves Jesus a little more than I do," he said, to laughter. "I used to laugh at those people who would fall on the ground praising. But actually they get it. They're the ones who get it." He sighed. "After all, when we compare ourselves to God, who are we?"

The crowd mumbled in a monotone: "NOBODY."

"Can I get an Amen?"

"AMEN!"

At the end of the sermon Sorensen indoctrinated the new members into the world of speaking in tongues, asking all who had not been baptized in the Holy Spirit to come forward and be anointed with oil. Those of us who had been baptized in the Spirit—and I had, of course, at the Encounter Weekend—were to come up and help the newbies. Specifically, we were supposed to stand behind them and catch them if they fell over with spiritual ecstasy.

I fell into the rear line, behind a pair of middle-aged new member women, and waited patiently. As Sorensen began anointing, the crowd all began to speak in tongues. Sorensen's tongues were like Fortenberry's—lots of lakakakashas and froooommms and see-bo-gralakashas, the same old *Temple of Doom* script. Sorensen's gobbledygook was fluent but not particularly inspired; he looked like a man who gave 80 percent in everything he did, even playing the desperate. When he glanced at me, I rolled my eyes back and started tongue-speaking on cue. I was tired; this time I went with the Soviet national anthem:

Through tempests the sunrays of freedom have cheered us
Along the new path where great Lenin did lead.
To righteous endeavors he raised up the peoples,
Inspired them to labor and to valorous deeds!

Sorensen nodded appreciatively at me; I smiled. Then he doused the woman in front of me with oil, and she fell backward, babbling nonsense; along with two other men, I caught her and laid her on the floor. She had a huge smile on her face. She was NOBODY.

• • •

BACK AT HOME, I sat at my desk, exhausted, and pulled my fortune cookie out of my pocket. It read:

There is no time like the pleasant.

On the other side of the paper there was a Chinese symbol. Next to it, in English, it read:

Milk.

SIX

Congressional Interlude II,

or

Democrats Seize the Reins

of the Derangement

IT'S THE FIRST WEEK of November 2006, and I'm reclining in a state of mild-to-heavy sedation in a large and lifeless Marriott Hotel suite in Pittsburgh, Pennsylvania. I'm here covering the midterm elections for *Rolling Stone* (specifically I'm here to poke a stick in the political corpse of Christ-humping senator Rick Santorum, who is about to lose his seat in a landslide), and while most of "progressive" America is popping the champagne corks, reveling in what looks like a stirring, throw-the-bums-out end to the Bush revolution, I'm feeling sick to my stomach.

The yellow legal pad covered with fevered scribbles lying next to me on the bed tells the story. My notes indicate that hours earlier, at 10:46 p.m., media demigod Barack Obama appeared on CNN, saying that the Democratic victory heralded "change" and a "new direction," adding that the party anxiously awaited the conclusions of the Baker-Hamilton report on the Iraq conflict. Later, at 11:58, Rahm Emanuel—slimy brother of even slimier Hollywood superagent Ari Emanuel—promises "change" and a "new direction." At 12:09 Harry Reid comes on the tube. His approximate quote: "All across America, from the deserts of somewhere to the streets of somewhere else, there is in the air the winds of change!" Roars, cheers from the crowd at this, then he adds: "We're headed in a new direction!" Reid points out that the Baker-Hamilton report should offer some insight into what to do about the whole Iraq business.

Seven minutes later, at 12:16, it's Nancy Pelosi's turn. "Never have we made it more clear that we need a new direction," she says. "Mr. President, we need a new direction!" She adds that she anxiously awaits the Baker-Hamilton report, which should help point the way forward in Iraq. At 12:24, someone asks Barack Obama, who is back on the air for what seems like the eight hundredth time tonight—the Dems are doing some serious brand-ID work this election—what he thinks the election results mean. Surprisingly, he says that it "confirms in my mind that the American people are eager to move in a new direction."

At 1:12 a.m., it's Dianne Feinstein's turn to speak. She says the elections are "a signal for a change in direction."

Apparently we need a new direction. We also need change. As for Iraq, that's a tough one, but let's wait for the conclusions of the Baker-Hamilton report, which might help us figure this shit out.

At some point in the midst of all of this, hurrumphing "political analyst" Jeff Greenfield comes on-screen. Commenting on the Democratic talking points, he has this to say: "They look to be very focus-group-tested for maximum appeal."

Says this approvingly, smiling, with admiration. I reach over to the night table, feel around for the bottle, eat the last of my pills . . .

Most of the people I know who follow politics are whooping it up today, reveling in the walloping defeat the evil Bushies suffered at the polls, but it's the other shoe that's about to drop that worries me. I can already feel in my bones what's coming. I've made quite a few friends among Democratic congressional staffers in recent years, most of them long-suffering political slaves laboring in windowless minority offices on the Hill—good guys most of them, sincere seeming, who'd tell me shocking tales of being ritualistically shat upon by the likes of Tom DeLay and Denny Hastert. They'd complain to me about the treatment their bosses suffered, sell it to me as crime against democracy, the People, and I'd buy most of what they were saying, because in most cases they were right.

Something tells me I'm going to stop hearing from those guys now. The phones are going to go cold. And I'm going to start seeing their bosses on TV with dumb grins on their faces and big erections in their pants, high on the smell of money and '08 White House invites.

No voter wants to believe he doesn't really matter, so he buys into the idea that there are two substantively different parties frantically competing for his attentions, the ideological fate of the country hanging on his decision every few years. It flatters the average citizen to think that way. The reality is that the dominant characteristic of our political system is the unchanging nature of the political consensus—while the two parties agree about most all of the important things, they disagree violently about the inconsequential stuff, providing the fodder and the drama for an endless political "struggle" that plays itself out in entertaining fashion every couple of years.

This business about waiting for the Baker-Hamilton report was a classic example. With popular discontent over the war raging, the Democratic Party still refused, technically, to come out against the war. It fudged the question of its original support for the invasion by claiming to have been misled en masse (despite the fact that even a small child could have seen through Bush's idiotic argument for the invasion back in 2002), and as for the future, it refused to make any promise to try to end the conflict. Instead, for the biggest issue of the election season, for a national vote that for most people is their only political decision in years, the Democrats avoided taking any stance at all, essentially saying, "We'll wait to see the conclusions of a random independent group of academics, and then we'll make our own decision." Basically, they punted and put the game in the hands of the defense.

The midterm elections might have marked the high point of the Bush revolution, the day the tide started receding, but it also marked the beginning of a new era. What followed would be a period dominated by the Democrats, in particular by the Democrats' skillful massaging of the war issue. It would be a period where the Democrats would prove absolutely that it is possible in America to govern entirely on the appearance of principle—while changing absolutely nothing.

ABOUT A MONTH after the elections I dropped in on a few friends in Congress, just to see how the power transfer was going. All over the congressional complex—in House buildings like Rayburn, Longworth, and Cannon, and Senate halls like Dirksen and Russell—minority staffers were moving into the bigger, plusher majority offices in the Capitol Building.

At one committee office I found a gang of young Democrats openly chortling at the Republicans' misery.

"You wouldn't believe those guys," said one. "They actually came by our office after the election and told us not to walk by their offices for a while, because it would hurt their feelings to be reminded that they have to move soon."

He shook his head.

"What a bunch of pussies," he said, chuckling.

When I asked what was on the agenda, they assured me that there were numerous ethics reforms on the way, but the bigger problem was that the Republicans had simply let their normal congressional housekeeping duties slide. They hadn't passed a budget before leaving town, forcing Democrats to put something together at the last minute to keep the agencies operating. That's how I left things that November—the Dems just moving in and immediately jamming their noses in the dreary muck of budget-building work. The last time I saw most of my "friends" on the Hill that season, they were looking haggard and sitting at desks overflowing with stacks of papers and budgetary requests.

Shortly thereafter I left town, and I finally went away to Texas for the winter, forgetting entirely about Washington politics through Christmas and the New Year. Occasionally, of course, I wondered what exactly was going on behind closed doors in those committee rooms back on the Hill. For six years ours had been a country dominated whole hog by Republican politicians, and the question of whether or not the Democrats upon returning to influence would represent a real opposition or a real alternative now loomed as the single weightiest question in American politics.

Shortly after the New Year I got a call from a friend in Washington, an aide to a certain unnamed congressman. I was in San Antonio at the time, splayed out in my boardinghouse bed, unshaven and more or less completely motionless, lazily watching an afternoon broadcast of one of Hagee's sermons. My cell rang and I brought it to my ear slowly, like a tree sloth.

"Uh-huh," I said.

"Hey, Taibbi," he said. "The fuck are you?"

"I'm in San Antonio," I said. "Praying to Jesus."

"Yeah, right," he said. "Anyway, get ready for a lot of bullshit."

"As in what?"

"As in the budget," he said. "They're doing a CR. It's absolutely crammed full of bullshit. Like you know how when you're packing, and you can't close the suitcase, so you jump on top of it, and it still doesn't close, and then finally you sit on it and you get your girlfriend to try to zip it up while you're sitting on it, and you're bouncing up and down on the suitcase and finally after like half a fucking hour the both of you manage to close it, but just barely?"

"Yeah."

"That's how much bullshit is in this thing," he said.

A CR is a continuing resolution. Basically, when Congress doesn't have time to write up a completely new budget, it passes a CR, which funds the government at roughly the same level as the previous year. Congressional leaders will write up guidelines for each CR; they may specify, for instance, that all programs in the budget are to be funded at the lowest number among the House, Senate, and final budget versions from the previous year. In other words, if last year's V-22 program is at $1 billion in the Senate bill, $1.2 billion in the House, and $1.4 billion after conference, this year the V-22 gets $1 billion. Old-timers of the budget process will tell you, though, that military programs tend to have pretty similar numbers across the board, while social programming may vary wildly from version to version—meaning CRs will end up naturally underfunding social programs compared to defense appropriations.

In any case, in the run-up to the release of the CR, the Democrats did a couple of things. The first was that Pelosi rammed through an "ethics bill," a thing called the Honest Leadership and Open Government Act, which was intended to be the Democrats' response to the Jack Abramoff/Duke Cunningham scandals of the Bush era. The bill prohibited lawmakers from knowingly accepting gifts from registered lobbyists or foreign agents and banned member use of corporate jets. Also, travel packages financed by outside interests would henceforth have to be approved by the Ethics Committee. This in theory was supposed to prevent the kind of skullduggery practiced by the Abramoffs of the world, who used golf junkets to Scotland and "fact-finding tours" to St. Thomas to buy government contracts and/or favors (like intervention in casino regulatory disputes) from members with a taste for luxury travel.

The second thing the Democrats did was pass a rules package containing what it called "earmark reform." At the beginning of each Congress, the House passes what it calls a "rules package," and the package is just that, a set of rules that govern how the House is going to operate. In this case, the rules package contained provisions that each bill passed by the House had to either contain a list of the earmarks included within (with the name of the member who requested the earmark listed next to it) or else contain a statement attesting to the absence of earmarks. Moreover, every listed earmark had to include a description of the earmark written by the requesting member, and that same member had to sign a statement attesting to the fact that he or she had not profited personally from said earmark.

If this all sounds confusing, it is. An earmark, to the un-initiated, is the basic currency of congressional corruption. Also called "state items," earmarks are simply budget items not requested by the administration and jammed into a bill during the budget process by an individual representative. Say Congressman X receives ten grand each election cycle from a cement-mixing company; if he wants to repay that company with a government contract, he ducks into the transportation bill during markups (i.e., while it is being put together in committee) or in conference and gets himself a $10 million highway project stuck into the fine print of the law.

Until now these little budget items were totally unregulated and a source of massive, endemic corruption. Lobbyists and corporate hacks leveraged private money into public works time and time again, as a word to the right committee chair or ranking minority member could get just about anything for anyone, and only the hundred or so people on the Hill who actually know how to read the budget will even know. The notorious "bridge to nowhere"—a $230 million bridge connecting Anchorage and the Knik area of Alaska, which is home to about 250 people—was a classic example of the kind of shit that happens when earmarks go unchecked. That earmark achieved a kind of fame, and unlike most earmarks (which for ages simply appeared anonymously in print, neither noticed nor tied directly to anyone), the Knik bridge deal was almost right away revealed to be the work of Senator Ted Stevens, one of the most powerful legislators in Washington. As the head of the Senate Appropriations Committee, a guy like Stevens could, until this year, basically give himself any contract he wanted, jamming bridges and roads and weapons bills into a bill markup at the last minute, like a kid scribbling ice cream and cookie requests onto Mom's shopping list.

The ethics bill and the rules package were intended to be linked, a matched set. With the ethics bill the Democrats addressed the means lobbyists and other interested parties used to gain access to lawmakers; with the rules package they addressed the means lawmakers used to execute the promised favors.

In theory.

In the weeks leading up to the Democrats' unveiling of the CR, the word coming out of Washington, at least in the major media, was that the bill would be the "cleanest" budget in years. Even conservatives were praising the new Democratic leadership. Here's an analysis of the upcoming CR by a pair of Heritage Foundation talking heads back in December of '06:

With a better sense of the electorate's anger over congressional corruption and profligate spending, incoming Speaker of the House Nancy Pelosi (D-CA) instead plans to extend the money-saving continuing resolution over the entire year and thereby strip all earmarks from this year's budget. In effect, and as some fiscal conservatives have urged, Pelosi intends to demonstrate that henceforth the budget of the United States

*government will be made in the United States Capitol, not in
the offices of the several thousand lobbyists who have hijacked
the process by selling earmarks to clients.*

The much-ballyhooed "earmark-free" CR became so axio-
matic that pretty soon prominent Democrats began to issue public statements praising it long before it was even a reality. Senator
Robert Byrd and Congressman David Obey, the appropriations
chairmen of their respective houses, issued a joint statement on
December 11: "We will work to restore an accountable, above-
board, transparent process for funding decisions and put an end
to the abuses that have harmed the credibility of Congress." The
Washington Post took these statements at face value and on December 12 became the first of many major news outlets to run
Congress stories with the phrase "earmark-free" or "earmark
freeze" in the headline: "Democrats Freeze Earmarks for Now."*

*Congresswoman Jane Harman on January 4: "We have already spent at
least $400 billion in Iraq and Afghanistan. But only about 9 percent of
those funds were approved through the normal appropriations process.

"The rest was passed in 'Emergency Supplemental' appropriation
bills not subject to budget caps or the normal congressional oversight process. These supplementals—because their numbers do not appear on the
budgetary bottom line—allow the White House to pretend it is maintaining a semblance of fiscal discipline. But our deficits are already spiraling
out of control and there is no way to bring the budget into balance without
taking the staggering war costs into account.

"The Bush Administration has claimed emergency spending is
necessary because the costs of a protracted war on terror are not known.
Nonsense. Both the Korean and the Vietnam wars were almost entirely
financed through the regular appropriations process—not emergency
supplementals.

"The White House will soon ask for over $100 billion in new emer-
gency war spending. Adjusted for inflation, that is more than we spent in
1968, the most expensive year of the war in Vietnam. And the lion's share
of that funding was done through the regular process.

"There must be no more blank checks for this president, and I predict this will be the last 'emergency' supplemental in the new Democrat-
controlled Congress."

A month or so later, on January 31, 2007, to be exact, the House passed the $463 billion CR by a huge margin, 286–140. Immediately Democrats rushed to take credit for the historically "clean" bill. Leading the charge was Rahm Emanuel, who chirped, "This is an earmark-free bill!" The *Washington Post* heard Emanuel and jammed his quote straight into a page 4 headline: "House Passes $463 Billion Spending Bill after Deleting Earmarks."

And yet, all that any of these reporters had to do was read the goddamn text of the CR to see that there were earmarks in there, big ones, not hidden in the slightest. Of course, I wouldn't have looked myself, had it not been for a friend of mine, a former Senate staffer turned independent budget analyst named Winslow Wheeler. A laconic, silver-haired gentleman with a salt-and-pepper mustache who seems always to have a wry smile on his face, as though living in a constant state of bemused disgust over the pork issue, Wheeler had been fired from the staff of New Mexico senator Pete Domenici in the early part of the decade for writing exposés about Defense Department pork under a pseudonym. Although he's been out of the Senate for years now, Wheeler is still intimately familiar with the pork/earmark process—in fact, he can even claim to have helped streamline the system.

As an aide to Domenici, he had been in charge of keeping track of the senator's earmark requests—cataloging them, tracking their progress through the various committees, and, most important, making sure they appeared in the final texts of the bills. "When I first got to Domenici's office, I was horrified that he had all of these pork requests in the defense bill," he says now. "And there was no systematic way of keeping track of 'em. It was just a pile of documents. Now, as a staffer I was supposed to keep track of these fucking things. And there were fifty, sixty, eighty of them, who knows.

"So being an organizational wimp I started putting them

in a table, keeping track of them. Here's the item, here's what the House Armed Services Committee did with it, here's what the Senate Armed Services Committee did with it, here's what the HAC [House Appropriations Committee] did with it, here's what the SAC [Senate Appropriations Committee] did with it, and so on."

Wheeler later explained to me that the table contained all sorts of information, including budget ID numbers, called PE numbers, and other info. "So in March," he said, "[Senator Ted] Stevens, the Appropriations chairman, he always wanted senators to send a letter stating what their 'state interest items' are—earmarks, in other words—and after the second or third year, I started including my Word Perfect table with Domenici's letters, to help the Appropriations Committee keep track of what the fuck each item was.

"Well," Wheeler explained, "Stevens loved that, and after that, he required everybody to include that table. So I guess that'll be my legacy."

When the Democrats' CR came out, I wrote to Wheeler and asked him to ID the earmarks in it for me. He wrote back and said there were several in the CR itself, including one on page 30, line 3, of the 137-page document. It read:

3   "(2) Of the amount made available in this sec-
4   tion for Research, Development, Test and Evalua-
5   tion, $217,500,000 shall be made available only for
6   peer reviewed cancer research activities, of which
7        $127,500,000 shall be for breast cancer research ac-
8   tivities; of which $10,000,000 shall be for ovarian
9   cancer research activities; and of which $80,000,000
10   shall be for prostate cancer research activities.

"That's what an earmark looks like?" I asked.

"Yeah," said Wheeler. "Well, that's one variety." He went on to explain that the cancer research earmarks were a nearly twenty-year tradition in the Congress, the by-products of an ongoing *War of the Roses*–style gender piss-fest between various members of Congress.

"It all started in the nineteen-eighties, when Pat Schroeder started sticking in 'women's health services' earmarks for breast cancer research," Wheeler said. "Then in the nineties, the boys got jealous and stuck in earmarks for prostate cancer. Then the girls went back and stuck in ovarian cancer. I'll bet you another lunch that we'll get testicular cancer next year, earmark reform or not."

All in all, there were about a half-billion dollars in earmarks in the "earmark-free" continuing resolution, which incidentally was sort of a canard to begin with. A CR is not a real budget; it is merely a mathematical formula that allows Congress to pay for government programs based on funding levels from, among other things, the previous year's budget. There are almost never earmarks in a CR itself; the earmarks are usually in the actual budget the CR refers to. So when the Democrats promised an "earmark-free CR," that was already funny—continuing resolutions, by nature, are almost always earmark-free anyway.

And yet in this case, the Democrats hit it both ways. They actually did put a half-billion dollars' worth of earmarks in this, their first CR, and then, in the defense budget anyway, they explicitly left in the earmarks from the previous year's budget. That is what the following passage from the CR means, when translated into human language:

> Amounts made available in this section are subject to the terms and conditions set forth in the Department of Defense Appropriations Act, 2007 . . .

Although the "earmarks" were said to have been removed from the budget, in fact the sums of money for the earmarks were left in the budget and distributed to the same agencies they had always been intended for. The money was still there, waiting to be spent—it just wasn't called an earmark anymore.

"It's an insult to Swiss cheese," said Wheeler. "I'll bet you that as we speak, staffers are calling agencies and saying, 'We want to make sure that you know that all the money from last year is still there.'"

And indeed, less than a week or so after the CR passed, word leaked out that a Republican staffer from the Senate Appropriations Committee had been circulating an e-mail request for earmarks for the upcoming Labor–Health and Human Services (colloquially known as the "Labor H") appropriations bill. The e-mail read:

> The Labor-HHS deadline for all requests will be April 13,
> 2007.
> This deadline includes any programmatic funding, project
> funding, bill or report language requests that your Senators
> would like to submit for the FY2008 LHHS bill.
> Please submit all requests by e-mail and deliver a hard copy
> to SD-156.

The "project funding, bill or report language requests" called for in this letter—that's Congress-ese for earmarks. The letter was irrefutable evidence that everything in Congress was back on the usual schedule. Appropriations season's coming up, send us your Christmas list. Incidentally, Santa moved; he's in the Democratic offices now.

SOME TIME LATER in the spring, the Democrats found themselves in a much-publicized bind. Charged with the responsibility of drawing up a budget for the unwanted Bush war, the Democrats—who had been elected on a mandate to end the conflict—were under heavy pressure to tie that funding to a timeline for withdrawal. And they initially did so, writing up an "Iraq supplemental" budget that made an exit timeline a precondition for funds disbursement.

That seemed like solid confrontational politics, except that the word soon leaked out that (a) President Bush planned on vetoing the supplemental and (b) the Democrats were almost certain to rework the budget the next time around, taking the timeline out. The whole withdrawal-timeline thing in this first pass at the war budget was therefore complete and total bullshit, a "message" sent to the president by a Congress that actually held all the power already. It would be cast in the press as an antiwar gesture; in reality it was a laborious piece of buck passing, the new Democratic majority trying to cast off its political mandate by pretending the president still held the cards. After all, the only real consequence of sending a vetoed budget back to the president (with a message to take it or leave it) would be the inevitable political fallout that would come from being slammed by Republicans for "failing to support the troops in harm's way" or whatever. The Democrats expected all of us to respect their boundless, ball-sucking dread of that kind of criticism, respect the fact that not more than five or ten of them have the decency to recognize that their political careers matter less than their duty to rescue young Americans and Iraqis from pointless deaths.

They also expected us not to notice that the supplemental had turned out to be a forum for reintroducing the old politics as usual. This time, the relevant clause was at the end of the bill. It read as follows:

EARMARKS

Pursuant to clause 9 of rule XXI of the Rules of the House of Representatives, this conference report contains no congressional earmarks, limited tax benefits, or limited tariff benefits as defined in clause 9(d), 9(e), or 9(f) of rule XXI.

I went back to see Wheeler in Washington. He'd promised to teach me how to read congressional bills so I could learn to spot the pork in them. And this one, he said through very hearty laughs, was as chock full of crap as any of them. So I grabbed the *Congressional Record* for April 24, 2007—Congress puts out a volume every day with a transcript of all floor dialogue that includes the texts of all relevant legislation—and sat down in his small office in downtown D.C.

The supplemental, he explained, was broken into two parts. The first part was simply the text of the bill, and in this case included about twenty italicized pages under the heading "Conference Report on HR 1591." The text of the bill summarized the contents of the supplemental in almost-readable prose, including the much-publicized section outlining the "benchmarks" the al-Maliki government of Iraq would have to follow in order to continue receiving military aid.

Wheeler directed me to ignore that section for now, however, and flip forward to a section called the "Joint Explanatory Statement of the Committee of the Conference." This was a much fatter section and had far less readable prose text; it was mostly numbers and tables.

"In any bill," he said, "you always want to look at the joint explanatory statement first. That's where you'll find all the stuff. Here, for instance, look at this . . ."

He flipped forward to page H3946. It was a table that read:

Explanation of Project Level Adjustments

(in thousands of dollars)

P-1	BUDGET REQUEST	HOUSE	SENATE	CONFERENCE
2 EA-18G Fund 1 EA-6B combat loss replacement	75,000	83,000 -367,000	75,000	75,000 0
4 F/A-18E/F (Fighter) Hornet (MYP) 3 F/A-18's combat loss replacements	16,000	208,000 192,000	16,000	208,000 192,000

(cont'd)

"When you're looking at earmarks," Wheeler said, "you just read these tables. Look at the column for the administration's request, then look at the last column, where it says 'Conference.' If the conference number is bigger than the administration number, you've usually got an earmark.

"Take a look at the number there for F/A-18's. The administration only asked for sixteen million dollars, most likely replacement parts. But you look over at the House number, and that number is two hundred and eight million dollars. And voilà, at the end, the final number is two hundred and eight million dollars. So by this you can deduce that Murtha's people in the House added three airplanes. That's a House earmark."

We flipped backward in the record.

"When you find an earmark," he said, "you can usually go back in the text of the bill and find a little section that explains a little bit what the fuck the actual earmark is. In this case, go back a few pages, and you find this:

AIRCRAFT COMBAT LOSSES

The conferees have agreed to fund procurement of aircraft to replace combat losses. The conference agreement includes funding for three F/A-18 aircraft to directly replace F/A-18 aircraft lost in combat and to fund a single EA-6B which is a functional replacement for an EA-6B Prowler combat loss.

"Notice anything odd about that?" he asked.

"Since when do Iraqi insurgents shoot down fighter jets?" I asked.

"They don't," he said.

"Then what is this?" I asked.

"That's a good question," he said. "I'd be interested to hear their answer to that, too."

The supplemental was full of stuff like this, crammed to the brim with earmarks military and domestic. A friend on the Hill explained his theory on what had happened. "The Democrats needed to hand out that one hundred and twenty-four billion dollars in gifts just to get the votes to pass the timeline. So you hand out some farm stuff, some Katrina stuff, some antidrought stuff, and maybe even some military stuff to various southern and western congressmen who were on the fence about voting for an 'antiwar' measure.

"Then they send that timeline to Bush, Bush vetoes it, and now the Democrats have to find a way to save face. So they'll send it back to Bush without the timeline, or with an 'advisory' timeline—but the price is that Bush has to sign off on the hundred and twenty-four billion dollars. Now you've got no timeline, and the antiwar vote the Congress was elected to cast isn't going to be there, but what you do have is one hundred and twenty-four billion dollars in new spending. It's beautiful. Rather than using the pork to leverage the timeline into law, they'll use the timeline to leverage the pork into law."

I called John Murtha's office to ask about the F/A-18s. His press guy, Matt Mazonkey, came to the phone.

"Matt Mazonkey!" he said cheerfully.

"Hi," I said. "My name is Matt Taibbi. I'm a reporter for *Rolling Stone*."

"Oh, hey, Matt! What's up?" he said, instantly adopting the buddies-for-life tone you often hear on the Hill from people you've never met and who, conversely, have never heard of you. I explained about the planes and asked if he knew the circumstances of those combat losses. I could almost hear him frowning on the other end of the line.

"What's this story about?" he asked, after a pause.

"The supplemental," I said unhelpfully. "I just saw this entry, and I was curious."

"Okay," he said. "Well, I, uh, don't know exactly when those planes were lost. But we'll get back to you, okay?"

"Yeah, okay," I said.

I called the Pentagon and the navy, even walked into the navy congressional liaison office, and made a series of requests for information about the combat losses. No one seemed to know anything. The last communication I received from the navy read as follows:

> *Matt,*
> *Wanted to let you know we are tracking this request.*
> *LT Bashon W. Mann*

GOLD Team Action Officer
CHINFO News Desk

Nobody ever got back to me about the planes. But the earmarks did end up staying in the final version of the supplemental, while the timeline had to wait for another day.

WHILE ALL of this supplemental stuff was going on, in early April, I went to a breakfast for a small group of reporters in the office of Bernie Sanders, the erstwhile Vermont congressman who in the anti-Bush fervor of the previous season had secured a startling promotion to the Senate. As a congressman Sanders had been a reporter's dream. A true independent who didn't rely on party money to win his elections—while Sanders caucused with the Democrats, he was technically an independent who relied upon his great name recognition and reputation in his tiny state—Sanders could be outspoken without fear of consequence. In years past he and his staff had been a great help in explaining the vagaries of Congress, including the ugly inner workings of the various committees. But Bernie was a senator now and he caucused with the majority party, which meant he had real power. It was not going to be possible anymore for him to play the role of an angry outsider. Moreover, when I'd dropped in on him a month or so before for an interview, he'd seemed overwhelmed by the differences between the House and the Senate. In particular he kept coming back to a story about his very first meeting with the Health, Education, Labor, and Pensions Committee.

At the meeting, the subject of the Head Start program had come up. Ted Kennedy, who runs the committee, had proposed a modest increase. Sanders wanted more—so he went and had a word with Kennedy after the meeting.

"The end result is that we got a 6 percent increase, instead of a 4 percent increase," he said. "Over a three-year period, that's five hundred million dollars more. What I'm finding out is it's just a different world. Not saying it's better, it's just different. If you want something, you just go talk to someone in the hall. It's all behind the scenes. Not like the House at all."

He tried to sound like it was a good thing, and it might very well have been, in terms of getting more money for a worthy-enough program. But the subtext of this story was Sanders expressing amazement that he could get $500 million just by talking to someone. As any human being would, he looked blown away by the reality of his situation. I left his office that day feeling like the conversation had turned weird at the end.

About a month and a half later, Sanders sent out invitations to a small group of progressive journalists for a breakfast at his Dirksen office. For those who hadn't had a chance to talk to him since his election, he wanted to reintroduce himself and remake a case he often made to reporters, appealing for the media's help in breaking the power monopoly in Washington. There were about ten of us there, and the list included a couple of friends of mine, including David Sirota and a former Sanders aide named Joel Barkin. We had pastries and coffee and after a few minutes of chatting sat down around a coffee table, with the senator planted in a central location on a couch. He immediately launched into a speech about trying to move the Congress in the direction of the public, handing out fliers with poll numbers to bolster his case. He told the same story about the HELP Committee meeting, Kennedy, and the $500 million. This went on for about a half hour, but when he opened up the discussion to questions, the reporters mostly blew off the senator's presentation in favor of questions about the war. Sanders looked miffed at first, then bit his lip and tried to meet the reporters halfway.

At the time, the Senate was in the midst of a controversial

vote over the Iraq supplemental budget; they were about to pass a version of the bill that included a timeline for scheduled withdrawal. It was well known that Bush was going to veto the bill and that the Democrats in the Senate would then be back to square one. The question on the reporters' minds was what was going to happen after the veto. Would the Democrats compromise and take the timeline out? What would Sanders do in that case?

The odd thing about this scene was that the reporters' consternation about the war was a mirror image of the public frustration over economic issues Sanders had given his speech about. The Senate was indeed far behind the public on the war; the public wanted the war ended now, no questions asked, while in the Senate the war was a political Gordian knot, impossible to take on directly. Sanders had called these reporters in to press them to pressure the Senate to be bolder and less politically calculating on health care, income disparity, and campaign finance reform, but ultimately he ended up defending the body's gradualist approach on the war. Before he knew it, the onetime idealist outsider was defending the "realities" of senatorial procedure.

Sirota, God bless him, kept haranguing Sanders to use the power of the filibuster to bully Harry Reid into keeping the timeline in. After all, apart from being able to get $500 million with an offhand conversation, each senator also has vast procedural power, and it seemed to be the judgment of the reporters in the room that Sanders should use that power on the war issue. I got the strong sense that the senator, just from a strategic standpoint, wanted nothing to do with talk like that; he wanted first to get his feet wet in the Senate and if he was going to take a stand on anything, it was going to be on one of "his" issues, like veterans' benefits or heating oil assistance, not the war. That made sense to me, but the people in the room wouldn't leave him alone.

"People say, 'Let's end the war right now,'" he said. "Okay, fine. How?"

"Well," said Sirota, "the *Washington Post* this morning is reporting that the new supplemental is going to have the timeline taken out, or reduced to a nonbinding, advisory timeline." He paused. "They're apparently doing this because conservative Democrats like Ben Nelson are threatening to not vote for any bill that has a timeline in it. Let me ask you this—can your side play a similar role in these proceedings? Or does the leadership only listen to the Ben Nelsons of the world?"

Sanders sighed. "That's a difficult question," he said. "I suppose you have to take it on a case-by-case basis. On the one hand, you don't want the president to get a great victory, but on the other hand you don't always want to be on the losing end—"

"Let me put it to you another way," interrupted Sirota. "In general, does the leadership listen to the conservatives like Nelson much more than people like you? Is there a way to play it like he plays it?"

Sanders looked grimly over at Sirota.

"Look, I've been here three and a half months," he sighed. "I like Harry Reid. I think sometimes you have to put yourself in his shoes. Sure, you can say to the Ben Nelsons, 'Ben, we don't want you to be in the coalition anymore.' And then what? You walk over to Mitch McConnell and say, Congratulations, you're the new majority leader. That's the reality of the situation. You want to do that? We can do that tomorrow."

"But—"

"So given that reality, what do you do? What do you do?"

The room fell silent. I looked down at my notebook. The word "reality" had been written about fifty times in the past hour. Every time he used the word "reality," it seemed, a little life went out of the room. Suddenly I was confused about something.

"Senator," I said, "isn't there a chance this whole thing could blow up in the faces of the Democrats? I mean, if they were planning on compromising all along, if they were always going to cave after the veto, then won't it look like they were just playing politics with funding for the troops this whole time? If you were always going to compromise in the end, isn't it fair to ask—what was this?"

Sanders sighed again.

"That's a good question," he said.

In the end the whole drama of the Democrat-controlled Congress publicly musing over whether or not to fund the war turned out to be a classic Washington mutual masturbation session, a prolonged exercise in favor trading and power maintenance that had as little to do with actually serving the desires of the electing public as a Martian zoning hearing would have. The "reality" narrative that even an honest guy like Bernie Sanders has to play along with to survive turns out to be no more rational or grounded in fact than the conspiracy narrative sustaining the 9/11 Truth Movement—in both cases you have a group of people whose community is defined by its members' common deference to a vast range of plainly bogus assumptions. Put five people who believe the Twin Towers were mined together in a room, and you have a 9/11 Truther meeting; put together five people who think they won't be able to golf in Scotland anymore if they vote "against the troops," and you have a caucus of Democratic senators. The fact that the internal logic—the "reality"—of congressional procedure has drifted so far from the needs and expectations of voters is highly convenient, of course, for the entrenched bureaucratic class in Washington; once you've created a situation where elected officials feel like they have to kowtow to this kind of artificial reality, you can find a way to mold that reality to the needs of the D.C. job-holding class and the financial interests supporting them.

Thus a Democratic Congress elected to clean up corruption and end a war will instead further the same corruption and continue the war, because that is what the people they are *really* beholden to expect of them. And if that Congress debates these issues publicly at all, the debate is mainly about how best to create the appearance of real action, i.e., how best to satisfy the voters' demand for a withdrawal without actually doing anything. Washington politicians basically view the People as a capricious and dangerous enemy, a dumb mob whose only interesting quality happens to be their power to take away politicians' jobs. The driving motivation of all Washington politicians is to quell or deflect that power, and this is visible even in such a terrible, immediate emergency as the Iraq war, when one would think that some kind of civic instinct would kick in, for five minutes or so at least. But no: instead, a newly conquering congressional majority armed with a fresh mandate essentially spent its first year in office trying to stay on the right side of public anger while maintaining business as usual; it was very plain that the party viewed its end-the-war mandate as a *burden,* not a privilege.

When the government sees its people as the enemy, sooner or later that feeling gets to be mutual. And that's when the real weirdness begins.

SEVEN

BIBLE STUDY

★ ★ ★ ★ ★ ★ ★ ★ ★ ★ ★ ★

I WAS LOSING CONTROL of my Christian mannequin. I'd snap awake during a service and catch him clapping his hands—or, worse, with his hands up in full Freeze-Motherfucker mode, a dumb smile frozen on his face, singing along:

To God . . . be the glo-r-r-r-y . . . To Go-o-o-d be the glo-o-o-o-ry . . . !

It was really becoming a problem. Before I came down to Texas, a female photographer friend of mine from Houston had cautioned me, "If you start going all Jesusy on us, we're going to come down and put a bullet in your brain."

"For my own good, I know," I said.

"Fuck that," she said. "For *our* own good. And don't for a minute think I'm kidding."

But here's the thing. Once you've spent enough time in this world, and sat through enough ball-numbingly dull sermons about The End of Everything and The Worthlessness of Me, you start catching yourself being very glad for the smallest reprieves. Specifically, after enough desperation and misery and corporate self-abnegation, and picking up the phone late at night to listen to fellow Christians wish openly that they can pray their way out of next week's bills, and drinking cheap powdered presweetened iced tea out of plastic cups in squalid stripmall chain restaurants with self-flagellating, past-middle-aged depressives who think Satan is the reason their kids don't call them anymore—after enough of that, a full-on, million-piecechorus, John Hagee Sunday spectacular starts to seem like a goddamned Rolling Stones concert.

Or so I told myself one Sunday, when—as I wandered aimlessly with the cattle flow of worshippers (or, to use the T. D. Jakes pronunciation popular around here, "wauwshp-s") into Hagee's megachurch—I caught my mannequin self actually looking forward to the Sunday service. I had a big postoperative smile on my face and was idly taking stock of the various odd sensual delights of Sunday worship: the cool sanitary air of the huge modern arena grazing my skin, the hypnotically faint organ music coaxing the crowd into its seats, the razor-sharp acoustics, the incipient promise of belting vocals and huge choral arrangements.

The realization that I was actually enjoying myself on some level hit me like an eighteen-wheeler. I was horrified, obviously, but I also realized that I had passed an important milestone on whatever journey it was that I was supposed to be taking.

I could clearly remember that when I first started coming to church months before, I couldn't even listen to the music we all sang along to during services. In fact, I wasn't even sure it was music; so atonal and emotionally neutral, it was music that didn't even attempt to engage and excite the senses. Instead it sort of just lapped over you, like a saline solution. Blah blah blah . . . the blood of Jesus . . . blah blah blah . . . the blood of Jesus . . . The music was so bad, in fact, that the empiricist in me spent weeks mulling over possible explanations for why and how the congregation spent so much time singing these horrid tunes.

I even considered that some sort of mass hypnosis was going on, that the repetitious chanting (mixed with some effects that I could see the church leaders clearly were manipulating, like the carefully timed dimming of lights) was some sort of clever way of numbing the brain and heightening suggestibility.

But now I could see that that wasn't really it at all. It wasn't the music that numbed you. It was the relentless, self-annihilating message of the church—the constant driving home of the idea that you were nothing, God was everything, and the End was coming—that did the numbing. Even if you weren't inclined to fight it, it was intellectually exhausting and depressed the senses. You felt freed from the guilty burdens of Self, but once Self was safely in its cage, you were left with nothing but meat and bones as tools for listening and enjoying. You were listening not with your ear but with your cerebellum, your brain stem—with your horseshoe-crab self. And suddenly music that couldn't have sucked worse a few months back sounds sweet, and inviting, and pretty, like it was written just for you, which incidentally it was.

I had come to church late that morning and so didn't sit down on the first floor with Laurie and Janine, as I usually did. Instead I went up to the balcony, whipped out my notebook and Bible, and prepared to receive the Wisdom. I sang some songs along with the crowd, and then Pastor Hagee trotted out a young female vocalist to sing a solo tune called "The Cross Said It All."

Churchgoing Matt purred; from the balcony, the vocalist looked a little like a young Linda Ronstadt (I would later see her up close and be troubled by the size of "her" Adam's apple). The tune had a stunning chorus:

> *He ain't never done me nothing but good . . .*
> *God used three nails and—two pieces of wood!*

I chuckled, wondering if the song's author had, like Salicri, thanked the Lord for that inspired rhyme. Then I sat down with the crowd and listened as Hagee ascended to the pulpit.

By any standard, Pastor John Hagee is an orator of unusual ability. His physical form is clownish; apart from the central-casting head of white, swept-back preacher hair, he has short, stubby arms and the body of a beach ball. He is one of those perfectly round fat men whose whole body seems like a plat-form for a straining top suit button that might at any moment shoot out skyward like a champagne cork. But when it talks, this beach ball has tremendous oratorical range, zooming back and forth from wry folksy humor to humility to booming fire-and-brimstone hellfire and back to humor again with effortless ease. When he asks for money, he sounds like he's asking you the time. John Hagee could, as they say down here in Texas, talk a dog off a meat truck.

Hagee started off slowly. He announced that today was the beginning of a new three-sermon series called "The Edge of Time." Right on cue, a flurry of helpers appeared out of nowhere to put up a billboard behind Hagee labeled "THE EDGE OF TIME" that contained several huge cartoonish illustrations, in-cluding the Four Horsemen of the Apocalypse and "the woman" of Revelation 12. The illustrations, as illustrations frequently do in fundamentalist Christian media, recalled the covers of Dun-geons and Dragons modules. Hagee explained that the sermon series was going to help reveal to us the mysteries of "God's clock" and unravel the "advanced mathematics" of the Bible, in this way helping us to understand that 2007 was going to be a "special year" in God's plan. I got the distinct impression that Hagee was hinting that something big was going to happen soon, End Times–wise.

Hagee spent this first sermon talking mostly about the Four Horsemen and this mysterious woman of Revelation 12. He read from the scripture:

1   Now a great sign appeared in heaven: a woman clothed
with the sun, with the moon under her feet, and on her
head a garland of twelve stars . . .
5   And she bore a male child who was to rule all nations
with a rod of iron . . .

Hagee noted that some people interpreted the woman in
Revelation 12 as being the church.

"But the church didn't give birth to Christ," he said. "Christ
gave birth to the church. It is not the church."

And he gave another reason why it was not the Virgin Mary,
as was commonly assumed. It was, however, Israel, and this had
something to do with some previous scripture involving Joseph
and Israel carrying eleven stars—only Joseph himself was the
twelfth star, or something like that. It was an awesome thing
to watch, the way Hagee just dove up to his neck in all of this
hilarious horseshit and passionately sold the audience on it
actually meaning something with a perfect deadpan delivery.
The audience cooed. He went back to the Four Horsemen and
pointed to the fourth horse.

"This is the Pale Horse," he warned. "He is the color of rot-
ting flesh. He will be given the power to destroy 25 percent of
the population. This is going to happen during the Tribulation.
You do not want to be here."

From here Hagee went into a long spiel about the difference between the Christ of the Gospels and the Christ of
Revelation. This is an important point for people who are not
fundamentalist Christians and want to understand them. The
Gospels Christ is basically a long-haired, touchy-feely hippie
who goes around being nice to people. The Christ of Revelation
is built like the Rock and roams the universe braining sinners
with lead pipes. Fundamentalists clearly prefer the Revelation
Christ. Hagee explained:

"In Matthew he is the lamb being led to the slaughter. In

Revelation he is the LION OF JUDAH! He is going to rule with a rod of iron!"

And when that rod-bearing Christ comes back, us unbelievers had better fucking duck:

"How is Jesus going to crush secular humanism and liberalism and anti-Semitism and atheism?" Hagee asked. "He is not going to ask the Supreme Court to put the Ten Commandments up in our courthouses. He is going to tell them, and they will bow down to him like children."

The crowd roared.

"And those judges who let men get married—he is going to cast them down into the pit of Hell to be roasted for all eternity like they deserve!"

I raised hands in a full Freeze-Motherfucker. Go Jesus! Waste those judges!

But just when it seemed that Hagee had his crowd right where he wanted them, he switched gears and began talking about Iran and Israel. Hagee is a subtle operator. Whenever he mentions the Iranian president Mahmoud Ahmadinejad, it is always moments after a long tirade about Satan. He will give hints about the Antichrist's identity—he is not an American, says Hagee, but he is a smooth talker.

"He will come preaching peace," said Hagee, "and he will sign treaties that he has no intention of keeping."

"Like Muslims!" someone behind me whispered.

And just as the crowd was ruminating over the possible identity of the Antichrist, Hagee switched gears and dropped a bombshell on the crowd. "Iran's president is planning a nuclear holocaust, and how our empty-headed leaders in Washington don't see that, I don't know!" he grumbled.

From there he went on for a while about Israel and Iran. I felt the energy leaving the hall. The people in this church come to services for help in dealing with their own problems, which of course are legion. They are there to find a reason for living amid the financial struggle, the constant battles with sin and despair, or romantic disappointment, loneliness, abuse, addiction. They could give a shit about Israel and they could give a shit about Iran. And so, while Hagee worked himself up into a frenzy about Iran, the crowd only cheered politely. This was true even at the climax:

"And now comes a new Hitler," roared the pastor, "and his name is Ahmadinejad. Iran MUST BE STOPPED!!!"

Polite clapping from the crowd.

Hagee frowned slightly. After attending these sessions, I could only say the man is a con man—a very good one, of course, but a con man nonetheless. His job is to deliver Middle American Christians in support of pro-Israeli policies. In Washington, John Hagee is a political operator whose influence stems from a close relationship with AIPAC, the Israeli lobby (which had Hagee give an address last summer) and various AIPAC-connected politicians like John McCain (who would later that year address Hagee's Christians United for Israel, or CUFI, group). There is talk that Hagee has been supported financially by certain members of the AIPAC board; one former AIPAC employee told me that Hagee had been the recipient of significant donations in the past. All outward appearances, therefore, point to Hagee as a canny operator, a run-of-the-mill kuntry preacher who found a Washington inside-baseball niche (delivering the Christian vote for Israel) and ran with it all the way to close access to Congress and the White House. Indeed, in 2005 and 2006, reports began to surface that Hagee's CUFI had held a series of "informal meetings" with White House officials about America's Middle East policy. In order to advance his agenda, Hagee hired a long-standing D.C. political operative named David Brog to lobby his cause on the Hill; Brog is a former chief of staff for Pennsylvania senator Arlen Specter, former Republican chairman of the Senate Judiciary Committee. All of this activity appears designed to further Hagee's aim of turning CUFI into a Christian AIPAC—which is a fairly strange and ambitious goal for a preacher whose congregation has probably never heard of AIPAC.

In that regard it takes some serious skills to get eighteen thousand Texan fundamentalists cheering, even robotically, for the Star of David. Hagee has those skills, but he can only take things so far. It's garden-variety domestic despair that keeps the flock coming in, and he can only leave that theme for so long.

So once he was finished with Ahmadinejad, Hagee quickly went back to the other Devil, the domestic Devil—and the crowd buzzed again, for the Devil is very real to these people. They see him everywhere, hovering over everything they love and need: their families, their husbands or wives, their jobs, their bodies.

"He intends to kill you physically!" shouted Hagee. "He intends to destroy your marriage!"

Behind me, the men and women of the congregation whispered their assent:

"Protect me, Lord!"

"Save me, Jesus!"

And he finished the sermon with the usual fire and brimstone, talking about how the Devil can try as hard as he wants, but he knows his is a lost cause, because he was already beaten at Calvary two thousand years ago. The crowd cheered; they never get tired of hearing this happy ending. And then there was music again, and the organ cranked back up, and we all filtered out of the church.

After services I went out for a cup of coffee with Janine and her little girl, who was coloring in a book as we talked.

"What did you think about the pastor's message?" I said. "About 2007 being a special year?"

"What do you mean?" she asked.

"I mean, I got the impression he was saying that something was going to happen in the Middle East, that maybe the Rapture was coming."

"Oh," she said. "I didn't get that. I just thought . . . you know, I wondered if 2007 would be a special year, too, but that's because I'm thirty-three this year. Christ was thirty-three when he died on the cross, you know."

"I know," I said. "And what did you think about what he said about Ahmadinejad?"

"Who?" she asked.

"Never mind," I said.

"You know, obviously, I think about the Rapture," she said, "but not that often. If it happens, it happens. I just try . . ."

"You're just trying to be the best Christian you can be right now, while we're still here," I offered.

"Exactly," she said.

OUR CHURCH had a clear hierarchical structure, one that placed Pastor Hagee at the top and then spread out to leaders of the "twelve tribes," which were like homeroom units within the church. Within each tribe there were smaller "cells," and each of these cells met once weekly, holding Bible-study classes and providing a sort of extended family structure that allowed each church member to have a real personal connection to the congregation. I imagined it was not dissimilar to Al-Qaeda.

Although the church itself claimed a different reason for having this cell structure—Reverend Sorensen, of course, had basically said that the cell structure gave the church an organizational framework to rely upon in the event of a terrorist attack upon the church building—I saw clearly that the cell/tribe structure was an absolutely necessary innovation, a bril-

liant way of transforming an utterly impersonal megachurch/
TV-preacher religious corporation into something even more
intimate than a backwoods, ten-pew country parish.

What the followers of Cornerstone craved more than anything was personal contact, a sense of being connected to something in the world, and the cell group, not the church, was what
fulfilled that need.

Through Laurie I'd joined a cell group and had begun going
to meetings. I'd been a bust at the first one, which had been just
a meet-and-greet at a member's house, a modest one-bedroom
ranch with Formica floors and slate faux-masonry walls
within earshot of a highway. Frightened by a clowder of fifty-
something housewives with crayon-thick eyeliner and Nancy
Reagan hairdos—and anxious to avoid their pious, potbellied,
truck-driving husbands—I spent the entire meeting clinging
to an octogenarian Japanese anesthesiologist named Hiroshi
Nakitomi, a stroke victim with memory lapses who sat mute at
the dinner table tranquilly clutching a cane with a saintly smile
on his face. I must have spent nearly forty minutes quizzing
the good old doctor about the types of anesthesia he used over
the years. Like all drug addicts, I have an unhealthy fascination
with this subject.

"You ever use methoxyflurane?" I asked. "I mean, what was
your go-to general?"

He looked at me and smiled. "Putting them out isn't the
problem," he said. "The trick is making sure they wake up."

He nodded, pleased with his joke. I laughed with him.

"How about trichloroethylene? When do you use that?"

"We used to use halothane," he said. "Of course, putting
them under isn't the problem."

"No?" I asked.

"No," he said. "The problem is making sure they wake up."

He laughed and put his hand on my shoulder. He smiled

again, a broad, kind smile. The doctor was losing it, but he was a good man.

"That's a good one," I said, laughing. "And what did you use in the nineties? Before you retired?"

"The nineties," he said, shaking his head.

"Right, the nineties," I said.

"I miss it, you know," he said wistfully. "I had fun being a doctor."

"I'll bet," I said.

"Of course, putting them under wasn't the problem . . ."

We went on like this for a long time. I started to notice eyebrows being raised around the room. It was weird enough for me to be a young, single man in this company of older married Christian couples, most of whom had grown children who had already left the hearth. And yet here I was, not only single but ignoring the host and hostess and accosting the only foreigner in the room with weirdly involved questions about chemicals. This was certainly about the least amount of effort I'd put into keeping my cover since I'd come to Texas, and I felt sure that I was blowing things on many levels. Moreover, as I later learned, there were rumors flying in the group that I was Laurie's new beau, and I can only imagine what kind of talk that inspired. So it was with some trepidation that I showed up at the next meeting, which wasn't just a social meeting—we were actually going to worship and praise and "get teaching."

I came late. This meeting was at the home of our cell leaders, Richard and Cassie Wiggle, who owned a biggish house on the north side of town.

Richard was a sloe-eyed fellow with a full head of silver hair and a faintly nautical-looking beard; he addressed the group in a gentle, Will Rogers speaking style, deferential and friendly. I guessed right away that Cassie wore the balls in this family. She was a prototypical southern power-housewife, dressed in an aggressive red permanent-press pantsuit (the southern house-wife version of a NASCAR racing outfit) over a garish mul-ticolored blouse that hung around her sun-splotched, sagging neck—which incidentally featured a Star of David pendant, a brazen and conspicuous symbol of her corporate loyalty to the church. Her eyes were keen bird-of-prey slits; seated as the group was for most of the night in a circle, her chair was just a shade behind Richard's, and from that vantage point she kept a careful eye on the whole proceeding. In discussions about scrip-ture, she would jump in and have the final word.

There were about twenty others there in Richard and Cassie's sunken living room, occupying a ring of folding chairs. Laurie had kept one open for me next to hers. I made my way around and took my seat. Dr. Hiroshi and his elderly, kindly wife, Frances, were on my other side. We exchanged a few nice-ties, and then suddenly a short, squat man, seated behind and to the left of me and wearing an awkward parted haircut that would have looked right in a 1987 Members Only commercial, began strumming an acoustic guitar.

"That's Reggie," whispered Laurie. "He does the music around here."

"Oh," I said.

"Okay, everyone," Reggie said. "Now, I want the men to stand up for their parts and sit down when they're done. Women, you stand up for your parts, same thing."

"What parts?" I whispered to Laurie.

"I don't know, honey," she said.

Reggie hit a chord and stood up. All the men followed.

"I've been re-deeeeemed!" he sang.

We sat down. The women stood up and repeated. I've been re-deeeeemed!

Reggie stood up again. "By the blood of the lamb!"

By the blood of the lamb!

They went on singing. It was the kind of song you could almost sing without knowing—you get a hint at the beginning, and you're off:

> *I've been redeemed, I've been redeemed*
> *By the blood of the lamb, by the blood of the lamb*
> *I've been redeemed by the blood of the lamb*
> *I'm filled with the Holy Ghost I am*
> *All my sins are washed away, I've been redeemed.*

> *And I went down, and I went down*
> *To the river to pray, to the river to pray*
> *And I went down, and I went down*
> *To the river to pray, to the river to pray*
> *And I went down to the river to pray*
> *I felt so good that I stayed all day*
> *All my sins are washed away, I've been redeemed.*

By then everyone was huffing and puffing from all the standing up and sitting down, but we went on:

"And that's not all," sang Dr. Hiroshi with the rest of the men, smiling at me.

And that's not all! sang the women.

"There's more besides!" sang the men.

There's more besides!

I figured I had it by then. I looked at the doctor and sang:

> *And that's not all, there's more besides*
> *I've been to the river and I've been baptized*
> *All my sins are washed away, I've been redeemed.*

The doctor hit the last note—the Sha Na Na bass ending:

> *I've ... been ... re-deeeemed.*

Everybody clapped and cheered. It was a pretty song, a song for kids—and these almost-elderly people were enjoying it like children. Once they all caught their breath, some shook hands or even hugged.

It was a weird scene, watching these empty-nest old parents moved near to tears by this children's song. But it wasn't their own kids they were remembering; it was their own childhoods. The church is a place where you can walk in and close your eyes and all the complex and inscrutable troubles of adult life are gone for a time. But you have to be careful to keep your eyes closed, because if you open them, what you'll see all around you are sad, middle-aged people with brittle hair and long faces, faces as old as your own, looking weary from that crooked road that God keeps promising will someday be made straight and trying to wish the world away with a children's song. Of course, if they all wish together, the wish comes true for a while.

At the end of each song the group stood with heads hung and eyes closed, and there was much whispering and incantation and even a little speaking in tongues: "We THANK you, Jesus . . . We do RECEIVE you, Lord . . . We praise you . . . Heal us, Jesus . . . Thank you, Lord . . . Froom-balakashaka . . ."

The whispering thing had originally been a big stumbling block for me. During preachers' prayers and after the singing of hymns, during any solemn silence in any service, you'll suddenly hear people in the crowd whispering aloud praise to the Lord—loud enough that folks can hear it a few pews in any direction. My first few times in church, I had a real problem with this, just as I had with the hand thing. At first, in church, I'd just whispered ever so faintly, so that only I could hear:

"Uh . . . thanks, Jesus . . . um . . . you rule . . ."

But now I was light-years past that time. My inhibitions in this area were almost completely gone. In fact, now, at Bible study, I found myself having a bit of a whisper-off with Laurie, who was of course a champion whisperer, not to be outdone by

anyone. Laurie scored terrific marks at all external verbal demonstrations of the Christian faith; it was the actual behavioral
tenets of the religion she had a problem with. But she had no
equal in whispering. When Laurie whispered praise to Jesus,
dogs would start barking blocks away.

"We THANK you, Jesus!" she whispered. "Lord, I thank
you!"

I peered at her, irritated.

"In the blood of Jesus!" I whispered. "I do RECEIVE you,
Lord!"

"Thank you, Jesus!" she whispered. "Thank YOU, Jesus!
THANK YOU, JESUS!"

Fuck! I thought, wincing and glancing sideways at her.

"Protect me, Lord!" I said. "Rom-balakashaka!"

Laurie didn't flinch. "Cooo-karakashakakakakakakakaaaaaa!"
she whispered. "Shom balakorososhaka!"

This went on for minutes. Finally, mercifully, Richard asked
the group, "Does anyone have a word they'd like to share, someone or something to pray for?"

A long-faced, sad-looking woman off to my right, seated on
a couch, stood up.

"I have something," she said.

"Okay," Richard said.

She nodded.

"I'd like to pray," she said, "dear Lord, to ask you to bring me
a letter tomorrow, dear Father, from the state of Texas, saying
that it's okay for me to drive a car again."

I thought about that one for a moment. I wanted to hear
why the state had revoked her license in the first place before
I prayed for her to be allowed back on the road. Maybe she'd
run over a crowd of blind children or something. The crowd,
however, exploded in prayer:

"Lift her up, Lord."

"Help her drive again."

"Hear her prayers, Lord."

"Embrace her, dear Jesus."

We went around the room. Most everyone had a prayer request:

"I'd like to ask you, dear Father, to lift up my son, who is going through a difficult time."

"Lord, lift up my mother and father, who are ill."

"Lord, please protect me on my trip upstate tomorrow, make sure that I arrive safely, without any problems on the highway."

There were a good dozen or so requests along those lines—and then we got to Richard and Cassie.

Richard cleared his throat.

"Lord," he said, "we pray today for President Bush."

It is a testament, I think, to the virginal purity of my atheism—my deep, unwavering faith in the nonexistence of this particular Christian god—that I did not even hesitate to spit out the asked-for prayers.

"Lord, protect the president!" I whispered. "Lift him up, dear Lord, and guide his every action! Protect him from slanderers and malcontents!"

"Guide him, Lord," whispered Laurie.

"Smite his enemies with disease!" I continued.

The crowd prayed enthusiastically. As if as one we all chanted in support of the former governor, and then also for the troops in Iraq, and we continued, right up until Cassie took her turn.

"Lord," she began, "I'd like to say a prayer for Israel, dear Father."

She looked up for a moment, then hung her head solemnly, looking deeply moved for Israel's plight all of a sudden. Cassie was all business, a good soldier who seemed to be doing what the church leaders asked her to do.

"I'd like you to guide her and to protect her," she went on, "not only from her enemies in the Middle East, but from those within Israel and in this country, dear Lord, who would ask her to give up any of her land. We ask you to save Jerusalem, dear Father, and to protect her from Iran!"

Cassie opened her eyes when she was done with her little speech and cast a glance at everyone in the room. Dutifully everyone in the group whispered the usual praise, but I detected the energy seeping out of the house. We were here to talk about our own problems, not Iran. And once Cassie was finished with her grim corporate duty—and that's so obviously what her anti-Iran prayer was that I don't doubt that even some of the other group members noticed it—the group went back to more usual prayer requests.

"Father, pray for so-and-so, who's in the hospital."

"Lord, I ask you to lift up my daughter, who's running with the wrong crowd."

"Father, guide me and protect me financially."

Cassie glanced at me in the midst of all of this. I realized that I hadn't prayed for anything. Not knowing what to do or say, I stepped forward.

"Lord," I said, "I'd like to say a prayer for my little cousin Katie, who's, uh, just now entering college . . ."

An alarm went off in my head. Just entering college? You idiot—it's February!

". . . who's just entering college a semester late," I continued. "Little Katie, dear Father, she calls herself an atheist now, and I ask you, dear Father, to lift her up and wash her in the blood of your only son, Jesus Christ, so that she may be healed of her addiction to drugs and inhalants, glues and such."

A woman off to the right of me stepped forward, like she wanted to say a new prayer. I cut her off.

"So, Father, I please ask that you cure my little cousin Katie of those addictions and lift her up so that she may return to school and resume a normal life and go back to studying again, and playing musical instruments . . ."

The crowd stared at me anxiously. I gulped.

"In particular the xylophone," I added finally.

There was an awkward pause. I took a deep breath and braced myself. Then the verdict came:

"Lord, protect this young lady!" whispered one man finally.

"Bind those demons inside her and cast them out!" said another.

"Save her, Lord!" said another.

EIGHT

Conspiracy Interlude I,

or

9/11 and the Derangement of Truth

EARLY ON THE MORNING of October 4, 2006, a friend of mine called, waking me up. When I hit the answer button on my cell, I could already hear him laughing.

"Dude," he stammered out, "you're being picketed!"

"What?"

"I just sent you the link," he said. "It's hilarious. The 9/11 protesters are picketing your office."

I crawled out of bed and slid into my desk chair, opened the link. It was an entry from the Official Loose Change Blog, and it read as follows:

> Edit: Just got this in from Luke . . . apparantly this article by Rolling Stone might be the catalyst for some blowback . . .
>
> Peaceful Picket @ Rolling Stone!
>
> Protest Magazine's 9/II Cover-Up!
>
> Wednesday, October 4th, 4–6pm
>
> I290 Avenue of the Americas (52nd St.)
>
> Recently, Rolling Stone Magazine featured yet another of

those uninformed, smarmy, know-it-all, "hit pieces" directed against our 9/11 Truth Movement. Appearing on its website and authored by Matt Taibbi, the article utilizes the usual mis-characterizations of our collective effort towards the truth of 9/11. What is intolerable though is that the writer stoops to personal attacks against those of us who doubt the official story of 9/11. Well, sorry establishment pseudo-hipsters, there are millions of us and we're not standing for it! We demand respect, if not for our sincere efforts, than [sic] for the truth of what happened that day. We'll see you in the street!

QUESTION AUTHORITY!

JUST GIVE US SOME 9/11 TRUTH!

"How would you rate the American media in their coverage of the events of the attack last September?"

"Well let's see, uh, shamefully, is a word that comes to mind," answered Hunter S. Thompson, Rolling Stone's best and most famous writer when speaking with Australian radio back in 2002.

Posted by Dylan Avery at 2:05 p.m.

"Jesus," I said into the phone. "I'm an establishment pseudo-hipster."

"The funny thing about that," my so-called friend answered, "is that you are."

"Fuck you," I said.

"Have fun at the meeting," he said, hanging up.

After the call I sat in my room for a minute, sorting it all out. The timeline of this whole ugly business began when I wrote a somewhat half-assed column for the *Rolling Stone* Web site on the fifth anniversary of 9/11, talking about what America did and did not learn from that event. In that column I made an offhand comment about the 9/11 Truthers, calling them "clinically insane."

It wasn't something I'd put a lot of thought into, just something that was in the back of my mind. I'd run into the "movement" over and over again in my travels for the magazine in the previous year; outside Cindy Sheehan's tent, among protesting Arab Americans in Dearborn, Michigan, at the site of a Kashmiri earthquake in Pakistan, at antiwar rallies in Washington. Each time I ran into talk about the towers being mined or felled by remote-controlled planes, I dismissed it as an anomaly. In fact, I had a mild ethical crisis over it when I covered the Cindy Sheehan story; because I was against the war and generally sympathetic to Sheehan's cause, I didn't want to have to mention in print that her supporters were abuzz with nut-job conspiracy theories accusing Bush of masterminding 9/11.

But the sheer numbers were so overwhelming—in one group of twenty Sheehan protesters I polled, there were fourteen who subscribed to some version of the Bush-did-it conspiracy theory—that I had no choice but to mention it in the piece.

It was the first time in my life that I felt forced to paint a negative portrait of a peace movement. It genuinely freaked me out when I eventually started to see my article linked up on a host of right-wing Web sites, used as ammunition against the antiwar crowd.

I ran into the same phenomenon several times after that. In Dearborn, where I went to interview Arab Americans who had organized to protest the Israel-Lebanon war, I was shocked to listen to well-educated, pious Lebanese Americans regurgitating 9/11 conspiracy theories like they were hard news. In particular there was a pair of college-educated sisters, Renee and Rannya Abdul-habi—both seriously religious young women who dressed in the hijab—who seemed fairly well informed about America's Middle East policy but in outer space when it came to domestic politics. Renee, the older and more politically active sister, could not be budged from her conviction that

Bush had bombed the Twin Towers and that no plane had hit the Pentagon.

What was interesting about the Dearborn trip was that when I arrived, virtually the entire community was abuzz about the arrests of a pair of young Arab American men, one of whom was unfortunately named Osama, who had been caught buying a large number of cell phones. The two boys, both of whom had been football stars at Dearborn High, had been immediately dubbed "terror suspects" in the big dailies and on television and tabbed the "Dearbornistan boy terrorists" by Detroit's Ann Coulter wannabe, Debbie Schlussel. The charges were dropped a few days after the arrests, and no terror connection was ever uncovered, but the damage, as far as the community was concerned, had been done. To them, this was another example of mainstream media racism and deception, of the media carelessly seizing an opportunity to railroad an Arab without cause. It was pretty obvious to me that, because of incidents like this, the Arab American community in the Detroit area had long ago stopped paying attention to the "mainstream" news and understood most of what they saw on television to be an unbroken string of deceptions and manipulations.

But I only thought about that later on. At the time, I still thought the 9/11 conspiracy stuff was a weird aberration, your basic Clinton-era black-helicopter paranoia reconfigured to fit disaffected lefties of the terrorism age, so when I mentioned it in that 9/11 anniversary column, it was just to score a quick punchline.

But almost instantly after the column went up online, my mailbox started filling up with hate mail. And what hate mail! If there is a consistent characteristic of the 9/11 Truth Movement, it's a kind of burning, defensive hypersensitivity, a powerful inclination to be instantly offended, which expresses itself in a tendency for its adherents to seem literally to leap out of their seats in anger even in e-mail form.

"Fuck you, you prick!" said one letter. "Left-gatekeeper cocksucker!" said another. "You're the one who's clinically insane," said a third. "I can't believe you call yourself a journalist." Numerous complainants promised to kick my ass. Even a column I'd written celebrating the death of the pope hadn't come close to inspiring this much invective.

About six days into this I called Jan Frel, my editor at AlterNet, and he mentioned, casually, that my 9/11 column was setting some kind of site record for comments. When I looked on the site I noticed that some of the comments touched on the actual subject I was writing about, but the vast majority were focused on that one "clinically insane" line. A sample:

Matt Taibbi, in denial or not, is misleading readers into
believing the government's fairy-tales concerning 9–11 and
everything that has followed. He doesn't ask "Cui bono?"
He tries to make us believe that it was simply those other
terrible people with box cutters who perpetrated 9–11 on
us—that despite increasing overwhelming evidence to the
contrary—that we are since 9–11 the poor victims of people
who hate us for our freedoms—yeah, right! What we collec-
tively are—are suckers for the "big lie" Taibbi is pitching.

AlterNet consistently plays the role of left-wing gatekeeper
by publishing articles such as this one. I wonder if AlterNet
could do some real journalism by giving a fair shake to the
9/11 Truth Movement. I think AlterNet is becoming part of
the problem, not the solution.

read "the new pearl harbor" by david ray griffin and rent the
film "network." there's no united states no middle east no
germany no japan no russia no china no iran no vietnam etc
etc there's just one big global governmet a shadow government the international finanical government which executed

a coup d etat on november 21, 1963 and orchestrated the attack on 9/11. its not a matter of winning any war its a matter of perpetual war.

The most insane conspiracy theory of all is to blame 9/11 on 19 Arab Muslims with box cutters led by a guy in a cave, outsmarting the the entire US Military, all of the US Spy Agencies and the US Government. As to the explosives that were most likely planted in buildings 1, 2 and 3 . . .

After scrolling through a couple hundred of these messages and looking through another hundred more or so in my mailbox, I lost my temper and tossed off a column thrashing the 9/11 "Truth" Movement. At the time I was, mistakenly, under the impression that the movement was an easy target. It seemed to me at the time that the only reason the 9/11 conspiracy theories were surviving on the Internet was that the movement's leaders had carefully avoided articulating their theories in full. I really thought that all anyone had to do was put all of the movement's claims together and the resulting summary would be so unbelievably ridiculous that people would actually be ashamed to defend them publicly. The 9/11 conspiracy theories seemed absurd on their face, the kind of thing that no person familiar with the mundane everyday corruption of Washington would ever take seriously, and I thought, mistakenly, that they would go away as soon as someone bothered to point out in public how retarded they are.

So I wrote something along those lines. But the response was twice, three times as vociferous as before. My in-box was deluged with hate mail of the white-hot-rage/die-cocksucker genus, and then, eventually, word of the protest hit me.

At the appointed time I walked across town and grabbed a hot dog across the street from our offices on Sixth Avenue, a block up from Rockefeller Center. It was a strange scene. Among other things, it was a bad time for a protest; the sun was just starting to recede, and it was late on a workday smack dab in the middle of a workweek. The crowd of about ten scraggly-looking protesters carrying placards and wearing black "INVESTIGATE 9/11" T-shirts could easily have been cameramen or techies lugging equipment from the giant NBC complex next door, and the suit-and-tie crowd was waltzing past them. After Falun Gong, you need a pretty good act to stop traffic in downtown New York.

I finished my hot dog, walked across the street, and picked out a pair of middle-aged men handing out fliers. One was slightly pudgy with an untucked shirt and curlyish hair, and the other had a big bulbous nose and glasses and the body of Woody Allen. Introducing myself as the guy they were protesting, I told them that I understood they needed a couple of hours to give their protest maximum exposure, but that I would be very pleased to sit down and hear their concerns in a nearby diner when they were finished.

Weirdly, the two men seemed very happy to meet me, enthusiastically shaking my hand even after I identified myself. I repeated the address of the diner and started to walk away. Curly Hair asked me my name again.

"I'm Matt Taibbi," I said. "You know, the guy you're picketing."

"Oh," he said. "Okay. Well, thank you," he said, shaking my hand again. He seemed very pleased to make my acquaintance.

A few hours later, I slipped into the Morning Star Café just down the block from my apartment. There were about five or six protesters there, including Curly Hair, whose real name was Les Jamieson. He was from the local chapter of 911Truth .org. They already had big plates of food in front of them and were munching happily. I sat at the end and ordered coffee.

It was awkward. I'm not sure exactly what was said at first, but I recall that after a stammering attempt on my part to start a discussion, all five or so protesters started speaking at once; I heard something about "heat levels" on my left and "video" on my right. Finally we settled down and Les started talking about some compelling 9/11 footage that some friend of his had, something about explosions, that the New York TV stations were "sitting on" and keeping from the public.

"Les," I said, "how do you think that works? Do you think a news director for Channel 2 says to the people in the archive room, 'Make sure this is locked away and no one sees it?'"

"Well, clearly, they're hiding it," he said.

"Okay," I said. "Do you think the guys from the TV stations are in communication with people in government, discussing what should and should not be aired?"

"All I'm saying is, they've got the footage, and they're not showing it," he said. "So there must be something going on."

Murmurs of assent all around the table. I changed the subject, asking them if they could just forget about the explosions and all the rest of it for now and name one piece of concrete evidence linking the government to the crimes of 9/11. From there a longish conversation started that seemed fruitful and pleasant—the tone of the discussion was respectful from both sides, and Les and his friends were making their case, even though neither side was convincing the other of much. I suppose on some level I was regretting the description of these nice people as clinically insane, but I also remembered that that's the thing about the Internet—there's an awful lot of white-hot insanity out there that is written by people who seem quite normal once they look up from their computer screens. Eventually Les concluded that the best evidence he could think of was the Project for the New American Century report that claimed that a "new Pearl Harbor" would be needed to get the public behind our expansionist policies in the Middle East.

"But that's not evidence of anything," I said. "It's a self-evident statement. Anyone could have said that before 9/11. I could have said it."

"But it's right there out in the open," said Les. "They said it. How come people in the press can't take a lead like that and—"

"A lead?" I said. "How is that a lead? Where does it lead to?"

There was a skittish, late-thirtyish woman sitting next to me with a long dark ponytail, I'll call her Mary, who had kept trying to bring the JFK assassination into the discussion. Mary had also said that the military was controlling the media, that "all this Brad and Jennifer stuff" was part of a plan to hide the truth. She interjected now.

"I think what he's asking, Les," she said, "is what the actual evidence is linking the government to the attack. What you're talking about is circumstantial evidence."

"And not good circumstantial evidence," I said.

"Yes it is," she said. "It's good circumstantial evidence. I would say it's very strong."

Les frowned. "Well," he said, "if you're asking for concrete . . ."

Just then a lean, bearded figure, dressed in an army jacket, stormed through the front door of the diner and made a bee-line straight for my side of the table. It was as if he'd studied my probable seating position beforehand; his entrance was executed with military precision. He pulled up a chair, spun it around to sit with the chair back facing forward, plopped down, and started barking at me in the frenzied, heavily accented English of a German film student sent to the emergency room for a meth overdose.

"Who zent you!" he screamed. "You left-gatekeeping scum! Who paid you off! Who made you do zis? You are vorking for zomebody! You . . ."

He kept screaming. I looked around the table in shock. The others looked down at their food.

"Hah! Who vas it! Answer me! Answer me now!"

"Jesus," I said. "Calm the fuck down!"

"I am not CALMING DOWN!" he screamed. "You vill give me ANSWERS!"

I reared back in my chair. I didn't know it yet, but this was my introduction to Nico Haupt, the so-called mad genius of the 9/11 Truth Movement, a feverish blogger who is credited with inventing the famed movement acronyms LIHOP (let it happen on purpose) and MIHOP (made it happen on purpose) and seems to be a ubiquitous presence at any 9/11 Truth function on the East Coast. Haupt is the movement mascot, the future propaganda minister of the Truth Republic. I would later look up his blog entries and find them to be masterpieces of conspiratorial paranoia and unintentional comedy. Among other things, they contain the usual salutations to the surveillance teams who of course are watching him at all times:

> Secretly on the payroll of some other weired intelligence?
> Not true, because I'm also constantly hungry. I still regret
> any kind of recruitments :)
> A personal note to the NSA, who's a regular log-in guest on
> my sites: I guess, you have to take the less comfortable way
> again and sniff my e-mails. You're still bastards for me, who
> betrayed this nation and the constitution. Shame on you
> and go to hell!

I also enjoyed his theories that someone "got to" Ed Asner, often listed as a 9/11 Truth supporter:

> I always was and always will be a big fan of Ed Asner's
> movies and TV series, especially "rich man, poor man". Last
> week, I was a bit disappointed that Asner "caved in" and
> basically made a u-turn, by writing that 9/II was based on
> negligence. I heard a different view a long while ago, even

personally from him on the phone. Someone else might
speculate, why this has happened now. Maybe someone
threatened Asner with some infos of his past?

Haupt's blogs are a great running account of the life of
a would-be revolutionary in the Internet age—sort of like a
MySpace version of Che's Congo diary. His writings are full
of little offhand personal tidbits left behind for his future biog-
raphers. "Or what about a romantic reason?" he writes one day
in 2004, apropos of nothing. "My girlfriend denied to marry
me . . . Maybe it's frustration, depression or that i'm constantly
broke." Later on, he confesses to bravery in the face of impending capture: "Maybe i'm scared that the Homeland Security will
arrest me as a 'terrorist'? Not at all."

In any case, Haupt had better hope he's a speed addict, because if he isn't, there are very few reasonable excuses for his
Raskolnikovian appearance. He spits wildly when he talks, and
he can't allow anyone to respond to anything he says. In fact, my
little meeting with the protesters basically broke up very shortly
after his entrance, because Haupt wouldn't let me or anyone else
shut him up for even ten seconds. After I said something about
needing evidence to accuse the Bush administration of planning the attacks, Haupt flipped and began demanding evidence
for absolutely everything that came out of everybody's mouth.
When someone asked me how I could explain Bush's failure
to prevent the attacks, I began by saying, "Well, this batch of
Republicans are the most incompetent, corrupt . . ."

"Where's your evidence for zat!" Haupt screamed. "Show
me evidence Bush eez corrupt!"

I sighed. "You think they knocked down the towers and you
want me to prove to you that Bush and his crew are corrupt?"

"Ver eez your evidence, you bastard!" he shouted.

"Well, there was the Jack Abramoff thing—"

"Bullshit!" Haupt screamed. "No proof!"

This was really getting weird. "He was convicted," I said. "Is that good enough for you?"

"Lies!" he screamed.

"Nico," Les whispered. "He was convicted."

"The evidence! Give me the evidence!"

At another point, when I tried to tell him that the issue of my being "paid off" was moot, since I write my online column for free, he just kept screaming, not letting me get a word in edgewise.

"Now it eez my turn to talk! You will listen! Vat about zee war games?" he screamed.

I looked around the table with a pleading expression. "Hey, can you get this guy to shut up?" I asked.

"Nico, please . . . ," said Les consolingly.

Nico ignored him and just kept screaming.

"You are a traitor to zee Constitution!" he bellowed, sticking a finger less than an inch from my nose. "An enemy of zee state!"

Hearing this German accuse me of being a traitor to the United States moved me immediately from stunned bemusement to genuine anger. "Stop spitting on me," I said.

Haupt kept screaming. Bits of food matter—from some previous meal, apparently, since he had not eaten here—were showering my sport coat.

"Hey, stop spitting," I said. "I'm not kidding."

"I vill spit on you all I like!" he shouted. "Go ahead, stop me! You vant to hit me? Hit me! Go ahead, hit me! Zen I vill have a story! Go ahead, hit me!"

Haupt was about two inches from my face. The whole restaurant was now staring. The manager of the diner, who had threatened to call the police early on in the confrontation, was now reduced to watching out of mere curiosity; there was nothing left for him to do but let this scene play itself out. The shower of spittle continued to rain on me as a torrent of incomprehensible accusations flowed from somewhere in the middle of Haupt's beard: "Controlled demolitions . . . war games . . . commission . . . traitors!" I couldn't even make out the individual words. Every cell in my body ached to twist his head off and roll it down Columbus Avenue, but I knew this was a bad solution.

"Okay," I said finally. "Let's go outside. You're not going to play nice, we'll just have to do this."

I went outside. Haupt, I could see through the window, stayed in his chair and smiled faintly, looking at the others for approval. For several minutes he refused to come out. I sighed. I was thirty-six years old, with an expensive dentist, and the prospect of getting into a fight with a deranged German conspiracy theorist on the corner of West Fifty-seventh Street suddenly seemed a more than unusually ridiculous way to spend an afternoon. I was actually relieved when Haupt slipped out the door and slithered uptown, away from me.

AFTER HAUPT LEFT, Les and his friends gathered their things and came outside. I walked with them to the subway.

"I'm sorry you had to see that," Les said. "He doesn't represent us."

Les was a nice guy. So were all his friends, actually. There was something very sad about the whole thing. On the way to the subway, we talked more about 9/11 Truth. I kept trying to explain my point, which was that there was no concrete evidence that the government had committed the attacks, and that if they wanted to be taken seriously, they had to come up with something solid. Moreover, instead of entertaining dozens of theories simultaneously, what real investigators do is follow the evidence and try to actually come up with a single theory of the crime. Narrow the field of view, not expand it. And part of that process involves asking why the alleged conspirators would do what the Truthers accuse them of doing. Why fly a plane into the towers and blow them up? Why crash a plane in the middle of Pennsylvania? Why shoot a missile at the Pentagon and say it was a plane? And so on.

"You're too concentrated on the why," said Les. "You have to concentrate on the what. And the what is a controlled demolition and a plane shot down in Pennsylvania."

"But why would they shoot down that plane in Pennsylvania?" I asked. "What does that do for them?"

Another of Les's friends, a long-haired guy named Mike, explained that the Shanksville plane, which was originally intended to hit the White House, had been delayed on the ground forty minutes by air traffic control. After the delay, he said, it would have been too obvious if they had just gone on and let it hit the White House. "That would have been just too unbelievable," he said. "No one would have believed they wouldn't have scrambled their air defenses for that long. So maybe they just shot the plane down to cover their mistake."

I didn't know where to start with that one. "Wait a minute," I said. "Are you saying that they had control of the airline and the air force, but not air traffic control? They could control every step of the process, but they couldn't keep air traffic control from delaying them forty minutes?"

"Actually," said a third of Les's friends, "if you read the transcripts, the people who come out looking the cleanest are the air traffic controllers."

I sighed. "But—okay, never mind."

"You'll see," Mike said. "I know a lot of people who started out like you. But sooner or later, they come around to the truth."

I smiled and said nothing. A few minutes later we shook hands and they got on the subway, headed downtown.

$\cdot\ \cdot\ \cdot$

How **MANY LIES** are too many? How much bullshit is the human organism designed to tolerate before it starts to malfunction? Is there a breaking point?

Mainstream American society has never been designed to confront difficult or dangerous truths. In fact, our mass media has corrupted the idea of objective truth so badly in the past five or six decades that it is now hard to tell when anyone is being serious about anything—the news, the movies, commercials, anything.

On the night after the diner incident I was watching television when I realized that this sort of thing was probably predictable. I was watching a "Can you hear me now?" Verizon commercial that featured a phony competitor to Verizon, with its own "Can you hear me now?" guy look-alike and a fake "support team" of cardboard figurines. My reaction to the commercial was a desire to decapitate everyone on-screen with a chainsaw—the healthy reaction, I think, to an intentional effort to dump obnoxious automated bullshit into my living room. But who has the energy to keep chainsawing all those heads off? How many lies can you fight off in a lifetime? Do they eventually creep into your head and spread the infection?

We probably took our first step into the danger zone back in the eighties with the notorious Joe Isuzu commercials, which were a clever attempt by Madison Avenue to capitalize on the American population's growing awareness that the claims of most television advertisements were transparent bullshit.

The Isuzu ads were a stroke of genius. Just when America was starting to figure out that there never really were four out of five real dentists who recommended anything, along comes Joe Isuzu, this parody of a mercury-tongued pitchman who comes on TV with a wildly overdone serpentine smile, claiming that an Isuzu truck could hold "every book in the Library of Congress" or had "more seats than the Astrodome." Isuzu was scoring honesty points, but the way they did it was by lying openly. The ads were a huge hit and the irony age was officially born.

The weird thing was that the new post-Isuzu ironic ads co-existed with ads of the same-old-bullshit genre. You had Joe Isuzu talking about using his trucks to haul two-thousand-pound cheeseburgers alongside cola ads that showed ordinary people looking like they were about to have huge heaving orgasms at the sight of a cold Coke, or be magically transformed into swimwear models after a couple of Diet Pepsis. You had open lies that were celebrated as such, veiled lies meant to be taken seriously, and then the ads would end and the news would come on and you would be presented with President Ronald Reagan—as skilled and telegenic a liar as politics has ever seen, Joe Isuzu's perfect Dostoyevskian double—getting up on TV and on the one hand lying through his teeth about Iran-Contra, and then on the other hand comparing Daniel Ortega to "that fellow from Isuzu."

Somehow, ordinary people were supposed to keep track of all this, make their own sense of it. Decades after Watergate, Vietnam, and the Kennedy assassination, Americans were forced to rummage for objective reality in a sea of the most confusing and diabolical web of bullshit ever created by human minds—a false media tableau created mainly as a medium to sell products, a medium in which even the content of the "news" was affected by commercial considerations. I'll leave it to someone else to break down all the different species of lies that by the early twenty-first-century Americans swallowed as a matter of routine—the preposterous laugh tracks in sitcoms, the parade of perfect-looking models used to sell products to the obese, the endless soap operas about the rich and the beautiful cruising the OC in Testarossas, marketed to a country in which 10 percent of the population lacks enough to eat.

It all got to be too much. Our political campaigns were reduced to an absurd joke, hollow image contests in which adult political commentators worried publicly about which candidate broke a sweat or looked at his watch during debates. In the late Clinton years government ground to a halt for almost two years in an utterly ridiculous and interminable national debate over a blowjob. The national press then stood by and did nothing while the country elected to the most powerful office on earth a man barely capable of reading—and if you ask me it was that set of circumstances, the outrageous presidential election of 2000 between a dingbat and a bore that was sold to the American people as a heroic clash of serious and qualified ideological opposites, that more than anything trained the population to dismiss as unserious anything the national media subsequently had to say about 9/11.

Thinking back now about 9/11—what were people supposed to think? It took about ten minutes after the towers fell for the lies to start. Well, actually it was about ten days. It was around then, on September 20, from the U.S. Capitol, that President Bush addressed the nation and offered this famous tidbit:

> Americans are asking, why do they hate us? They hate what we see right here in this chamber—a democratically elected government. Their leaders are self-appointed. They hate our freedoms—our freedom of religion, our freedom of speech, our freedom to vote and assemble and disagree with each other.

Bush's famous explanation for 9/11 was a new low in American politics. It was a lie, obviously, but it wasn't even a good lie. We were watching, live, the last stage of a fifty-year decline in the performance standards of the White House's propaganda professionals. Once upon a time, in the days of FDR and Truman and Ike, the president was like a cross between Superman and God, the descendant of George Washington, who could not lie. Then Kennedy was shot and the Warren Commission came along (bringing with it a whole cottage industry of Kennedy mudslinging) and we learned that if the president was not a liar exactly, he was sure getting a lot of pussy that he never told us about. Then came Nixon and Watergate, and by the mid-seventies America learned to check its silverware case every time the president finished giving a televised speech. Nixon's fall coincided with the CIA hearings and the awful revelations of all manner of crazed government behavior—exploding cigars for Castro, foot powder planted by the CIA to make the dictator's beard fall out. Northwoods. Gulf of Tonkin. By the middle of the decade, America knew: not only was its president a crook, but its government was a criminal enterprise, a potential suspect in any heinous unsolved crime. Who killed JFK, MLK, Malcolm X? Who conspired to assassinate Salvador Allende? You knew who the first suspect was.

This was too much for people to handle. After Carter, with his dreary, not-always-convincing attempts at honesty, America decided that even if it knew its president was a fraud, it could live with him, so long as he was a skilled fraud. To the rescue came Ronald Reagan, whose virtue was that he told lies that were enjoyable, uplifting. Reagan was the first president who was rewarded at the polls for the quality of his fictions. He shared this trait with Bill Clinton, a bullshitter of Shakespearean dimensions who carried America all the way through the nineties with an orgiastic smile on his face. We knew Clinton was a liar and a pussy-killer, but we didn't mind. Two-hundred-fifty-odd years after "I cannot tell a lie," Clinton's reign defined presidential truth as a statement that was legally defensible in theory and also vetted by the best and most expensive lawyers on the planet, i.e., "I did not have sex with that woman."

So America went from being a place where the president set the standard for truth and forthrightness to being a place where the president was expected to lie always, and at all times.

But the one thing throughout this period that Americans could always depend on, even after Nixon and the collapse of public faith in the president's morals, was that the lies the American president told would always be the very best lies that science, computerized research, and Washington's most devious spooks could produce. Our president may lie, but he will lie effectively and spectacularly, with all the epic stagecraft and lighting and special effects available to the White House publicity apparatus. He is never a hack, never a half-assed, off-the-cuff, squirming, my-dog-ate-my-homework sort of liar. Or at least he wasn't until George W. Bush came around.

"They hate our freedoms" was possibly the dumbest, most insulting piece of bullshit ever to escape the lips of an American president. As an explanation for the appalling tragedy of 9/11, which was the culmination of decades of escalating tension between the Arab world and the West, it was insufficient even as a calculated effort to snow an uneducated public—it was too stupid even to hold up as that. And yet when he said it, Bush was not savaged by the mainstream media for blowing off the biggest security question of our time. The Washington press corps did not line up to pelt him with mushy pineapples for insulting their intelligence. Instead, he was cheered as a hero by members of both parties and virtually all the country's commercial media, which engaged in a kind of frantic race to see who could more enthusiastically compare Bush's speechmaking to that of Winston Churchill. Worse still, the mainstream media followed Bush's lead by coming up with its own, more verbose, versions of Bush's analysis.

"THEY HATE OUR FREEDOMS" was only one of a number of preposterous lies mainstream society was expected to embrace after 9/11. The Iraq invasion and the reasons for it were only the most obvious. By 2003 or 2004 any American with even

half a brain could only assess the performance of his government via a careful weighing of its various lies and contradic-
tions. An educated person understood that the weapons of
mass destruction (WMD) business was a canard and that
there had to be some other reason for the invasion of Iraq; indeed, even in the weeks before the war began, commentators
across the country were already judging (and in some cases
supporting) the war plan based entirely on what they guessed
the real reasons for the invasion were. A classic example was
Tom Friedman of the *New York Times,* who even as he boosted
the war never took the WMD business seriously, imagining
instead that Iraq had always been a kind of geopolitical Hail
Mary, designed to transform the region.

But President Bush was a man on a mission. He had been
convinced by a tiny group of advisers that throwing "the long
bomb"—attempting to transform the most dangerous Arab
state—is a geopolitical game-changer.

It is not a good sign when even your supporters don't even
bother to take your cover story seriously. And yet that was the
position the Bush administration was in by 2003–4. No one
except his most dug-in Republican loyalists took anything his
people said or did at face value. When the administration sub-
mitted its "Clear Skies" plan to Congress, who among us didn't
automatically know that it was a giveaway to polluters? Or that
"Healthy Forests" was somehow going to result in more trees
being cut down? America by the early years of this century
was a confusing kaleidoscope of transparent, invidious bullshit,
a place where politicians hired consultants to teach them to
"straight talk," where debates were decided by inadvertent
coughs and smiles and elections were resolved via competing
smear campaigns, and where network news programs—subsi-
dized by advertisements for bogus alchemist potions like En-
zyte that supposedly made your dick grow by magic—could
feature as a lead story newly released photos of the Tom Cruise

love child, at a time when young American men and women were dying every day in the deserts of the Middle East.

The message of all of this was that Americans were now supposed to make their own sense of the world. There was no dependable authority left to turn to, no life raft in the increasingly perilous informational sea. This coincided with an age when Americans now needed to understand more of the world than ever before. A factory worker in suburban Ohio now needed to understand the cultures of places like Bangalore and Beijing if he wanted to know why he'd lost his job. Which, incidentally, he probably had. Now broke, or under severe financial pressure, with no community leaders, no community, no news he can trust, Joe American has to turn on the Internet and tell himself a story that makes sense to him.

What story is he going to tell?

NINE

PEAK EXPERIENCE

★ ★ ★ ★ ★ ★ ★ ★ ★ ★ ★ ★

THERE WAS a weird scene at Bible study on an otherwise un-
eventful evening. A new guy had joined the group, let's call him
Ron. Ron was overjoyed to be in the group. He had the glow
of a person hitting an early peak in his Christian experience,
although he was still very much a person to be pitied; he'd had
a family tragedy many years before. But throughout the Bible-
study session he kept raising his hand and making it plain to
everyone how thrilled he was to be here with all of us.

"You know," he said, "we all of us are in the Body of Christ,
not just here in San Antonio but all over the country, and I can't
tell you how happy it makes me to be here sharing this time
with all of you. I feel such love in my heart and I can really feel
the spirit of the Lord in here tonight. I can even feel it on my
skin!"

He tapped the exposed skin of his arm. Ron was a white-
haired, shortish man in his fifties, with a mustache and glasses,
the formerly wayward younger brother of a longtime group

member, now a full-blooded Christian on the Right Path. He'd been Lost and was so happy to be Found again, he couldn't be silent about it. The crowd ate him up.

"We're overjoyed to have you here, too, Ron," said Richard, scratching his beard.

"Thank you," he said. "God bless you."

The meeting went on. The "Bible lesson" turned out to be a reading of Deuteronomy 19, which to me seemed like a fairly arcane and legalistic section of the Bible, involving God's instructions with regard to "cities of refuge." In biblical times, if a man were to kill someone accidentally, he was supposed to flee to a city of refuge, where he would be safe from any family members who might be inclined to seek retribution against him. He was to remain there until there was a judgment against him by a court. Of course, if the killing was not accidental, the "manslayer" was not supposed to go to the city of refuge, but should be executed. The primary point that our group leader Cassie wanted to make with this lesson was that we modern Christians do not have to physically flee to a "city of refuge," but instead can simply take refuge in the Lord by turning to him at any time. Your basic meat-and-potatoes "God is always there for U" sermon.

However, there was a secondary point of the lesson, and that is that the guilty should indeed be executed.

"If the manslayer did it with premeditation, he's got to be put to death," said Cassie. "Because God is for capital punishment—let's not have any doubt about that."

"Hallelujah," said someone from the crowd.

"Let me tell you," continued Cassie, "we are so far from those times. I mean, how long do people stay on death row nowadays? Twenty-five, thirty years? It's ridiculous."

"Ridiculous," I agreed.

"I think the thing about that," said Richard, "is that God so values life, that when someone takes a life, the only thing that's going to satisfy him—he's so offended that the only thing that will make it right for him is if that person gives up his life."

"Amen," muttered the group.

"Amen," I said. Why object now?

Ron was frowning during this time. He raised his hand. Richard called on him.

"You know," he said, "you know, lately, we've been having so many of those cases where people on death row go free because of DNA evidence . . ."

The crowd murmured. I could see eyebrows rising all over the room. I wonder where he's going with this, I thought. Ron looked up and seemed nervous all of a sudden; he went on.

"I think the thing is, we've got so many of those liberal judges now . . . And when you've got jury trials, and people are sitting on the jury trying to decide these cases, I think that people who are good Christian people, it's easier for them to make a rational decision about these things. I think that people who are in the world, who aren't with Christ, it's hard for people like that to make a rational decision. About cases like that, I mean."

He looked up. I had absolutely no idea what the fuck he was talking about, and I'm pretty sure no one else did either. But this group was not much for arguing; this group was about "testifying," and testimony, for those to whom the concept is foreign, does not involve much rigorous debate. You give your opinion, you tell your story, everyone claps and pats you on the back and nods in agreement, and then the group moves on. That's what happened here. Ron made no sense, but everyone nodded like they agreed with him, and that was that.

The meeting went on, through the reading of scripture, more "teaching," communion, etc. Finally, at around 9:00 p.m., it broke up. I made a beeline across the room to talk to Ron.

"Hey," I said.

"Oh, hi," he said. "Really nice to meet you."

"Nice to meet you, too," I said. "I was just wondering—what did you mean about those DNA tests?"

"Oh," he said, his smile disappearing. "I just meant—you know, they've been releasing people from death row, because of DNA and all."

"Right, but what do you mean about that? Do you—do you not believe in the death penalty?"

I asked this in almost a threatening voice, like I was asking if he was gay. I didn't want him to think *I* was soft on the death penalty, so the best way to accomplish that, I figured, was to put him on the defensive, like I was an inquisitor trying to weed out a heretic. Incidentally, this was also amusing.

"Oh, no," he said instantly, looking frightened. "I'm definitely for the death penalty."

"Then what about those DNA tests?"

"Oh, well, it's just—a lot of mistakes are made. By liberal judges."

I frowned. "Okay," I said. "The people who are on death row by mistake are there because liberal judges put them there?"

"Right," he said. "I just think—there are people who aren't in Christ who can't make rational decisions about these things."

"But Ron," I said, "aren't liberal judges usually against the death penalty?"

He frowned. "I guess, yes."

"So you're saying," I said, "that liberal judges who are against the death penalty often make mistakes by sending people to be executed by the death penalty, which they're against?"

He looked at me and a new expression—suspicion—came over his face. "Um," he said, "I guess what I was saying is—wait, are you a Democrat or a Republican?"

I smiled. "Oh, I'm a Republican, of course," I said.

"Me too," he said, sighing in relief.

"I just didn't understand what you were talking about," I said.

"Oh," he said. "Okay. I guess I was just saying, people make mistakes. It does make you think sometimes, though."

"Yeah, sure," I said, frowning again. "But I'm still totally for the death penalty."

"Oh, me too," he said.

I smiled again. I felt sorry for the guy, but Jesus—what a pussy. So afraid of being labeled a political dissident that he has to keep his doubts and his rational opinions hidden behind some half-assed tirade against "liberal judges."

I had already seen this same phenomenon at least a dozen times. For most churchgoers it isn't a conflict, but there are a few who struggle at times with the political orthodoxy that somewhat unexpectedly goes hand in hand with the religious orthodoxy they so enthusiastically volunteered for. Many of these people don't mind being an ever-saluting soldier for God, but they chafe a little at some of the other restrictions. I knew one churchgoer who admitted that he smoked marijuana on occasion, and he even tried to convince me that it was harmless and just something that he did "to relax" every now and then—but when I went silent he quickly insisted that he only used it according to a doctor's advice, and that he abhorred drug abuse, etc., etc.

I shook Ron's hand and peered at him queerly. "Well, you have a nice evening," I said. "It was nice to meet you."

"You, too," he said, tapping my shoulder. "God bless you!"

"God bless you, too," I said, walking out.

BY THE MIDDLE of March, after many months in the church, I was finding it harder and harder to drag myself to church events. On the one hand, playing the role of a good Christian—a superficially good Christian—had become not merely easy but effortless. I was no Joel Osteen, but I could handle most biblical conversations by then, was able to pray out loud convincingly in a group in a pinch, and at any rate had mastered a blank, beatific, whacked-in-the-face-with-a-pine-plank expression that seemed effective in conveying an air of simple, sincere devotion to folks who might otherwise have been curious about what I was doing there.

But on the other hand, I was having an increasingly difficult time swallowing certain aspects of the experience. There was a deep-seated viciousness and intellectual violence interwoven into the church ideology that I simply didn't understand, which at times made it hard for me to play my part.

There were a great many things about the church that I could readily understand and identify with—the genuine warmth and sense of community that we all felt at the Bible-study meetings, the easy intimacy with other members of the church, the sense of belonging and being a part of something, the feeling of relief that comes with the knowledge that you don't have to figure it out all by yourself, that at least some of the answers are there for you.

I understood these things. I didn't have to fake the friendliness, the emotional connectedness. At the Bible-study meetings I could see clearly that this chance that people had to get together and be welcomed and listened to and appreciated by others was a source of tremendous comfort, that it was an antidote for loneliness and rejection. When I saw poor confused Laurie singing and dancing with the group, or Frances and old Dr. Hiroshi holding hands as they read their Bible together, I didn't have to fake a smile. I could feel the "spirit of gladness" coursing through the room. And even though I don't believe in God, I felt I understood something about their devotion. I could even see the ragged existential poverty of the unbeliever's journey of self-discovery as compared to the warming, collective Walk with God that Christians experienced. When Matt Taibbi woke up alone in a Texas boardinghouse, with every thought that bounced through his head, with every minute of the endless asinine dialogue with himself that passed pointlessly into the out-box of history, he became stranger than he was before, more alienated from the rest of humanity. But when my Christian friends woke up and bounded out of bed to dust their furniture, that other voice in their skull was God's; they were part of the same ongoing conversation the rest of their friends were having. And when those same Christian friends met for Bible study later that evening, it was like they had already been talking all day long.

But these same friends of mine had a powerful appetite for stories about killing and hating, and that I didn't get. There was one Bible-study meeting I went to at Richard and Cassie's house that nearly bowled me over. To set the scene: a typical Bible-study meeting at the one-story suburban home of the cell leaders, chit-chat to start, cookies and key lime pie in the kitchen. I grabbed a soda, chatted with the doctor and some other folks. Laurie came over and mentioned a neighbor had gone through eye surgery, but she seemed upbeat. Everything was normal. We got together, sang, whispered the usual incantations, and everyone seemed positive. But when we got to the prayer requests, Cassie coughed up a whopper.

"Lord," she said, "I ask you to lift up Scooter Libby."

Libby had just been convicted that day.

"I ask you to comfort him and deliver him from the spirit of vengeance," she said. "Do not let him try to take vengeance, Lord, even though he might want to. Take vengeance for him."

She frowned as she spoke the word "vengeance," and the room buzzed with each mention of the word. The implication was that it was going to be really, really hard to resist the urge to take vengeance on his behalf, and everyone in the room seemed to feel the spirit of this request. This was one area where Christians of this sort do not mind admitting that they have a hard time obeying God's instructions. Vengeance is mine, I will repay, saith the Lord—and while they understand this command in Texas, they struggle with it. And frankly, they like to advertise their struggles with it.

"Take vengeance upon his enemies, Lord," she continued. "And please, take away his spirit of vengeance, and give him instead . . ."

She paused for a long time. The room fell silent. Cassie, who was normally a very composed woman who never missed a beat, seemed lost—her hawk eyes were closed, and people began to look up from their prayer and stare at her quizzically.

"Give him instead," she said finally, "a pardon."

The crowd whistled in approval.

"Amen!" said someone near me.

"Grant it, Lord!" said another.

"Pardon him, Lord!" I said, though silently recoiling. I just didn't get the anger, the buzz that the word "enemies" had aroused before. I wasn't tuned in to where that was coming from. Weren't we all happy ten seconds ago?

We went on to read from Deuteronomy 20, a section concerning the laws of warfare. Cassie spoke about that for a while, then used that topic as a chance to examine 2 Chronicles 13.

This was the story of Jeroboam and Abijah, and the story was a theme that the church had examined very frequently even in the few short months I had been in Texas—an outnumbered force of Israelites seemingly headed for crushing defeat, but suddenly rallying and whipping ass with the help of the Lord. Pastor Hagee had sounded a similar theme from the book of Ezekiel, seeing in the story of Ezekiel's faithless servant a metaphor for the spineless opposition to the Iraq war. In the scripture Cassie sent us to, Jeroboam had rebelled against God and caused Israel to be split into northern and southern sections, with the south being called Judah, led by a God-fearing Abijah.

Well, Jeroboam had eight hundred thousand men, while Abijah had only four hundred thousand. But when it came time for battle, Abijah kicked his ass.

"God just killed them all," said Cassie with relish. "It says here that he killed five hundred thousand choice men of Jeroboam. They weren't ordinary men."

"Choice meaning special," said Richard, interjecting. "They were like special forces. Like Green Berets."

The crowd cooed. I heard Laurie say, "Wow."

"Right," said Cassie. "They were special, but God just killed them dead. Five hundred thousand of 'em."

Another man in the crowd raised his hand.

"Yes?" Cassie said.

"It says in my Bible they were 'chosen' men," he said.

"Yes?"

"Well, God chose them all right," he said. "He chose them to die."

"That's right," said Cassie. "He sure did."

Jesus, I thought. This is creepy. We went back to Deuteronomy 20 and the rules of warfare. There was a section there about what to do with conquered cities. We read from a section at the end:

15 Thus shalt thou do unto all the cities which are very far off from thee, which are not of the cities of these nations.

16 Howbeit of the cities of these peoples, that the LORD thy God giveth thee for an inheritance, thou shalt save alive nothing that breatheth.

"Again, notice how God kills absolutely everyone," Cassie said, smiling. "He leaves alive nothing. Everything has to die."

A hand across the room raised.

"Even the animals?" Laurie said.

"What?" said Cassie.

Laurie gulped. "I mean," she said, "I can see how you have to kill all the humans, but why do all of the animals have to die? They can't contaminate—"

"NOTHING THAT BREATHES," Cassie repeated. "Just look at what it says. Kill everything that breathes."

"Mmm-hmm!" said someone in the room.

"Amen to that!" said another.

"God means business," came a third voice.

"But the—" Laurie began.

At this point we devolved into a discussion of Saul's disobedience in making an offering, how Laurie's thinking was similar to Saul's, in the sense that she was deciding for herself how she wanted to worship God. From here we moved on to a discussion of Sennacherib, the cocky Assyrian (read: Arab) king who showed up in Israel in the middle of the book of Kings boasting about how he was going to waste everybody. "He did a lot of talking," said Cassie, "but he soon found out what this God was about. God destroyed him."

"Mm-hmm," said yes-man Richard.

And there was more and more of this, and finally we got to a section of the book of Romans in which the concept of defeating evil with good was discussed. "We have to defeat our enemies with love," Cassie grumbled. "Now, I know that's really hard to do sometimes, but . . ."

"Does that mean that I have to put a picture of Nancy Pelosi up on my wall?" grumbled Reggie, the guitarist.

The room exploded in laughter.

"If that's what it takes," laughed Cassie. "Now, I know how hard that is . . ."

"That would be impossible for me to do," said one man.

"Don't know if I could," said another.

The jokes went on and on. This part I understood by now.

This was a sort of Church of America, where the religious and political orthodoxies were inextricable. You could no more protest on behalf of Nancy Pelosi here than you could question the wisdom of God. It was groupthink in the classic sense of the word, with the rants against Pelosi and against Libby's "enemies" an essentially exactly parallel version of the Two Minutes' Hate. But I couldn't find a way to get off on it the same way they did. Like Orwell's protagonist Winston, I was in trouble because to be a convincing hater you really have to feel it. And when you don't feel it, you give off a kind of stink. I was stinking pretty hard that night and had to scoot out the door as soon as the meeting broke up, even though Richard tried to engage me in conversation.

"So, Matthew, how are things going?"

"I'm fine," I said. "Gotta run, though."

"Where are you working these days?" he pressed, squinting at me.

"Um," I said, "I've been tutoring kids . . . Those Mexicans have trouble with the language—terrible grammar—listen, I've really got to go . . ."

A few days later I went to church and met Janine before a meeting of Joshua's Generation, which was a sort of Sunday Bible class for thirty-somethings ministered by Matthew Hagee, the porcine son of the lead pastor. I hadn't seen her for a while, and we passed an awkward few minutes as we got reacquainted. Rebecca and Brian, a couple from Janine's Bible-study group whom I'd met while visiting one night with them, hovered nearby and seemed to be watching us closely. I had the distinct feeling that Rebecca was grading me on some kind of mental scorecard.

"So, did you decide to go to the Men of God program?" was the first thing she said to me.

"Huh? What?" I said.

"The Men of God program," she said flatly. "We passed out a sheet at the meeting."

My mind raced. Men of God, right—the junior Promise Keepers–type deal for Cornerstone men. For anthropological reasons I wanted to go, but doubted I'd be able to, owing to an assignment in D.C. I was being packed off to.

"Um, I don't think I can make it," I said.

"I see," she said, glaring.

We went into the chapel—Joshua's Generation met in a small chapel on the Cornerstone grounds, much smaller than the basketball-stadium-sized sanctuary and about the size of a neighborhood church. It even had stained-glass windows to bring out the small-town feel, although the stained glass looked somehow too new. The four of us slid awkwardly into a pew, Janine first, then me, then the watching Rebecca, then her doofus husband, Brian.

The sermon began. In the previous times I'd seen him, Hagee the younger had seemed to follow the Bush model of political heredity, being both dumber and more vicious than his dad. This would be no exception.

He began slowly, asking the crowd if there was anyone here who was concerned about global warming and the environment. Stupidly, unconsciously, I raised my hand. Still not completely awake, I turned to look at Janine, smiled, and then actually saw my hand raised.

Fuck! I lowered it right away, but Rebecca caught me. Pastor Hagee then snorted and said something about being tired of being told that using nonrecyclable cans was destroying the world. I am not of the opinion that that is true, he said. Doesn't sound right to me, he said. Then he mentioned the Oscars from the previous weekend, and the Oscar Al Gore received for his documentary, *An Inconvenient Truth.*

He asked if anyone had seen the excellent speech by our

former vice president, spitting the words "vice president" out like they were dead flesh. When the chapel filled with hisses, he plowed on. "I felt a need to rebut this individual," he said, and proceeded to rail against Gore, the environment, and global warming for a half hour.

"These environmentalists," he said, "they're trying to tell you that somehow all of these terrible things are going to happen because of us. Something WE did.

"They want to tell you," he went on, "that it was America that did something bad, because they want to be able to tell us what we did wrong and send us a bill for it. China burns coal like—they burn so much coal, like it was nothing. But it's all America's fault, of course. If you ask anybody who knows whether America is a polluter, they'll tell you, America is the cleanest country there is."

"Amen!" shouted the crowd.

"Now," he said, "why do they want you to believe this? Because they want to control what you do. They want to control where you go, what countries you go to, what cars you drive. They want to use the environment as a way to control the world!"

"Amen!" I shouted.

"I'll tell you what they want to do," he said. "They want to use the environment to force America to reduce its population. And how do they want to do that? Through abortion."

I was ready to cheer for that, too, except that I couldn't figure out what the fuck he was talking about, so I kept my mouth shut. There were more Amens, though. Encouraged, the portly pastor now looked down at his pulpit and read from a bunch of paper sheets.

"*Time* magazine says that the Sierra Club and others met with environmental leaders in Brazil in 1992 to discuss how to use the environment to reduce the American population from

175 million to 75 million, to control us. This was 1992. How many environmental laws have they passed since then?"

I frowned. Come on, people, I thought. First of all, in 1992, the population of the United States was already well over 200 million. There's no way such an article could possibly have existed. And indeed, when I went back and looked later on, the only mention in *Time*'s Earth Summit coverage of population control that I could find—amid otherwise massive and voluminous coverage of the summit participants' proposals for greenhouse gas restrictions, sustainable development policies, preservation of genetic material, species protection, air quality, and dozens of other issues—was an item about how "in what is perhaps the worst example of bureaucratic obfuscation, the text at one point endorses the promotion of appropriate demographic policies—the nearest negotiators could come to confronting the explosive issue of population control."

The idea that someone at the Earth Summit was proposing cutting the American population by more than half ought to have struck even these people as absurd. Beyond that, the whole idea was counterintuitive. Not even environmentalists think the American population is threateningly large—not compared to Bangladesh, India, and China. But more interesting to me was the fact that Hagee felt so comfortable offering up these absurd fictions; he must have known that no one was going to call bullshit or bother to look up his "facts."

Hagee went on. "Then there was a law they tried to pass last week," he began, "to make it mandatory to check for birth defects using amniocentesis. Now why would they want to check for birth defects? What is the only reason you would want to know if a baby has birth defects before birth? To abort. To abort."

I looked that one up, too. The Genetic Information Non-discrimination Act—which I had to assume was the piece of legislation he was talking about, since no other bill involving genetic screening popped up in Congress that week—was a law that I suppose could have, in the abstract, encouraged abortions. But it certainly had nothing to do with requiring prenatal screening. All the proposed bill would do is prevent health insurers and employers from discriminating on the basis of genetic information gleaned from medical tests. The general point of the bill was to alleviate concerns people might have about getting themselves or their fetuses tested for birth defects. Hagee didn't have to misrepresent this bill—he could have said quite honestly what it was and still have been correct in saying that it encouraged abortions. But what's interesting is that he didn't do that; he just went the fictional route.

Next he went after global warming, denouncing it as a bunch of bosh.

"These people, what they do is, they tell you that something is a problem when it isn't," he said. "That is how they control you. And who else does that?"

"The Devil!" some voices shouted.

"The Devil, that's right," he said. "You know who else? Hitler did that. What did he say Europe's problem was?"

"Jews!" the voices cried out.

"The Jews, that's right. Now, were the Jews a problem in Europe?"

No! No!

"Of course not," he said. "Of course the Jews weren't a problem. And that's exactly the same thing they're doing with global warming!"

"Hear hear!" shouted Brian, Rebecca's husband, clapping enthusiastically.

"Amen!" I shouted.

Hagee smiled.

"They say we're all going to die because the ice caps are

going to melt," he snorted. "No we're not. We just gonna get wet—IF they melt."

The crowd roared.

"They want you to be afraid that aerosol is going to contaminate the planet," he went on. "So what? Don't worry about it. The earth belongs to God. And God . . ."

The crowd finished the rest of his sentence along with him:

". . . did not instill us with an attitude of fear!"

"Aerosol," he sneered. "Aerosol destroying the earth. Ridiculous. Why, if aerosol could kill, everyone on the set with Jan Crouch of TBN woulda been dead a long time ago!"

Janine laughed out loud at that one, clapping her silly little hands. For the first time since I'd met her, she was pissing me off. The TBN joke wasn't even that funny.

He went on for a little while longer, then abruptly ended the sermon. Janine and Rebecca, as we filed out, immediately started babbling about something that had absolutely nothing to do with global warming or the environment or anything. It was as if the whole sermon had passed straight through their skulls. I interrupted and asked them what they thought of the sermon. Janine shrugged, then asked me what I thought.

"Me?" I said. "Oh, I'm stoked. I feel like going out and polluting right now!"

She laughed. "Polluting right now," she said. "That's a good one."

No it isn't, for fuck's sake! I thought.

They then dropped the subject again and went right back to their gibberish. Rebecca started showing us some prayer journal she kept containing her "thoughts," which I was afraid even to look at. Her handwriting was perfectly round, like a fourth-grader's—the booklet had a little picture on the front (it wasn't a unicorn, but it was something of that ilk), plus a scriptural quotation. I could barely hear what she was talking about—my head was spinning from Hagee's sermon. As I struggled to keep my focus, straining to listen to the two babbling Christian ladies—one a housewife, one angling to be one—something came to me in a flash. I remembered suddenly a vicious argument I'd had with my father once when I was a teenager and I felt he wasn't taking me seriously as a grownup. It was an incomplete thought, something about feeling free to be angry because I felt I wasn't being listened to anyway. If no one's listening to you, why not let it all hang out? Why be fair? Why be measured? And suddenly something clicked. If you're here, why not hate an environmentalist? Why not hate him out loud? Like he would ever come here anyway to do anything but laugh. Fuck him and the horse he rode in on! Fuck them all!

Or not? In a flash the "clicking" disappeared and I was back to feeling disoriented and confused. Janine was saying something to Rebecca.

"I used to keep my thoughts in a diary, too," she said. "And I used to organize my prayers. I used to ask God for things. I remember this one time, I asked God for a car. I just pictured to myself what kind of car I wanted, exactly that kind of car, and I prayed and I prayed and I asked God for that car, and he delivered it to me!"

"You see!" Rebecca said. "It works!"

"Of course it works," Brian said. "It always works. We just don't always see it—but we know it."

"How did God give you the car?" I asked.

"What do you mean?" she asked.

"I mean," I said, "did you see an ad or something?"

Janine told a story about a friend of the family selling it to her.

"But it was exactly that car," she said.

"A used Buick Regal?" I asked. "That's what you prayed for?"

"Well, I mean, it was in good condition," she said.

"Well, in that case, of course," I said.

Janine smiled. We all stood around for a few minutes longer, and then after a time Janine asked me if I wanted to join her family at a bowling alley. Her daughter, her dad, and some other folks were there. She invited Rebecca and Brian, too, but they clearly didn't want to go.

"We, uh, have to go to Wal-Mart," said Rebecca.

"Uh-huh," said Janine.

"Get some things," Rebecca said. "There's a list . . ."

We left them behind and went to the bowling alley, where we shared Diet Cokes, chatted, and bowled a string with her family. I explained to her, as we went up to the counter to get our bowling shoes, that where I came from, they bowled something called candlepins, with a skinnier sort of pin and a smaller ball; when she asked where that was, I said New England. To which she asked me if I meant someplace outside of America. I said no, explaining that New England meant Massachusetts, Connecticut, Rhode Island, Maine, New Hampshire, and Vermont.

Still nothing. Finally I mentioned the New England Patriots, and she nodded, understanding. Oh, I see, she said. We went back to the lane and bowled. About halfway through the game, I leaned over to where she was sitting.

"Did I ever tell you the story about my college roommate?" I said. "He was an environmentalist. Used to volunteer for the Sierra Club."

"The what?" she said.

"The Sierra Club. It's an environmentalist organization."

"Oh," she said. "Yuck."

"Yeah, he was a real jerk," I said. "Always telling people what to do, what kind of food to buy, complaining about their garbage, accusing them of polluting. Always complaining about the air not being clean enough and such, saying there were all these poisons in the air. Really silly stuff. But the really obnoxious thing was, he used to drink beer and pee all over the place when he got drunk."

"That's disgusting!" she said.

"It was awful," I said. "He'd just walk into a room, whip it out, and start peeing all over the rug. He'd be like, I dare you to stop me! He even did it in class once. There was one time—you're not going to believe this, but he even did it at a wedding. He was drunk and after yelling at everyone at the wedding about all the wrapping paper and all the trees they'd killed to make it, he just walked up to the wedding cake right during the part where the bride and groom were dancing, and he just unzipped his pants and peed all over this huge ten-layer wedding cake. Even the little wax statue of the newlyweds fell over. And even after that he was still telling us what jerks we were for polluting. He was really obnoxious."

"He sounds like it," she said.

"The thing is," I went on, "after the wedding thing, we realized something was wrong with him. Psychologically wrong, that is. Eventually they had him committed. They sent him away to a mental institution. But he was still really badly behaved even there."

Janine was looking over at the bowling alley. "I think you're up," she said.

"But apparently he got out of his room one night," I continued, ignoring her. "Seriously, I just heard about this for the first time a few years ago, I had fallen out of touch with him. I heard he got out of his room at the institution and he went downstairs to the kitchen. And somehow he crushed both of his hands in the door of a walk-in freezer. Broke all the bones in both of his hands!"

"Um—"

"And the worst part is, they took him to a hospital to get fixed, but guess what happened? He got a staph infection in both hands. Eventually, they had to chop off both of his hands at the wrist. Amputate, that is. So now he's walking around with no hands."

I mimed a pair of stumps.

Janine looked at me and gasped. "That's . . . wow. I guess he can't pee on stuff anymore. Well, I mean, he can, but he can't aim."

"He can't aim, that's right," I said thoughtfully as I took my turn. "It's kind of funny, when you think about it, considering how he used to be. Obnoxious and all."

"Yeah!" she said. "That's such a wild story!"

"Anyway," I said offhandedly, "he's a Christian now."

"Oh, well, that's good!" said Janine.

"Yeah," I said. "At least the story has a happy ending."

She walked up to the lane and bowled. Right down the middle, pins flying.

"Strike!" she said, clapping.

TEN

Conspiracy Interlude II,

or

The Derangement of the American Left

THE 9/11 TRUTH MOVEMENT is not easily defined. The simplest definition of a Truther is probably someone who believes that the U.S. government shared some complicity, whether direct or indirect, in the 9/11 attack. In a broader sense, most Truthers believe the culprits to be a bund of neoconservatives that includes Bush, Dick Cheney, and Paul Wolfowitz and is organizationally represented by groups like the Project for the New American Century (PNAC). These neocons first secured the White House by means legal and illegal (with the Florida fiasco of 2000 greatly aiding their rise to power) and then set into motion a plan to launch a series of wars in the Middle East, a plan that involved either covertly aiding or actively participating in the bombing of the World Trade Center.

Regarding the actual events of 9/11, the theories espoused by Truthers vary significantly. Some believe in little more than the matador-defense LIHOP theory (in which Bush & Co. simply allowed the attacks to happen), others believe that the

Pentagon was hit by a missile instead of a plane, while still others believe that the "planes" that crashed into the towers were not planes at all but high-tech holograms or video tricks (the "no-planes" theory). But almost all Truthers seem at least to accept one central idea, which is that the collapse of the towers was caused not by the planes but by a controlled demolition, planned long in advance and timed to coincide with the impact of the hijacked jets.

As proof of motive, Truthers, like the ones I met in the diner, often point to a document called "Rebuilding America's Defenses," a policy paper about future defense strategies crafted by PNAC in September 2000. In particular, Truthers highlight a passage late in the document that reads as follows:

> Further, the process of transformation, even if it brings revolutionary change, is likely to be a long one, absent some catastrophic and catalyzing event—like a new Pearl Harbor.

This single passage is considered a smoking gun in 9/11 Truth circles. The amazing thing is that the "transformation" envisioned in the PNAC document has absolutely nothing to do with the launching of energy wars in Mesopotamia or the institution of repressive domestic security laws like the Patriot Act. In fact, if you actually read "Rebuilding America's Defenses," what you find is a rather drab and conventional conservative policy paper seemingly written by a group of people who played too much Risk as kids, one that indulges heavily in masturbatory and oftentimes wildly inaccurate speculation about the shape of future military conflicts around the world and America's ability to fight and win them. It is a paper about reconfiguring the cold war fighting force for the challenges of the twenty-first century, and while it spends a lot of time worrying about maintaining American preeminence, there's no evidence in it for anything like the evil plan Truthers insist is in there.

So a "new Pearl Harbor" was needed to justify the invasion of Iraq? Not according to "Rebuilding America's Defenses," which not only did not argue for a need to overthrow Saddam Hussein, but confidently asserted that little needed to be done to ensure security in the region. "Kuwait itself is strongly defended," the paper's authors conclude. "With a minor increase in strength, more permanent basing arrangements, and continued 'no fly' and 'no drive' zone enforcement, the danger of a repeat short-warning Iraqi invasion . . . would be significantly reduced."

The paper moreover argued that the strong ground presence in Kuwait obviated the need for increased naval activity in the region. "With a substantial permanent Army ground presence in Kuwait," PNAC writes, "the demands for increased Marine presence in the Gulf could be scaled back as well."

The paper made a wide variety of suggestions with regard to its vision for a "transformation" of the armed forces, including but not limited to:

1. Reducing the size of the National Guard.
2. Reducing or eliminating spending on aircraft carrier programs.
3. Reducing or eliminating spending on the Joint Strike Fighter.
4. Instituting a global missile defense system (this is heavily emphasized in the paper).

Yes, the paper argued for increased spending on defense, using the age-old Republican trick of showing how defense spending as a percentage of GDP had fallen in the Clinton years. And yes, the paper argued vaguely for an increased emphasis on building capability to fight "constabulatory" wars to police potential challenges to American preeminence. But when they talked about America needing a "new Pearl Harbor" to "transform" the military, what they were talking about was transforming the old cold war military designed for combat against the Russians in Europe into a new, modern military designed to fight localized wars across the globe against nonstate actors like terrorists and rogue groups, particularly those that might acquire long-range missiles.

Yet after 9/11 occurred, did this "transformation" take place? Did we reduce the size of the National Guard? Reduce spending on aircraft carriers? Remove carrier groups from the Gulf? Institute a global missile defense system? No. In fact, in some cases, 9/11 actually scuttled these very plans. Condoleezza Rice, for instance, was scheduled on 9/11 to give a speech at Johns Hopkins outlining the need for missile defense—but the speech was postponed. A year later, Rice finally gave her Johns Hopkins speech, but this time only mentioned missile defense, which by then had fallen off the Washington radar completely, in passing. If PNAC and its neocon villains bombed the Trade Center in order to institute a missile defense system, they sure gave up on their dreams pretty quickly.

Moreover, the actual sentence so frequently referenced in the document is taken completely out of context. If you read the entire passage, you'll find that it says that the "transformation" is probably going to take a long time. "Domestic politics and industrial policy will shape the pace and content of transformation as much as the requirements of current missions," it reads. "This report advocates a two-stage process of change—transition and transformation—over the coming decades." They then go on to outline "transition" and "transformation."

Does this sound like the work of a group of people planning the "next Pearl Harbor"? Or was this laborious outlining of the decades-long two-stage process just a clever cover story, designed to throw readers off the trail of the senselessly candid admission about a "new Pearl Harbor" made two sentences previously? Any way you look at this, it's lunacy.

But beyond that . . . what the fuck? Only a generation born and raised on the Internet could possibly believe that the motive for a political mass killing would be paraded openly in a document like "Rebuilding America's Defenses." Who would think that the likes of Dick Cheney and Paul Wolfowitz would openly confess their motives for a monstrous criminal conspiracy in a position paper? How could anyone think such a thing would even get into print? Did Dick Cheney sidle up to report authors Thomas Donnelly, Don Kagan, and Gary Schmitt after a meeting and mumble something like, "You know, I think this World Trade Center thing is a go. Write us up a paper saying that the only thing we need to transform the military is a new Pearl Harbor or something."

Or was it the other way? Did Donnelly, Kagan, and Schmitt write their paper first, only to have Cheney/Wolfowitz/Bush read it later and think, Dangit, they're right! We do need a new Pearl Harbor! And then immediately start hitting the phones, calling their munitions people, arranging fake passports and stick-on beards, etc.

Because if you seriously believe that this paper is evidence of motive, it has to be one or the other. Either they used the release of this policy paper as an occasion to confess spontaneously to their own criminal conspiracy for absolutely no reason whatsoever, or they first published it and then were suddenly and innocently inspired by their own literature to a previously unimagined plan that less than a year later would turn out to be the most monstrous—and most seamlessly executed—crime in American history. No other explanation makes sense.

"Rebuilding America's Defenses" is cited everywhere in the 9/11 Truth world. It was mentioned prominently in the seminal Internet documentary *Loose Change*. It's been referenced by all the major priests of the movement: Alex Jones, John Pilger . . . Hell, leading 9/11 "scholar" David Griffin even named his 9/11 conspiracy book *The New Pearl Harbor.* Yet not once anywhere do any of these people explain why a group of extremely rich and powerful people bent on murdering thousands of innocent Americans would decide to voluntarily shine a light on their evil plan in a publicly circulated document a year before the attack.

But this kind of thing is all over the 9/11 Truth Movement. The movement is really distinguished by a kind of defiant unfamiliarity with the actual character of America's ruling class. In 9/11 Truth lore, the people who staff the White House, the security agencies, the Pentagon, and groups like PNAC and the Council on Foreign Relations are imagined to be a monolithic, united class of dastardly, swashbuckling risk-takers with permanent hard-ons for *Bourne Supremacy*–style "false flag" and "black bag" operations, instead of the mundanely greedy, risk-averse, backstabbing, lawn-tending, half-clever suburban golfers they are in real life. It completely misunderstands the nature of American government—fails to see that the old maxim about "the business of America is business" is absolutely true, that the federal government in this country is really just a low-rent time-share property seasonally occupied by this or that clan of financial interests, each of which takes its four-year turn at the helm, tinkering with the tax laws and regulatory code and the rates at the Fed in the way it thinks will best keep the money train rolling.

The people who really run America don't send the likes of George Bush and Dick Cheney to the White House to cook up boat-rocking, maniacal world-domination plans and commit massive criminal conspiracies on live national television; they send them there to repeal PUHCA and dole out funds for the F-22 and pass energy bills with $14 billion tax breaks and slash fuel-efficiency standards and do all the other shit that never makes the papers but keeps Wall Street and the country's corporate boardrooms happy. You don't elect politicians to commit crimes; you elect politicians to make your crimes legal. That is the whole purpose of the racket of government. Another use of it would be a terrible investment, and the financial class in this country didn't get to where it is by betting on the ability of a president whose lips move when he reads to blow up two Manhattan skyscrapers in broad daylight without getting caught.

But according to 9/11 Truth lore, the financial patrons of democratic government were game for exactly that sort of gamble. According to the movement, the Powers That Be in the year 2000 spent $200 million electing George Bush and Dick Cheney because they were insufficiently impressed with the docility of the American population. What was needed, apparently, was a distraction, a gruesome mass murder that would whip the American population into a war frenzy. The same people who had managed in the 2000 election to sell multimillionaire petro-royalist George Bush as an ordinary down-to-earth ranch hand apparently so completely lacked confidence in their own propaganda skills that they resorted to ordering a mass murder on American soil as a way of cajoling America to go to war against a second-rate tyrant like Saddam Hussein. As if getting America to support going to war even against innocent countries had ever been hard before!

The truly sad thing about the 9/11 Truth Movement is that it's based upon the wildly erroneous proposition that our leaders would ever be frightened enough of public opinion to feel the need to pull off this kind of stunt before acting in a place like Afghanistan or Iraq. At its heart, 9/11 Truth is a conceit, a narcissistic pipe dream for a dingbat, sheeplike population that is pleased to imagine itself dangerous and ungovernable. Rather than admit to their own powerlessness and irrelevance, or admit that they've spent the last fifty years or so electing leaders who openly handed their tax money to business cronies and golfed in Scotland while Middle America's jobs were being sent overseas, the adherents to 9/11 Truth instead flatter themselves with fantasies about a ruling class obsessed with keeping the terrible truth from the watchful, exacting eye of the People.

Whereas the real conspiracy of power in America is right out in the open and always has been, only nobody cares, so long as *Fear Factor* and *Baseball Tonight* come on at the right times. A conspiracy like the one described by 9/11 Truth would only be necessary in a country where the people are a threat to actually govern themselves effectively.

But none of that even matters nearly as much as what 9/11 Truth says about the mental state of the population. The whole narrative of the movement is so completely and utterly retarded, it boggles the mind. It's like something cooked up by a bunch of teenagers raised on texting, TV, and *Sports Illustrated* who just saw *V for Vendetta* for the first time and decided to write a Penguin History of the World on the strength of it. A genius on the order of a Mozart or a Shakespeare would be hard-pressed to dream up the awesome comedy that is the alleged plot from the point of view of the plotters. If there was such a conspiracy, remember, something like the following conversation would have had to have taken place:

April 1999, World Trade Center building 7, New York, NY. A secret meeting of the Project for the New American Century. In attendance are Dick Cheney, Paul Wolfowitz, Douglas Feith, Irv Kristol, and . . . others. Cheney, standing at the head of the table and glaring downward, addresses the group:

CHENEY: Gentlemen, we stand at a crossroads.
KRISTOL (*whispering to Feith*): I love it when we stand at a crossroads!
FEITH (*giggling*): Me too. But I never know what to wear.
CHENEY: Do you assholes mind?

KRISTOL: Sorry, Dick.

FEITH: Me too.

CHENEY: Okay. (*clears throat*) As I was saying, gentlemen, we stand at a crossroads . . .

KRISTOL (*in Bill Murray fashion, mimicking suspense-movie soundtrack*): Dunh-dunh-dunh!

FEITH: Dunh-dunh-dunh! Dunh . . . duh-duh-dunh!

CHENEY: Oh, for fuck's sake.

KRISTOL (*laughing*): Okay, seriously, Dick, I'm sorry.

FEITH (*still laughing*): Duh-duh-duh . . .

KRISTOL: Shhh!

FEITH: Okay, okay. (*to Cheney*) No, it's okay, Dick, you can go on.

CHENEY: You're sure? No more jokes to make? Guys want to do your goddamn Katharine Hepburn impersonations or something?

KRISTOL (*channeling* On Golden Pond): Come on, Norman! Hurry up! The loons, the loons!

FEITH (*whispering*): Shut up, for Christ's sake! (*to Cheney*) Our lips are sealed, Dick. Honest.

CHENEY: Okay. Jesus. As I was saying, I think we all know about Marion King Hubbert's projections about the future of oil reserves. We all know the deal: in every oil field there comes a time when half of the field's reachable oil has been extracted. After that point, exploitation becomes more and more expensive; as time goes on, it requires more and more energy just to extract one barrel of oil. Eventually, oil extraction becomes uneconomic, which is to say it requires a barrel of oil's worth of energy to extract a barrel of oil. When that time comes, gentlemen, our oil-based empire is fucked. And the clock begins ticking in that direction once we pass that halfway point with the world's oil reserves. Once oil "peaks,"

America—an empire whose power is based almost entirely upon its oil dominance—will officially be on the decline.

FEITH: Yeah. And it doesn't help that the only reason the dollar is worth more than the peso is that OPEC still trades in dollars.

CHENEY: Exactly. Without oil, we're like Bangladesh with fat people. And here's the problem: that fail-safe point is upon us. I think we all know that oil production in the lower forty-eight states peaked in 1970, that Alaskan oil production peaked in 1988, Russia around the same time. Saudi Arabia may be just years from peaking, and in any case our political situation there is tenuous at best. Our guys at Halliburton now estimate that worldwide oil and gas production from existing reserves is declining by about 4 to 6 percent every year.

WOLFOWITZ: So what's your point? We're all old anyway. Who cares what happens twenty years from now?

CHENEY: The point, Paul, is that the American empire as we know it will collapse within twenty to thirty years unless we find massive new supplies of oil and find them fast. By 2010 we're going to need to find fifty million additional barrels of oil per day. And there's only one place where we can get that much oil . . .

KRISTOL: Sweden!

FEITH: Of course. Let's invade! I hate those speed skaters anyway.

CHENEY: No, you assholes, not Sweden. Iraq. It's the only major oil-rich state whose reserves haven't mostly been exploited. There's probably seven million barrels a day minimum just sitting in those fields—and the worst thing is, unless we get in there soon, it's all going to go to the French, the Russians, and the

Germans, since Saddam will sell to all of them long before he deals with us, assuming his UN sanctions get lifted at some point.

WOLFOWITZ: My God.

CHENEY: So it's clear we've got to get in there. Are we agreed on this?

ALL: Agreed.

CHENEY: All right. Well, I've got a plan.

WOLFOWITZ: We get George elected in 2000 and go in, right? Tell the public Saddam's in violation of his UN restrictions or some shit like that? He is anyway, isn't he?

CHENEY: No, that would never work. The public would never stand for it.

(*Everyone bursts out laughing.*)

CHENEY: Seriously.

WOLFOWITZ: Oh, wait—you're serious?

CHENEY: Absolutely. No, I think the way to go is to cook up some kind of justification. Something that will really get the public behind the invasion.

FEITH: I know! We go to the UN, show bogus photos of Saddam's secret store of chemical and biological weapons, evidence of his nuclear weapons program. Tell the world he's planning to attack.

CHENEY: No. Not emotional enough. I mean something really hot.

KRISTOL: It could be a human-rights thing. Some emergency, like he's gassing Kurds again or something. That worked for Clinton in Kosovo. I mean, who gave a shit about Albanians, right? I wouldn't know an Albanian if I caught one in bed with my wife. But that whole rape-camp thing was good enough by a mile to start that war.

CHENEY: No, no, that's not vivid enough, not *Band of*

Brothers enough. We need the people all lathered up, their mouths full of spittle, howling for blood, like pit bulls. You guys need to think to scale, think big, think like Michael Bay.

FEITH: Michael Bay, Jesus. Okay, okay, what then?

CHENEY: We attack the World Trade Center.

KRISTOL: Perfect! And blame it on Saddam!

CHENEY: No, we bomb the World Trade Center and blame it on Osama bin Laden.

FEITH: Oh. How?

CHENEY: Easy. First, we cultivate nineteen suicidal Muslim patsies from a variety of Middle Eastern countries, I'd say mostly from Saudi Arabia. We bring them to the U.S., train them at U.S. flight schools. They should be high-profile terrorist suspects who are magically given free rein by the security agencies to travel back and forth to various terrorist training camps to study passenger jet piloting. Actually, that process is already under way now. Our friends in the Clinton administration are seeing to it that four groups of Arab men are being brought along by the FBI and the CIA.

WOLFOWITZ: How is it that the Clinton administration is already helping us with this, when we haven't even planned this yet?

CHENEY: They just are. Okay?

WOLFOWITZ: Okay, fine. And what do we do with these hijackers?

CHENEY: We sit idly by while they plot to hijack a series of passenger jet planes and crash them into the World Trade Center, the Pentagon, and the White House.

WOLFOWITZ: And how do we get them to do that?

CHENEY: We just do. You see, we worked with these people back in the old mujahideen days in

Afghanistan. So naturally we're still thick as thieves with them.

FEITH: Oh, of course. So we get them to fly into these buildings. And the impact from the planes will bring down the World Trade Center.

CHENEY: No, Doug, dammit, you're not following me. The impact from the planes most certainly won't be sufficient to knock down the towers. We know this because we've privately conducted studies that show that the towers will easily be able to withstand impact by two jets loaded to the gills with jet fuel. That said, the jets will likely cause skyscraper fires hot enough to kill everyone above the point of impact; we're going to have to assume, of course, that the exits from the higher floors to the lower floors will be mostly blocked after the collisions. So assuming we crash the planes about two-thirds of the way up each of the towers early on a business day, we're looking at trapping and killing a good three, four, maybe even five thousand people on the upper floors.

FEITH: Fantastic. I love killing people in the finance industry. It's too bad the people on the lower floors will get to escape.

CHENEY: It is too bad—especially since we're going to blow up the rest of the building complex anyway.

FEITH: We are?

CHENEY: Yes. You see, the way I see it, our best course of action is to first crash planes into each of the towers, trapping and killing those thousands on the upper floors of each building. After the impact, of course, the people on the lower floors will find their way out of the building and onto the street, where they will achieve relative safety—at which point we'll finally detonate the massive network of explosive charges

we've secretly hidden in the buildings in the weeks
and months prior to the attacks.

FEITH: Wait, why did we do that again?

CHENEY: Because the buildings wouldn't have fallen
down unless we did.

WOLFOWITZ: But why do we need the buildings to fall
down?

CHENEY: Because the events of the day will be
insufficiently horrifying and impactful without the
building collapses.

FEITH: So why don't we detonate the charges earlier, so
that we can kill the people on the lower floors, too?

CHENEY: That's a good question. At some point we
have to sacrifice effect for believability. You see, if
the planes crash into the buildings and the buildings
collapse immediately, everyone will be suspicious and
they'll be onto the presence of the explosives. So what
we have to do is let the planes crash into the building,
give the jet fuel time to start fires that will "soften"
the building core, and then we detonate the charges.
Afterward, we'll be able to argue that the fires
coupled with the impact actually caused the buildings
to collapse.

FEITH: Why will we be able to argue that? Didn't our
studies show that impact and fire alone wouldn't have
caused the buildings to collapse?

CHENEY: Those were our secret, far-more-advanced
studies, done with secret, far-more-advanced military
technology. The vast majority of the world's civilian
structural engineers, however, can be counted on after
the incident to conclude that the buildings collapsed
due to a combination of fire, impact, and the
knocking off of fireproofing from the building beams.

FEITH: Why can they be counted on to conclude that?

CHENEY: Because that's what our secret research shows their not-secret research will show! Jesus Christ, work with me on this, will you?

WOLFOWITZ: I think I get it. We crash the planes, kill everyone above the impact of the planes, let the people underneath the impact out to safety, then collapse the buildings about an hour or so later using the explosives that we pointlessly incurred months' and weeks' worth of career- and life-threatening risk to covertly plant in a building complex visited by hundreds of thousands of people every week.

CHENEY: Exactly! The actual deaths will mostly be caused by the planes. But we'll incur the massive additional risk simply to destroy the building for effect, because it will look cool and scary on television.

FEITH: I'm still confused about the our-studies and their-studies thing.

CHENEY (*sighing*): What's the matter, Doug?

FEITH: If we know the planes won't collapse the buildings, isn't it possible that other people after the accident will figure out that the planes didn't collapse the buildings?

CHENEY: Yes. But those other people will be a tiny minority of mostly nonscientists who'll deduce the whole plan by researching the matter on the Internet. But we can count on their groundbreaking, visionary research being ignored by the mainstream scientific community, which will continue to insist the planes caused the collapses.

FEITH: Why can we count on that?

CHENEY: Because the mainstream science community, like the whole of the corporate media, the Congress, the Democratic Party, even the mainstream leftist

political opposition, will naturally be in either
conscious or unconscious assent with our plan.
Most scientists, you know, depend in some form or
another on government funding. So they'll be highly
motivated to sign off on our dastardly mass-murder
plot, since they know their salaries—some of these
people make almost a hundred thousand a year, you
know—ultimately depend on our ability to secure
fifty billion additional barrels of oil per day by 2010
by fooling the population into invading Saddam
Hussein's secular Iraq by faking a terrorist attack
against the World Trade Center at the hands of a
bunch of Saudi religious radicals loyal to the Afghan-
supported terrorist leader Osama bin Laden.

WOLFOWITZ: No, I get it, I really do. It all makes sense.

CHENEY: Also, we have to knock down WTC 7, this very
building, in order to get rid of the evidence. I think
it goes without saying that we'll need a command
center for these operations, and I can't think of a
place that would be better or more appropriate than
an office right next to the point of attack. From
these very offices, gentlemen, we will coordinate the
military war exercises that will be held in this region
on that very morning, war exercises that will so
thoroughly confuse our own military that they will be
unable to identify and intercept the hijacked planes
we will be sending at the towers like so many deadly
guided missiles.

KRISTOL: But, Dick—how can we be sure that the air
force won't find a way to intercept the planes anyway?

WOLFOWITZ: I'll answer that, Dick. Irv, the best way we
can guarantee that will be to issue stand-down orders
in addition to implementing the war games.

KRISTOL: I see. We order the war games in order to

stymie the air force intercepts we don't control, but just in case those fail, we'll control the air force intercepts.

CHENEY: Now you're catching on.

KRISTOL: And the control center for those war games and for all our other plans, including the demolition, will be right here. These rooms are secret and utterly impenetrable to the general public at the moment, but after the attacks they will be vulnerable to forensic inspection by whichever city or federal agency goes through the wreckage of this doomed building.

CHENEY: Exactly. That's one of the reasons I thought we should choose this space. If we chose some other spot as a base of operations—a warehouse in Queens, say—we might be able to keep it secure forever. But if we set up here, we can be sure some snooping official will end up poking around in the ruins. And we want that, it adds intrigue to the whole deal. Because it goes without saying that we won't be able to control all the cleanup agencies, except those that might be inclined to find our bomb fragments. Those we can count on one hundred percent.

KRISTOL: Right, but still, we have to really be sure we destroy everything here. Especially all the papers and computer records of the conspiracy plans, which we will naturally leave behind, banking on the fact that they will be destroyed in the hellish conflagration.

FEITH: Guys, I'm lost. You're saying we have to detonate this entire building in order to cover up the evidence of the crime?

ALL: Of course.

FEITH: Why don't we just not leave the evidence behind and not blow up the building? Why should there be any evidence to leave behind at all?

CHENEY: Doug, you're not being realistic. You always have to leave evidence of covert operations behind for the public to maybe find.

WOLFOWITZ: Well, except that we never have before.

CHENEY: Right, except for that. (*A phone in the middle of the conference table rings. Kristol picks it up.*)

KRISTOL: Hello? Who's this? Oh, hey, Larry. *A gast in shtetl!* I'll put you on speaker! (*cups phone, presses speaker button; addresses others*) It's Larry Silverstein, the WTC landlord.

SILVERSTEIN: Hey guys! *Vos makht ir?*

CHENEY: Not bad, Larry, how goes it?

SILVERSTEIN: *In dr'erd afn dek!* Just awful! But we get by, you know.

CHENEY: What can we do you for, Larry?

SILVERSTEIN: Oh, hey, well, a little birdie told me that you guys were planning on blowing up my building complex and blaming it on Islamic terrorists!

CHENEY: We all have our hobbies, Larry.

SILVERSTEIN: Well, naturally, you have my assent. Anything to grease the wheels of international capitalism. Also, as a landlord, I love seeing my tenants burned to death and jumping out of high windows on live television and that sort of thing. Plus, I'm a Jew, you know, I have horns. Paul, how's your family?

WOLFOWITZ: Oh, Larry, don't ask. Clare just last week popped her bursa sac building a sukkah. But does anyone live a life without troubles these days?

SILVERSTEIN: Things just keep getting worse and worse, you're right there. Listen, fellas, about that building complex . . .

CHENEY: Yes?

SILVERSTEIN: Do you think you could make sure that the

WTC 7 building goes down, too? See, the thing is, I just signed a new insurance deal with Industrial Risk Insurers; this could all work out very nicely for me.

CHENEY: Larry, it's such an amazing coincidence, we were just talking about that. As it happens, we need to destroy the building to get rid of the evidence anyway. So say no more about that, we'll take care of it.

WOLFOWITZ: Well, say no more until it happens. Then you might just want to casually mention near a PBS camera that you're planning on "pulling" the building.

SILVERSTEIN: What does "pulling" mean?

CHENEY: Well, it's not a demolition term, but some will say it is. We're thinking you might just want to make a little admission in that direction.

SILVERSTEIN: Before my insurance investigation is concluded? At exactly the time when such an admission would cost me my entire settlement? Consider it done!

ALL: Thanks, Larry.

SILVERSTEIN: You bet, fellas! See you on the links. *Mazel tov!* Oh, hey, Paul . . .

WOLFOWITZ: Yes?

SILVERSTEIN: Pull my finger, Paul! Pull it!

WOLFOWITZ: You bet I'll "pull it," you mensch!

SILVERSTEIN: Later!

(*Silverstein hangs up.*)

CHENEY: Well, that worked out well. I guess the only things left to really worry about are the other two planes. What do you guys think?

KRISTOL: Well, one plane. I'm thinking with the Pentagon, we send a missile or a drone into the building, then just tell everyone it's a plane. Just to fuck with people.

FEITH: Is this going to be one of your basic take-the-real-
plane-to-a-remote-military-base, kill-the-passengers,
then-fake-their-cell-phone-distress-calls-using-
advanced-voice-recog-technology deals?

KRISTOL: That's what I'm thinking. Keep it simple, in
other words.

WOLFOWITZ: Now I'm confused. We hire patsies to fly
into the World Trade Center, but for the Pentagon,
we don't use patsies?

CHENEY: No. We use patsies, but just not to fly the plane.
See, the patsies we choose for the Pentagon job won't
actually have enough piloting skill to maneuver a
plane into the Pentagon. So what we'll do is take a
real passenger flight, hijack it, and take it to a remote
location—say, Wright-Patterson Air Force Base in
Ohio—and then kill all the passengers on board,
including the patsies, with poison gas.* Then, instead
of using that plane, we'll either shoot a missile or
use one of those Global Hawk drone planes to crash
into the Pentagon. Then we tell everyone that it

---

*Most Truther sites try to avoid speculating about what happened to the
passengers of what turned out to be Flight 77, but the theory that the
plane and its passengers were removed to a secret location and executed
is bandied about a lot. I found one site that explained away the presence
on Flight 77 of Barbara Olson, wife of solicitor general and friend to
George W. Bush Ted Olson, by speculating that Olson was in on the
plot to kill the passengers from the start: "For all we know Babs was in
on the plot from the beginning and was even prepared with a suitable
gas mask to protect her from the poison gas that killed everyone else
onboard. If so, it is not unlikely that she is 'making the bunker homey'
for the 'housewarming' when Bush and the Gang all arrive to ride out
the apocalypse they have initiated. Or, she could have had a little plastic surgery and is waiting for Ted (who has recently quit his job) on
that nice Caribbean Island they always wanted to retire to. They 'meet
and marry' and everyone is glad to see that Ted has found love again!"
www.cassiopaea.org/cass/boeing.htm

was actually the missing plane that crashed into the Pentagon.

WOLFOWITZ: Why don't we just get patsies who can fly a plane? Isn't that what we're doing in New York?

CHENEY: It's so hard to find skilled patsies these days.

KRISTOL: Plus, Paul, it'll be simple. All we have to do is go to the crash site afterward and deposit pieces of airplane wreckage, landing gear and so on, at the appropriate places.

CHENEY: That's perfect. I know exactly where we can get some airplane wreckage, too. There was an American Airlines jet that crashed in Colombia in 1995; we can take pieces of that plane and just sort of drop them on the lawn when no one is looking.* You know, just like in *The Great Escape*—drop them through a pantleg while whistling and looking off into the distance, and just sort of kick them around in the burning wreckage.

KRISTOL: Or even better, we can drop them on the lawn from a circling C-130 after the crash.† Just have

---

*The Cali, Colombia, flight is often presumed to have been cannibalized to play the role of the wrecked Flight 77. From Aftermath News: "James Hanson, a newspaper reporter who earned his law degree from the University of Michigan College of Law, has traced that debris to an American Airlines 757 that crashed in a rain forest above Cali, Colombia in 1995. 'It was the kind of slow-speed crash that would have torn off paneling in this fashion, with no fires, leaving them largely intact,' [he said]." http://aftermathnews.wordpress .com/2007/06/23/new-study-no-boeing-757-hit-the-pentagon

†Leading 9/11 Truther Jim Fetzer came up with this one: "In fact, debris begins to show up on the completely clean lawn in short order, which might have been dropped from a C-130 that was circling above the Pentagon or placed there by men in suits who were photographed carrying debris with them."

someone leaning out the cargo bay with big pieces
of fuselage, dropping them strategically in between
the rescue workers. We can do the same thing with
the body parts; we'll just take some of the bodies,
barbecue them with jet fuel, and just sort of toss bits
of them here and there around the site.

CHENEY: That works for me. What I like about that is
that it's so simple.

WOLFOWITZ: Okay, let me back up. Rather than just
finding some patsies who can fly—which is exactly
what we'll be doing in New York—we instead seize
an actual passenger flight and remove the passengers
to a remote location and kill them, disposing of the
plane later. Then we attack the Pentagon and kill
one hundred or so of our own people with either a
missile or a Global Hawk drone plane, banking on
the probability that no one will see a plane shooting a
missile in broad daylight in the nation's capital. Then,
after we execute this attack on the Pentagon, we go
back to the site and cleverly rearrange the evidence
to make it look like a plane crashed there, including
planting the samples of DNA of all the people we
killed in Ohio or whatever. I'm not saying it doesn't
sound like a good plan, but can I ask why we're doing
this? If we can't find a patsy who can fly a plane, why
not just not crash a plane into the Pentagon?

CHENEY: What do you mean? But a plane crashes into
the Pentagon. That's part of the plan.

WOLFOWITZ: Right, but since it's our plan and we
can change it, why don't we just scuttle the entire
Pentagon operation? We've already got the money
shot with the towers—why do we need to go
through all the trouble of finding hijackers who
can't fly, nurturing them in the womb of ineffective

government surveillance, getting them on a plane full of passengers, and then faking the deaths of all these people, telling the world they died in a plane crash that was actually a sinister attack using our own technology? I mean, so many things can go wrong. You've got to get people to sign off on the DNA reports, you've got eyewitnesses with weird stories, you've got inconsistent radar data, you've got to put stuff there for the dogs to find . . .

CHENEY: Don't worry about the dogs. We've got the dogs covered.*

WOLFOWITZ: Oh, well, okay. But still—why not just skip the whole thing?

CHENEY: Are you suggesting that instead of executing hundreds of sinister, secretive, murderous subplans that all must go off flawlessly together to create a single underpublicized deception, that instead of that we just blow it off and go with the much larger and more spectacular World Trade Center event?

WOLFOWITZ: Right. Either that or find patsies who can fly.

CHENEY: Hmm. Interesting. What do you guys think?

FEITH: I don't know, Dick. It seems much easier just to go with the whole fake-the-flight, kill-the-passengers, fake-the-cell-phone-calls, pass-off-the-missile-attack-as-a-plane-crash thing. I can't think of any simpler way to do this plan than that.

KRISTOL: Yeah, Dick, frankly, neither can I. I like your plan better. It's so much more . . . cloak 'n' daggerier!

CHENEY: Well, it's settled, then. Paul, you cool?

---

*From FreedomFiles.org: "If you look at the pictures of the dogs doing searches at the Pentagon for body parts, they all have blanked faces, like there is nothing there to find." www.freedomfiles.org/war/pentagon.htm

WOLFOWITZ: Hey, I trust you guys, you know that.

FEITH: Well, that worked out well. I mean, there are a
few loose ends, but . . .

CHENEY: Look, the point is, we do the towers and pin it
on bin Laden. That leads us to invade Afghanistan. A
year and a half later, we invade Iraq.

FEITH: And we blame the whole WTC thing on Saddam.

CHENEY: Right, and . . . wait, what? No! No, actually
we never make that connection, because none exists.
I figure we can just say he's in violation of his UN
restrictions, and that will be a good enough reason to
invade. He is anyway, right? In violation, I mean?

WOLFOWITZ: I think you're right, he is!

Of course one could go on and on in this direction. To read
9/11 Truther lore is to enter a world where criminals commit
dastardly acts without motive, where even brilliant Machiavel-
lian politicians like Dick Cheney repeatedly take the path of
most perilous resistance to achieve their nefarious ends, where
simplicity of criminal plan is eschewed as a matter of principle,
where everyone who is not actively involved with exposing the
conspiracy can be considered a solid suspect for mass murder.

ELEVEN

PRACTICE, PRACTICE, PRACTICE

★ ★ ★ ★ ★ ★ ★ ★ ★ ★ ★ ★

IN EARLY MARCH I woke up in the middle of the night with an idea—literally woke up laughing. As it happened it was a Sunday, in the predawn hours. I looked down at my forearm, chuckled, then went back to bed.

Within a few hours I was dressed up and back in church, sitting next to Laurie and Janine and a few other familiars, watching on the dual church JumboTrons as Pastor Hagee played a few homemade public service announcements. One of these was a spoof of Apple's "Get a Mac" ad campaign—those irritating "offbeat" computer ads where effete hipster actor Justin Long ("Mac") tries endlessly, against a seamless digital white-screen background, to console the hapless pudgy humorist John Hodgman ("PC"). In the "hilarious" church version, the two characters were "Man of God" and "Man of the World"—with the Man of God a cool, together cat and the Man of the World a helpless, flailing dickwad with a comb-over.

"I live according to the holy values and principles set down

in the Bible, the revealed word of God!" was the kickoff statement of the suave Man of God.

"I get my values from pretty much anything and everything
that I read and see, with no direction or guidance whatsoever!"
moaned the goofball Man of the World.

The audience roared with laughter. Someone behind me, I
swear, slapped a knee. Laurie, sitting next to me, chortled out
loud.

"Oh, that is funn-ny!" she said.

"Hilarious!" I agreed. "First-rate stuff."

She looked down at me.

"Are you okay, honey? Something wrong with your arm?"

I was scratching my left forearm furiously.

"No," I said. "I'm fine. Just a little itch."

She shrugged. "Okay, then," she said. "I hope you're okay."

I smiled. I felt firmly in my element by now. I had even
been baptized in the church, an amusing if sensually unpleasant
ceremony. Hagee farmed out the orientation process to a fifth-
string pastor named Larry, an aging, bitter old curmudgeon
whose mangled beet-red face was a mess of exploding capillar-
ies. Larry's crushed-cauliflower nose passed air to his lungs very
spottily, and as a result the old meanie's speech was almost completely incomprehensible, which made his narration about our
impending spiritual journey into grace somewhat less enthrall-
ing than it might have been. In a cramped second-floor storage
room, he kept telling stories about what a mean drunken prick
he used to be before he found God, and how after he was saved
he became just a flat-out frickin' awesome individual. Everyone
in the room looked bored. It didn't help that he had a cold and
kept sneezing and hacking in the windowless chamber, causing,
I noticed with some amusement, some Mexican children in the
front row to recoil continually from his speech.

"I tell ya, I was one mean ole boy," he rambled. "But then

I found Jesus, and I completely changed. You'll change, too. You'll be just like me." Then he sneezed again.

I looked around the room. A few couples, a few teens, but lots of loners like me. Single men with bad skin and sad eyes. One very skinny young man with a wavy 1970s hairdo smiled at me. He doesn't fit here, I thought. A few minutes later, when Larry led us to the changing room, I noticed that same young man; with his shirt off, he looked emaciated, like a concentration camp victim. We each then put on cheap blue polyester ceremonial cloaks and descended a set of wet stairs toward the baptismal pool, which was strategically located just behind the church pulpit in the main chapel. Skinny Man was behind me and tapped my shoulder.

"Your first time?" he asked.

A very strange question, when you think about it. I wondered if there had ever in history been an instance of someone having a second go at defiling the baptismal ritual for journalistic purposes.

"Yah, first time," I said.

"Me too," he said. "How did you come to this decision?"

"It was either this or *The Sopranos*," I offered.

He nodded. "My mother's making me do this," he said, ignoring me. "I'm actually a Catholic."

"Oh," I said.

"She thinks it will help," he said.

"With what?"

He stared meaningfully at me.

"My . . . illness," he said finally. "I'm anemic."

"Oh," I said. So that's what they call it down here. "What kind of anemia? Iron-deficiency anemia?"

"I don't know," he said mysteriously. "It's some kind of anemia, though."

He smiled affectionately at me. I almost wished I were gay. I would have asked him out. It seemed like a perfect setup: two closeted Texans, finding true love in line for the fundamentalist baptism that won't quite be enough to save us from Hell.

"I see," I said. "Well, I hope this helps."

He shrugged. "Me too, I guess," he said.

We went down a few more steps. In front of us, in plain view of the whole congregation, little children bathed in spotlights were reciting their line—"My name is X, and I accept Jesus Christ as my personal savior"—before being plunged into the water by Larry, who unpleasantly was also half-clad in a blue cloak. It was a bad effect; he looked like a cross between a druid and Klansman. Anyway, the adults ahead of us in line were all practicing their lines in whispers; so was I, and so was Skinny Man. Once he got it straight, he tapped me on the shoulder again.

"Like I said, this was my mother's idea. I wonder if that water's cold."

I stepped down into the pool. "Not bad, actually."

I splashed the water a little. This whole scene was like something out of a bad porn movie. I wondered about my new friend's health and felt sad all of a sudden.

"Well, good luck," he said finally.

I nodded, stepped forward into the bright light, took one look back, and waved. Now in the pool, I looked out at the congregation. Several thousand good Christian faces stared back at me. I looked for Janine and Laurie but in the end focused for some reason on an old couple in one of the front rows who were staring impatiently at me with eyes like drills, their denture-filled mouths clamped tightly. They had been smiling when the kids were being baptized.

Feeling pressured, I looked down; on the lip of the pool I could see, written on what looked like a piece of tape, a script:

"MY NAME IS _____ AND I ACCEPT JESUS CHRIST AS MY PERSONAL SAVIOR."

I shrugged and leaned over to the microphone:

"Hello," I said. "My name is Matthew Collins, and I accept—"

Splash! Larry's fat virusy hand clasped my forehead and plunged me under the water. Chlorine shot up my nose. I stood up. I was born again. Larry nudged me off to the side. I dried myself, then trudged back to the locker room. Some big fat guy I'd never seen before was also in there getting his street clothes back on. He shook my hand. So did another guy, and another guy. We all changed in silence, and within five minutes I was back on the freeway.

That was that. I celebrated my spiritual rebirth with an order of the worst fish 'n' chips of all time at a Hooters off Route 281. A huge-titted brunette waitress approached me and started chatting me up. Hmm, I thought, maybe there really is a God. I stopped fighting with my fish husk for a minute and turned the charm on.

"So, listen," I said, grinning. "My name is—"

"Would you like to buy a Hooters calendar?" she asked, batting her eyelashes at me. "We have a special discount tonight."

I sighed. Whether you're after Heaven or pussy in this country, it's all the same freaking mechanized car wash. When I waved off the waitress, telling her I didn't need a calendar, she copped an attitude.

"No, honestly, I just want to finish my meal," I said. "You see, I just got baptized."

"Okay, whatever, mister," she snapped. I could hear her orange satin hot pants squeaking as she made her escape. Sawing through the rock-hard wreckage of my last piece of dark-browned fish batter, I thought, At least I'm saved now.

I WAS ZOOMING through the process. It was strange, the way it worked. I had gone to Phil Fortenberry's retreat and a few days out of the retreat I had been asked, like everyone else who went, to be a life coach at the next retreat. Then I bumble through the baptismal assembly line and before the water even has time to leak out of my ears I'm being pushed into evangelical instruction. In this organization, when you get called up to the Show, they stick you in the lineup right away. Volume, volume, volume! We had Sunday school classes on street evangelism, and in case you missed those, you had another go-around in your cell meeting.

When I showed up to mine that week—I was visiting a new cell group, one recommended by Janine, at yet another antiseptic one-story white-people house on the north side of town—I discovered a sloe-eyed balding man named Joe in his late forties or early fifties coaching a smallish group of what looked like Texan versions of yuppies to overcome their fears of evangelism. Joe was a telemarketer, or at least that's what he said. His expertise was the cold call, and he wanted all of us to stop pussyfooting and start throwing our irons in the spiritual fire. Gathered in a circle on the freshly vacuumed cream-colored wall-to-wall carpet of his lifeless den, he challenged us in his droopy, Miss Othmar voice:

"What," he said, "is the biggest obstacle to your evangelism? What are you afraid of and what are you concerned with and what is keeping you from . . ."*

"I feel like I don't know what to say," drawled a woman across the room. "I walk up to 'em and my mind just draws a blank."

"Okay," Joe said. "Draws a blank. Let me write that down."

"Not having the answers to questions that they ask," said a man to her right.

---

*I'd noticed that a lot of people in Texas didn't finish their sentences. Because of a Zelig-like habit of imitating people around me—picked up, probably, from having changed schools a dozen times as a kid—I'd actually started doing it myself. At the time of this prayer meeting I actually had the letters "FYS"—finish your sentences—written on my thumb as a reminder.

"Okay," Joe said. "Answers to questions."

"Rejection," piped in a third voice.

"Hostility?" I ventured.

"Hostility!" said Joe, writing dutifully on his notepad. "Okay."

A few more hands raised. A spiffily dressed black fellow, obviously a business professional, worried aloud about company policies against such conversations. Another man confessed that he could never quite find the right "segue" into the conversation. More and more people told their reasons why they couldn't spread the Word—until Joe finally broke it up:

"Okay," he said, "those are excellent, all of them, and of course they have to be excellent, because they are your personal concerns. But they are each one something that has Satan's grip on us because of—what's my favorite word about what Satan does?"

"He deceives!" the group called out.

"That's right, he deceives!" Joe said. "He deceives you that you're going to be attacked, he deceives us that the time's not right, he deceives you that maybe the boss is listening and there's a rule against it, he deceives you that there's some kind of fear or anxiety that comes over us."

I wrote down in my notebook

SATAN DECEIVES!

with "Satan" triple-underlined in junior-high-scribble style. Janine looked over at me. I held up the notebook and gave her a thumbs-up. She smiled nervously and looked back at Joe. It occurred to me that she couldn't read my writing at that distance. Maybe she thought I'd written something else, like I HAVE AN ERECTION!!! Rattled, I slammed down the notebook and looked back at the group leader.

Meanwhile, Joe had turned on his giant-screen television and popped in a DVD. Next thing I knew, I was looking at the preposterous face of former television sitcom star Kirk Cameron. I slumped in my chair. The church had been steadily force-feeding us lessons from a video evangelism series called The Way of the Master, starring the aforementioned Cameron and another like-minded Christian lunatic, a demented Sonny Bono clone with a Fuller-brush mustache and a British accent name Ray Comfort.

The series is a sort of Beavis and Butt-Head–style PG-rated love story in which the two earnest, constrictively dressed Christians go out into the world and regale happy pedestrians with threats of Hell until they lumber away from the cameras looking confused and miserable. It's a solid program, and what really makes it fly is the performance of Cameron, the former *Growing Pains* star who's joined Hal Linden, Stephen Baldwin, and Mel Gibson as onetime Hollywood luminaries who shorted out in the limelight, disappeared from view for a time, and re-surfaced years later wearing reenergized, meaner-than-Hitler evangelical personas. You just haven't seen Christian evange-lism until you've seen video of curly-headed overgrown child actor Cameron sliding up to some well-dressed, too-polite Los Angeles homosexual, grinning at him with that maddening, fosh-Muppet face of his, and saying, "By your own admission you're a lying, thieving, murdering adulterer who's doomed to go to Hell!"

The Way of the Master exposes American Christian fun-damentalism at its most idiotic and infuriating. The entire gazillion-part lesson series is geared toward teaching Christian charges a single trick. According to the Bible, we find out, ev-eryone is going to Hell. You see, we have these things called the Ten Commandments, and if you violate any of the Ten Com-mandments, God sends you downstairs for the big burn. These Ten Commandments prohibit, among other things, adultery and murder.

But I haven't committed adultery, you protest—but that's

where you'll be wrong, because it's written right there in Jimmy Carter's favorite passage, Matthew 5:28, "But I tell you that everyone who gazes at a woman to lust after her has committed adultery with her already in his heart."

Okay, fine, but I'm not a murderer, you say. Wrong again! It's right there in the first epistle of John, chapter 3, verse 15: "Everyone who hates his brother is a murderer." If you've ever hated, and everybody hates somebody, then you have murdered.

Therefore, everybody is a murderer and everybody is an adulterer and everybody is going to Hell, unless they get saved. It's perfect, a completely seamless formula.

Christians are immensely proud of this neat little trick. They love the way that, no matter how you twist and turn things, you're going to Hell. It's just the coolest thing. And they love watching videos of people like Cameron sneaking up on unsuspecting godless pedestrians in the doomed Sodomite capitals of American culture and asking them if they've ever lusted after anyone or hated somebody. Why yes, they answer, of course I have, not suspecting that friendly little Kirk Cameron is about to drop the mother of all surprises on their stupid unbelieving heads—well, then, if you've hated, you're a MURDERER and you're GOING TO HELL! Now how do you feel, unbeliever? Think you might change your mind now?

Amazingly, the trick works absolutely every time in the videos. Christians coo over this like junior high boys who swear by some karate move one of them learned from a tenth-grader who's got a green belt—you know, if a guy tries to punch you here, you can just grab his wrist like this and then flip him like that and then hit him with a back round kick before he lands. Cool! Awesome! They then spend the next three years waiting for a chance to use the move at recess until eventually puberty kicks in and they forget about it completely and start focusing on getting girls. Eighth-grade boys, in other words, grow out of this sort of thing, but Christians can stay impressed by this crap until they're gray and walking with canes.

Anyway, during the showing of the video I was seated closest of all to the TV, which faded for a moment and then faded back in with the image of a trickling, tree-lined stream. A twangy, cheery acoustic guitar soundtrack chimed in as the camera panned down to the mustachioed co-host Ray Comfort standing in a friendly pose by the rushing water.

"Alright!" he said. "I'm going to lead Kirk through these four stepping stones across the sca-a-a-ry waters of personal evangelism! That is, sharing his faith with a non-Christian. Kirk, what are you doing hiding behind that bush?"

Camera pans over to Cameron, who is crouching ludicrously behind a bush on the other side of the river.

"I'm a-scared!" he shouted. "I've never done this before, I'm nervous!"

The room erupted in laughter. On-screen, Comfort smiled.

"Folks," he went on, "most of us are scared when it comes to personal evangelism! If you're hiding behind a bush or in a cave of inferiority, let me tell you a secret. I had an inferiority complex before I was a Christian. I was called Beet-Root Face in school!"

Beet-Root Face? I was about to laugh, but Janine looked over at me and I quickly straightened back up.

"I would go red at the drop of a hat," Comfort said. "But when you're a Christian, you've been commissioned to take a gospel of everlasting life to a world that's in a shadow of death! I mean, the issue is so important, we can't afford to hide behind a bush! Kirk, save us! Come out from behind that bush! Remember, I can do all things in Christ, who strengthens me!"

"I can do all things in Christ, who strengthens me!" shouted Cameron.

"Come on, what are you scared of? What's your fear?"

"Well, I'm just kind of a shy person," Cameron repeats.

"So am I," Comfort reiterated. "But remember, I can do all things in Christ, who strengthens me!"

On and on it went. Eventually, as one might predict, Cameron manages to cross the "scary waters of personal evangelism." He achieves this by jumping on the "four stepping stones," represented by the acronym

W
D
J
D

which is easily enough remembered by the phrase "What did Jesus do?" But in fact WDJD stands for:

Would you consider yourself a good person?
Do you think you have kept the Ten Commandments?
Judgment. If God were to judge you by the Ten Commandments, do you think you would be innocent or guilty?
Destiny. Do you think you would go to Heaven or Hell?

It was an easy formula to remember, a simple concept and an even simpler pitch. When the show was over, we went around the room and discussed some possible methods for beginning witnessing conversations. There was much talk about the opportunities afforded by encounters with the likes of bank tellers and store cashiers. One woman even talked about calling a plumber and cornering him once he was under the sink. "I just don't want him to think that I . . . ," she began, and looked up at us; too late, we were thinking it. Anyway, the collective loneliness of the group was striking—almost no one had good ideas for how to meet people. It was even suggested that we use chance telemarketing calls as an opportunity to try to convert the telemarketers.

Later on in the meeting we broke down into pairs—boys with boys and girls with girls, of course, so there was no risk of hanky-panky—and practiced witnessing to each other. Joe for some reason chose me, the new guy, as his partner. I guess he wanted to get to know me. But after nearly an hour of Kirk Cameron on top of many months of relentless indoctrination, I was increasingly impatient with the entire scene. I was not about to allow anyone to flip me and hit me with a back round kick, at least not with this silly nonsense. So in the "training session" with Joe, I decided to take my mask off, just for a few minutes.

He got himself into character by rocking back and forth in his chair, then finally extended his hand.

"Well, hello, there," he said. "My name's Joe."

"Matt," I said.

"Matt, let me ask you something," he said. "Would you consider yourself a good person?"

"That's not for me to say," I said unhelpfully.

His smile waned. "What do you mean?"

"I mean that it's not my job to decide whether I'm a good or a bad person," I said. "It's my job to try to be good. Whether or not I succeed is a matter for someone else to determine. After all, if I could answer that question myself, the act of asking it would be meaningless."

He stared at me, then looked at his WDJD card. There was nothing on there about this answer. He looked back at me suspiciously.

"I'm just saying," I said, "that this is something a secular person might say."

"Oh," he said, frowning. "Well, okay then. Let me ask you, Matthew, have you ever told a lie?"

"Sure," I said.

"What would that make you?" he asked.

"A liar, I suppose."

"And have you ever lusted after someone?"

"Sure," I said. "I suppose you might even say that I've committed adultery. In my heart and even in fact."

He smiled. Now we were getting somewhere. "Are you aware that you've broken the Ten Commandments?"

"I am," I said.

"And if God were to judge you according to the Ten Commandments, do you think you'd be innocent or guilty?"

"That's an irrelevant question," I said, "because I don't believe in God."

He frowned. "But say you did—"

"I can't," I said, "because I don't."

"But it's written in the Bible—"

"Yes, I know, but, you see, I don't care. I don't believe in the Bible."

Joe glared at me. This wasn't helping.

"I can see you're going to be a hard-ass about this," he complained.

"A what?" I said, reverting to my Christian state, pretending to be mortified by the word "ass."

"A—I mean, you're not making this easy."

"I just wasn't sure what word you used," I said. "I didn't hear."

"Nothing," he said defensively. "I didn't say anything."

I shrugged. "It's just hard, dealing with nonbelievers," I said. "I never know what to say when people say they don't believe. If they're not afraid of burning in Hell or having their arms pulled out or whatever, what can you say? W, D, J, D—none of the letters work."

He thought about that. "You're right," he said. "I know."

"It's just—it's tough."

"Yeah, it is."

We sat there staring at each other for an uncomfortably long pause. Finally he clapped his hands.

"Well," he said, "I guess we should switch places."

"Good idea," I said.

"Let's pretend we're in Miami Beach," he said. "I'll be a tourist by the pool. You try to convert me."

"Okay. Miami's nice."

He reclined in his chair and whistled. "Wow," he said. "Just look at all those bikinis!"

He gestured toward the "bikinis," actually the other side of his den. I looked over. Three pairs of dumpy role-playing housewives. But Joe was really in the role.

"I sure would like to get some of that action!" he said. "How about you? Would you like summa that?"

I looked back at Joe with alarm. He was really imagining those bikinis. Momentarily I was offended for God's sake. We were in decent company, after all.

"Oh, I'm not interested in sex," I said sternly. "I'm a Christian."

Joe slumped, looking subdued again all of a sudden. "Right, right," he said. "Of course."

The meeting ended shortly thereafter. I stopped to see *We Are Marshall* on the way home, then studied my evangelical materials, preparing for my first day saving souls.

"**WHAT'S WRONG** with your arm?" Janine asked a few days later, as she and I and Laurie walked from the Rolling Oaks Mall parking lot toward the entrance of Dillard's department store. Each of us was carrying Bibles and stacks of little Bible tracts and evangelical icebreakers—little "Million Dollar Bills" with gospel messages on the back, New Testament answers to the "billion-dollar question" about where we all go after we die.

"It's nothing," I said, scratching furiously. "Just a rash or something."

"Mmm," she said.

The Rolling Oaks Mall is one of San Antonio's newest and most opulent, a huge spread on the northeast corner of the 1604 highway loop. It has an odd design, with a series of big teapot domes with spires dotting its roof.

"Wow, those really do look like boobs," I said, looking up.

"I told you," said Laurie. "They're just trying to get the male customers."

"It's amazing what this world has come to," I said, shaking my head.

We chose the mall as a target site for our first day out evangelizing more or less by process of elimination. The original plan was to hit a gun and tackle store off the McDermott Freeway, but when Laurie and I showed up there I was immediately spooked by the sight of security trucks cruising the parking lot. We ended up going inside, where I spent six bucks in a target-shooting gallery.

Later Laurie and I met up with Janine and her daughter at a Taco Bell and settled on "The Boobs" as the target location.

By the time we got to Dillard's we were all deeply nervous. Laurie and Janine decided that we should stop and pray before we went inside. So the three of us stood in a circle holding hands, with hanging heads, in between the two sets of heavy glass entryway doors in front of the giant department store. Mortified, I clasped both hands lightly and sent my mind racing for a quick prayer I might be able to say in order to fake my way through this scene. Laurie, meanwhile, had begun her recitation:

"Lord," she said, "we ask that you bless us with a spirit of strength and courage."

Waves of shoppers were entering and exiting the store, and each was staring at us. One little child pointed at me, and her mother quickly yanked the kid by the hand and dragged her out to the parking lot—spiriting her child safely away from us, as though we were emitting sulfur fumes.

Janine was up next and had begun her prayer. Janine's prayers were always strange, original, and poetic. "Lord," she said, fidgeting as a shopper nudged her aside, "I ask you to bless us with your rain. Rain on us, dear God!"

A young man burst through the door behind us. When the door flew open, the handle nailed me right on the coccyx bone. Worse, I was panicking at the thought of actually praying out loud in this doorway. I wasn't sure I could do it.

"Your turn, honey," Laurie said.

I bit my lip. "Can I pray later?" I said.

They frowned. "Why?" said Laurie.

"I just feel shy," I said, wincing.

This didn't go over well—the women eyed me strangely—but eventually we shrugged it off and loped through the store. I was walking funny after taking that blow and also momentarily captivated by a store ad for the "Cabernet Full-Figure Deep-Plunge Seamless Bra" that featured a distracted russet-haired beauty and a ridiculously long cleavage line. Again, perhaps I had been in the church too long, but the ad just seemed way over the top. Children shop in this store, I thought.

Christ, I'm losing my mind.

As we walked through the store, Laurie and Janine were talking about the "Million Dollar Bill" icebreakers we were about to use.

"Whose face is that on the bill?" Laurie said.

"I don't know," said Janine. "Matt, do you know?"

"It's Enrico Fermi," I said, still staring at the bra ad.

"Who?"

I looked at the bill again. Actually the husky bearded figure in the picture was Charles Haddon Spurgeon, a nineteenth-century icon of the fundamentalist movement, probably the

world's first megachurch preacher. He once preached to twenty-
three thousand people at the Crystal Palace in Victorian Lon-
don. They handed us this stuff in church without telling us any
of it—I'd had to look it up the night before.

"Enrico Fermi," I repeated. "He founded Grace Bible College."

"Oh, that's nice," said Janine.

"I'm nervous," said Laurie.

"Me too," I said.

"Me too," said Janine.

In a few minutes we were in the food court. Janine and
her little girl sat down at a table. At the moment of truth, Janine couldn't actually approach anyone and decided to assist in
the venture by offering prayer support. So she sat at a table in
front of the China Super Buffet and began whispering prayers
to herself.

Laurie, on the other hand, immediately started accosting
strangers—she was a natural. She hit a whole crowd full of
shoppers and had them eating out of her hand in about eight
seconds. Laurie had a lot of good qualities. She was fearless and
easy with people. Her tragedy was that while these were wonderful traits to have, they didn't help her self-esteem. She would
make friends but not be soothed by them, so then she would
have to make more. For a few minutes I stood behind her, just
mumbling under my breath, and then I fumbled the snap with
my first solo try, inspiring laughter from Laurie when I invited
a young man with a Limp Bizkit–style chin beard to come visit
Cornerstone.

"You're not supposed to invite them to the church," she
said.

"I'm not?"

"No," she said. "Just go by the program."

"WDJD," I said, smacking my head in exasperation.

"That's right, honey," she said. "You'll get it."

She went off again, this time hitting a crowd full of teens over by a sporting goods store. I would later learn that one of the teens in this crowd was wearing a hat with an anarchy symbol on it, which would lead Laurie to conclude days later that they had been Satanists. Anyway, I sighed, sucked it up, then marched down toward the other end of the food court. For a moment I paused and stared out at the river of plump shoppers with glazed eyes. I was about to be hit with a major surprise—the lamer my religious come-on was, the more people would respond to me.

I could scarcely even start my rap with half of these people before they started reading back to me the transcripts from their latest group therapy sessions. It was like none of these people had ever had a friend before. No creature on earth is more inclined to public verbal diarrhea than a modern American; whether it's the AA culture, or the post–Me Generation emphasis on "finding yourself," or all those neo–Woody Allens confessing to their therapists, or just too many damn people fantasizing about telling the audience of *Oprah* what influenced their latest album ("In the fourth track, I'm trying to share the sacred message of His Holiness the Dalai Lama . . ."), we live in a country where people believe implicitly in their right to bore the living shit out of absolutely everybody within haranguing distance with tales of their miserable, lonely, and inevitably self-deluding searches for personal fulfillment in the emotional desert that is our crass commercial culture.

It's like a sacrament in the American religion of the Self—the seminal post-Oscar Charlie Rose interview where you talk about Truffaut and your battle to overcome your glue addiction. You know the one I'm talking about—since in the national fantasy we're all celebrities, we all get to have our Cuba Gooding/Rod Tidwell moment tearfully confessing our love for Jerry Maguire to ESPN's Roy Firestone after we sign our inevitable $11 million deals (nirvana, in the American religion). That's why it's always dangerous to ask a stranger in America about himself, because the likelihood is that he's been practicing his "Ralph Knobshlutz Reveals All!" interview in his head for years.

When I asked one gothed-out girl in front of Java Jo'z whether she thought she was a good person or not, she immediately confessed to me that she'd been on Paxil and that it was "helping with her impulse control," which was great because before she started on the drug, she'd just say anything that came into her head, which affected her relationship with her mom, which on the other hand was actually getting better lately, etc., etc. A youngish housewife then told me she had trouble forgiving people because she had been abused ("I have triggers that make the bad thoughts come back"), and that although she was "in a good place right now" she'd like to see some literature because she liked to "work on herself." None of these people had a discernible filter. The few men I approached were even quicker to tell all.

"You're absolutely right," said one older man in a PING golfer's hat. "I've got to start getting back to church. I've been backsliding since my divorce."

"Well, this is your opportunity to get right with the L—"

"And then I started drinking, too," he said. "I never used to drink that much before. But at least I know I have a problem now, you know what I mean? But I'm beating it now, God willing, so long as I go to my meetings."

I stepped back a little. "Um," I said.

"I tried to blame everyone in my family for my drinking but me," he went on. "Everyone was responsible but me. I'd tell myself that it was my wife's fault for not giving me my space after work. Then I'd tell myself I was okay because I'd like give up vodka for beer for a few weeks . . ."

This guy was like a walking ONE DAY AT A TIME bumper sticker. I frowned. "Yeah, I hear you—"

"The thing is, I went through all the steps, I admitted that a higher power can help me, and I accepted God's power over me," he said. "Anyway, I may not come to your church, but I appreciate what you're doing, it's important. People need to know they can't do it alone."

My God's OK, your God's OK. As long as his name is Jesus. I sighed, spotted an oldish Hispanic woman, and walked over, deciding to make one last try.

"Excuse me, can I ask you something?" I said.

The woman looked up and said nothing. I looked down at the letters WDJD written on my hand and recited:

"Would you consider yourself a good person?"

The woman was probably in her late forties and looked like she had a few hard mothering years behind her. She was carrying an Image Trends-wear bag.

"I don't know," she said finally.

"Have you ever told a lie?" I asked.

"Yes," she said.

"Do you know that it's against the Ten Commandments to lie?"

She hung her head. "Yes," she said.

"Okay," I said. "Now, have you ever hated anyone?"

She stared at me with blank eyes, confused.

"Because you know," I said, "the Bible says that if you've hated, it's like committing murder in your heart."

She looked away for a moment, then looked back.

"I have done many bad things," she said.

"Well, God's going to forgive you for that," I said. "But first, you have to—"

"I did this thing with a car," she said.

I looked at her carefully.

"What kind of thing with a car?" I asked.

"I drive the car away," she said absently.

"Away from what?" I asked.

"I have to go," she said, and started to walk off.

"Wait!" I said. "Away from what? What did you drive the car away from?"

She glared back at me and hurried down the mall aisle.

A few minutes later I walked over to Janine's seat in the food court.

"I'm trying," I said, "but it's tough sledding out there."

"We'll do better someday," she said.

THERE WAS no next time. Other business took me out of Texas, and after a while I became increasingly sloppy, continually forgetting to water the Matthew Collins plant. I was in Washington one afternoon in the reception room for Massachusetts congressman Jim McGovern when Laurie called. I picked up; she wanted to have lunch. I told her I couldn't, I was at the gym. Later on I got sick and decided to go home to New York for a few days' rest. Laurie called repeatedly; I just lay there in bed, piles of Japanese and Thai food containers on my desk, letting her call go to voice mail. I missed one cell meeting, then the next. I was a lapsing Christian, but in what direction was I lapsing? To nowhere, to nothingness. As absurd as the church was, it was an improvement over my actual life because there was at least a pretense of meaning there. Back in New York, I was just eating and taking up space, a depraved postmodern creature on the job, carrying pebbles up the media anthill. As I convalesced in my Midtown apartment, I began, weirdly enough, to feel a strong urge to get back to Texas.

Finally I recovered and booked a trip back to San Antonio. When I arrived, I pulled out of the freezer a cone of henna tattoo mix that I'd bought from an Indian family some weeks before. Using a tourist's guide to Israel I'd bought in D.C., I traced a brown blotch on my left forearm in the shape of the

Holy Land. Later that day Laurie called and invited me to lunch—she sounded bad. We made a date for the next day.

I found the restaurant—coincidentally, yet another Chinese place, this one a sit-down joint—and walked inside. We talked for a while about Laurie's problems. She was having some issues at work; a client was trying to stiff her out of a real estate commission. The client was a fellow Christian, someone she'd met through the life coach orientation. "And she calls herself a Christian," she said. "Of course, in reality, they always turn out to be the worst ones."

She got sad after that, then, a few minutes later, returned to her story about her conflict at work. She went on about it; it really was a sad story. The poor woman was being shunned by people from the church, and much of it was her own fault, because she didn't know how to keep quiet, how to be political. It was typically ugly human-being stuff, the kind of thing that happens in all communities, Christian and non-Christian alike, but what was so difficult about it was Laurie's belief that the church was supposed to be a refuge from this sort of thing. That it turned out not always to be so was, I could see, very painful for her.

My heart sank as she looked at my arm. I'd told her over the phone that I'd seen a Jewish doctor in Houston and that he'd pointed out to me that my "rash" was exactly in the shape of Israel. My plan, originally, had been to show my "rash" to our cell group and then later announce that God had told me it was a sign, and that I should move to the Holy Land. Then Matthew Collins would disappear to Israel.

When I first came up with this plan in the middle of the night some weeks back, it seemed to make literary sense. Having this strange born-again imposter disappear back to the Holy Land by means of some absurd and weirdly banal maybe-miracle seemed like the correct play here, comedically. But that was in a vacuum, dealing not with real people but with uncomplicated Christian villains. But most of these people were just plain sad, and pulling this kind of stunt was turning out to be meaner than even I was willing to be. Listening to Laurie tell her terrible story, I was beginning to wish I'd kept my sleeve rolled down.

"Do you think it's a sign?" she asked.

"I don't know," I said.

"Maybe it means Jesus is coming," she said, a tear falling down her cheek.

"Maybe," I said.

"Because I'm ready," she said, sniffling. "Are you ready?"

Jesus, I thought. This is awful.

"I don't know," I said honestly.

"Isn't it wonderful?" she said, smiling. "With things in this world so bad, at least we Christians are ready for the next one."

She dabbed her eyes with a napkin. This was too much. I got up to go to the bathroom, splashed my face with water, took a deep breath, then came back. Stopping in front of our table, I smiled. In front of Laurie, on the check pad, were a pair of paper fortune-cookie fortunes, surrounded by a mess of yellow crumblets. Laurie had been unable to resist eating the forbidden cookies.

When I sat back down, she saw me glance at the pile.

"I didn't read the fortunes," she said quickly, wiping her mouth. "Honest. I just ate the cookies."

"That's alright with me," I said. "Seriously."

"It's alright?"

"Sure," I said. "I think so."

She didn't sound convinced. A few minutes later, we got up and left the restaurant. My time in Texas was up.

TWELVE

Conspiracy Interlude III,

or

The Derangement of the Peace Movement

AFTER MY INCIDENT in the diner with Nico Haupt and the other Truthers, I was, for quite some time, obsessed with the movement. I couldn't get it out of my head. I would stay up late at night surfing Truther sites and trying to wrap my head around some of the theories. I found myself trying to put myself in the shoes of someone like University of Minnesota professor emeritus Jim Fetzer, a onetime leader of the movement (and head of the Scholars for 9/11 Truth) who among other things was the guy who came up with the theory about conspirators dropping 757 parts onto the Pentagon lawn from a circling C-130. I wondered where exactly a philosophy professor from Duluth imagined people like Dick Cheney and George W. Bush would go to find soldiers willing to lean out of a massive cargo plane midflight and drop huge chunks of metal onto a crowded crime scene. Clearly he thought this was not much of a problem, logistically speaking.

Another writer, a noted JFK conspiracist named Jim Marrs, speculated that former New Jersey governor Thomas Kean was an obvious choice to head the massive coverup exercise known as the 9/11 Commission because he sat on the Council on Foreign Relations, a "secret society," as Marrs called it. He wrote this matter-of-factly, as if could be taken for granted that groups like these were little more than tightly knit bureaucratic communities of like-minded assassins. I then saw this assertion repeated religiously all over the Web—Kean naturally led the coverup, he was in the CFR, after all.

Gradually it began to dawn on me that very large numbers of people, perhaps millions,* had no problem accepting the idea that a milquetoast career pol like Tom Kean would just casually salute and say "Jawohl!" when asked to cover up the biggest mass murder in American history—just because he sits on the Council on Foreign Relations! This sort of thing was everywhere on the Internet: 9/11 Commission member Jamie Gorelick was a board member of the oil drilling firm Schlumberger—so naturally, she's in on it! Fellow commission member John Lehman had been Reagan's secretary of the navy, so naturally he was on call, willing to play his part in the plot. Even James Meigs, the magazine writer who wrote a lengthy article debunking the movement's science claims, was subsequently labeled part of the conspiracy because, among other things, he worked for the "Hearst-owned" *Popular Mechanics.* If you had a connection with an oil company, a Wall Street bank, a security agency, a Republican presidential administration, a commercial media outlet, or a conservative think tank, you were in on the plot.

This enthusiastic belief in the pure, almost mathematical

---

*A Scripps Howard poll in the fall of 2006 indicated that 36 percent of Americans believed that it was either "very likely" or "somewhat likely" that the U.S. government either consciously allowed the 9/11 attacks to happen or helped actively in the commission of the attacks. "Thirty-six percent adds up to a lot of people. This is not a fringe phenomenon. It is a mainstream political reality," commented *Time* magazine.

precision of the conspiracy, with its unshakable faith in the unthinking, automatic participation of these long lists of faceless
members of the cultural establishment, all coldly eager to get in
on the killing of thousands of innocent Americans—it freaked
me out. Among other things it seemed like an almost perfect
mirror image of the Christian extremists on the other side of the
political spectrum, who similarly believed in the same childlike,
unquestioning sort of way in the satanic inhumanity of liberals
and nonbelievers. Jim Fetzer believing the army to be full of
soldiers willing to rain fuselage parts on Washington was no
different from Matt Hagee believing the world scientific community to be teeming with men and women anxious to impose
government-mandated abortions on the planet as a means of
controlling the population. It was hard to imagine how either of
these people managed to keep calm as they walked the streets,
knowing they might at any time be sharing the sidewalk with
some veins-in-his-teeth member of the Godless Man-Eating
Conspiracy.

Or was it me? Was I losing my mind? To make absolutely
sure, I spent much of November 2006 calling structural engineers and architects and pestering them with questions about
9/11. Most of the ones I spoke to seemed ready to reach through
the phone and snap my neck in half for even bothering them
with the dreaded "controlled demolition" theory. "Let me ask
you a question," hissed Mir Ali, a professor at the University
of Illinois School of Architecture. "If you get sick and you need
an operation, where do you go? Do you go to a restaurant? A
bicycle store?"

"Um . . . ," I said.

"It's the same with this," he snapped. "How many of these
people are structural engineers? How many? You people, always
you are calling me!"

"But I'm not one of—"

From there he veered off into a long tangent about the fireproofing in buildings, and from there into a rant about fire in a building consuming oxygen and creating a vacuum. "The air outside the building wants to rush in, do you understand?"

"No," I said. "I have no idea what you're talking about."

"Well, then, how can you say you know what caused the building to collapse?"

"I didn't," I said. "I'm calling about someone else's theory about—"

But he was off on another tangent by then, ranting angrily into the phone. I got similar responses from more than a dozen other engineers and architects, all of whom said that no one in the field took the controlled demolition theory seriously. "Oh, man, not this again," said Matthys Levy, a Vermont-based engineer and author of *Why Buildings Fall Down*. "I'm not going to end up on the Internet again, am I?" An architect friend of mine helped out by asking me to look at my own problem logically. "The key thing you have to ask yourself is who the people in the movement are going to believe," he said. "If you tell them you talked to ten of the country's leading guys in the field, and they all told you the planes caused the collapses, will they believe you? If the answer is no, what are you going to do—talk to ten more?"

"That's a good point," I said.

"Just give it up, man," he said. "This is an American controversy. No one ever gives up or admits they're wrong. It keeps going until it's time for the next argument."

Sadly, he was right, because I couldn't give it up either. Instead of just ignoring the hate mail I was continuing to get, I started answering some, leading to several uncomfortably long exchanges with total strangers who seemed to have limitless amounts of time on their hands. I began to mark the passage of time by the tenor of the letters that came into my in-box every day. The Democrats' midterm electoral victory, for instance, had its own species of letter. "Hey 'dickwad,'" read one. "You still feeel [*sic*] that *Loose Change* has helped the republicans win votes? get a clue, fucking traitor-asshole." I remember NFL week 5 of the 2006 season very well—an uninspiring Patriots-Dolphins game—because I spent half the day fending off a particularly infuriating letter-writer named Tim Woodill. The Woodill exchange drove me up a wall; the discussion kept going in circle after circle. The exchange is worth recalling because it shows how ridiculously far off into metaphorical hell these discussions can get. At one point, for instance, I kept asking him just to tell me what he thought happened on 9/11, but he refused.

"As for demanding that 9/11 Truth advocates furnish an affirmative theory of the crime," he said, "that is a little like the police refusing to investigate the burglary of your house until you tell them who did it, how they got in and where they stashed the loot."

Huh? No it isn't, I said. It's like asking police to say, "We think the burglar entered through the front window, raided the bedroom first, took a glass of milk from the kitchen, left through the garage, and fled on a bicycle." In such a case, I said, "the evidence speaks—the front window ajar, the footprints leading up the stairs, the spilled milk on the floor, the milk droplets in the garage, the bicycle tracks in the woods."

He wasn't convinced. "Except in this case," he shot back, "the police have cleaned up all the evidence, wont [*sic*] show you any of the crime scene photos and used their presence in your house to rifle through your personal possessions so that you have no idea what the burglar took and what the police may have confiscated themselves. Finally it turns out that the burglary suspect was an ex-cop who used to work for the guys investigating your case."

I spent about twenty minutes staring at that passage, trying to make sense of it. Was Osama bin Laden the ex-cop? Which possessions was he talking about? I was beginning to feel like the metaphorical house we were talking about was actually this correspondence—was it the cops or the burglar who took out the trusses that held this metaphor together? I was still working it out when I saw the conclusion of his letter. "I guess I can understand why you don't want to debate me on this," he wrote. "We both know that in a straight debate I'd kick your ass.

"Regards, TJ Woodill."

So ended about six thousand words of angry correspondence. I sat there with that curt farewell staring me in the face, eyes blank, not knowing what to do. Now I was losing my shit. I tried to avoid the computer for a few days, but soon enough I was back at it, debating with none other than Jason Bermas, coproducer of the seminal Internet documentary *Loose Change.* This correspondence lasted even longer and drove me even crazier. *Loose Change,* made by a couple of twentysomething kids from Jersey and featuring a catchy electronic soundtrack to go with an admittedly first-rate use of conspiracy-theory rhetorical innuendo, is a slick piece of shoestring-budget filmmaking, the kind of thing that should win a prize, if there were a prize to give out for best use of two thousand dollars to scramble the brains of mental fourteen-year-olds. But the movie is also a classic example of post-9/11 Internet journalism, where the fact-checking process is limited to finding a link, any link, however old, to support your story. I couldn't be sure, but it seemed like these guys had made one of the decade's most influential films without making a single phone call to check a fact.

Before long I was calling people all over the world trying to see if any of the stuff in the film was true. For instance, *Loose Change* makes a point of "reporting" that many of the hijackers were reportedly seen alive after the attacks. If you looked closely, however, the sources they cited—in one case the *Los Angeles Times,* in another the BBC—they were all very old stories, dating to less than a week after the attacks. As I subsequently learned, all of these supposed sightings were simple misunderstandings, based upon similarities with Arab names and cases of mistaken identity, in which the authorities, for instance, mistook one Waleed al-Shehri for another. The same sources that *Loose Change* quoted had all long since corrected the misunderstandings. The Saudi embassy, which had been the source for the *LA Times* story cited in *Loose Change,* laughed about the whole thing. "For God's sake, they're all dead. We settled this question ages ago. We even have DNA tests to confirm it," said Nail as-Jubeier of the embassy in Washington. The guys at *Arab News* were flabbergasted by the call. "They're just as dead as they were four years ago," one of the editors said. There was simply no way any of this stuff had made it into the movie unless they hadn't checked their facts.

So I asked Bermas if he'd made even one phone call on that score. His response:

"Yes phone calls were made to organizations such as CNN, the BBC, and other media outlets," he wrote. "However many of us do not have the privilege of being employed by The Rolling Stone [*sic*], so when asked about the legitimacy of an article or the possibility of licensing footage we would either be completely ignored or someone would 'get back to us.'"

These guys thought the "9/11 Commission Report" was shoddy, yet the sum total of their journalistic research was "No one returned our calls"!

We went back and forth for a while; meanwhile, I was still being deluged with angry mail and I was beginning to develop a strange sort of permanent migraine headache from staring at sites like PrisonPlanet.com and 911Truth.org. I started talking at great length about 9/11 to friends and relatives who clearly weren't in the least bit interested in the topic, and the slightest provocation would get me dialing anyone and everyone in search of immediate answers to my 9/11 questions. Bermas, for instance, at one point sent me a letter berating me about the notorious (notorious in Truther circles, that is) "missing twenty-eight pages" that had been redacted from the original congressional report about 9/11, pages that Truthers believe contain "missing evidence" of the involvement of a foreign power in funding the terrorists. The Truthers, you see, believed that the "foreign power" was probably Pakistan, and that was significant because Mahmoud Ahmad, the chief of the Pakistani intelligence agency ISI, was actually in Washington, meeting with Senator Bob Graham and onetime CIA director Porter Goss, on the morning of 9/11.

The whole thing struck me as absurd; if there was something suspicious about Bob Graham meeting with Mahmoud Ahmad, then what smoking-gun evidence could anyone possibly hope to glean from a redacted congressional report that had been written by . . . Bob Graham! In a frenzy by this point, I called the now-retired Graham (whom I'd last run into in a highly uncomfortable meeting while working for the Bush campaign undercover in Florida) and asked if I could ask him a few 9/11 questions. He was very polite and seemed to think this was a normal press inquiry, but his tone quickly became nervous when I started rambling about the Truth Movement and *Loose Change* and Jim Fetzer and a bunch of other names he'd never heard of. "What's, uh, the 9/11 Truth Movement?" he asked. "And who did you say you worked for?"

"It's, uh . . . Well, listen, what foreign country were you talking about in that report, anyway?" I asked, ignoring his second question.

Graham said he was talking about Saudi Arabia, that the commission had found evidence that Saudi Arabia had supported at least two of the hijackers financially. I asked him: Did he think that this hinted at U.S./Bush administration complicity in the planning of the attacks?

"No," he said. "That's absurd."

Then what did he mean?

"I think the Bush administration was anxious to protect its

relationship with Saudi Arabia. I think they were covering up Saudi Arabian involvement," he said. "Dating back many years the U.S. had an agreement to provide security to Saudi Arabia in exchange for a free flow of petroleum. They just weren't ready to jeopardize that relationship. That's what that was about."

"Right," I said. "Well . . . thanks."

"No problem," he said. "Who did you say you worked for again?"

"Um, well, usually I work for *Rolling Stone*, but not in this case," I said. "I was just sort of curious."

"I see," he said nervously.

"You know, Senator, we met once," I said. "In Orlando. I carried your luggage."

"I see," he said again.

"But the thing was, we never got to finish talking, because I was undercover and I had to revert back to my, uh, secret identity," I said.

"Mm-hmm, ri-i-i-ght," said the retired senator.

Graham couldn't get off the phone fast enough after that. When he finally hung up, I sat in my room—I was in Texas by then, ensconced in my new life as a member of the Cornerstone Church—and suddenly it occurred to me that I had adopted all the characteristics of a 9/11 Truther. I was living almost full-time on the Internet, my personality had twisted in an extremely unpleasant missionary direction, and I was now more intimately familiar with names like Mahmoud Ahmad and Hani Hanjour than I was with the affairs of my own family. I used to think a lot about things like football in my spare time—now I was running over the historical details of 9/11 even as I went to sleep.

I started going to 9/11 Truther meetings under a pseudonym. My real self was under there somewhere, but it was becoming alarmingly easy for me to deal in these environments. Technically I was still what they would call a debunker or a "left gatekeeper," a defender of the "official story," but in a weird way I found myself in some of these gatherings getting legitimately impatient with the slow tactics of the movement. After all, I thought, if you really think that the government murdered three thousand Americans, shouldn't you be doing more than holding sit-ins and organizing discussion groups? And so, at some of these meetings, I started to hear "Lee Smith"—my alter ego—calling for immediate action.

"We've got to call Henry Waxman!" I shouted at a meeting of the Austin Citizens for 9/11 Truth. "Now that the Democrats have Congress, he's in charge of the Government Reform Committee. He's got subpoena power. He can get the documents we need, the information they've been hiding from us!"

What the fuck am I talking about, I wondered. It also suddenly occurred to me that my "disguise" was incredibly stupid. I had shaved my head bald and put on a pair of thin pane glasses. I looked like Emma Thomspon in *Wit*, only with stubble.

"Anyway," I said, eyes darting left and right, "I just think now is the time to act. We've got to get people together and hit Congress, let 'em know we're here."

The moderator, a soft, curly-headed teacherish type named Geoff—the kind of guy who would have been a perfect physical fit as an activities counselor at a substance abuse retreat, passing out volleyballs to upper-class drunks—stood at the lectern and scanned the crowd. "Okay, well, that's certainly a good idea," he said, mock-clapping. "We do have to organize. Anyone else have a comment or a question? Yes? You in the back?"

There were about twenty-five people in the small church where we were meeting, mostly middle- to upper-class whites but of varying ages. Most of the people had come alone, although there were a few pairs. Attire was solidly post-hippie/film school, lots of ruffled hair, black T-shirts, olive tones, goatees—a crowd you'd expect to see at a Werner Herzog film festival.

A microphone was passed to the man in the back. He looked

older, I guessed mid-forties, largish, dressed in work clothes. He grabbed the mic and stood up.

"Thanks," he said. "Yeah, I just wanted to say that I think it's important for everybody to remember that what's going on right now is that they're provoking a war between the mono-theists. They're setting the Christians against the Moslems, so that they'll wipe each other out. Then the Luciferians'll move in."

"Exactly," shouted a woman on my side of the church. "It's the Antichrist. It's all in the Bible."

"Hmm," said Geoff. "I don't know. That's an interesting comment, though. I appreciate that. Anyone else?"

A redheaded man in his early forties in the back stood up. "I have one thing to add," he said. "Listen, they've got the courts. They've got the media. We still have the Internet, but they're looking for ways to take that away, too. I mean, they'll take that away, eventually. What I'm saying is that we have to find a way to communicate after they take that away. We've got to be prepared!"

Light murmurs, applause.

"Okay, thanks," said Geoff. "Preparation is good, I agree. Thank you."

It went on like this for a while, then the Q&A broke up so that the group could watch a Truther film called *Everybody's Gotta Learn Sometime*. The film was a hodgepodge of boiler-plate 9/11 Truth assertions, i.e., that the 9/11 Commission in-vestigation was a massive coverup, that the 9/11 hijackers had ties to the FBI and the Republican Party, that the Twin Towers were brought down by controlled demolitions and not by crash-ing airplanes, etc. It also had some new stuff in there, including a deft little tie-in to Jack Abramoff—according to the film, hi-jacker Mohamed Atta was seen on Abramoff's floating casino in south Florida prior to the 9/11 attacks. There were also long clips culled from various dystopian films that were often shown as "background material" at Truther gatherings, the Truthers generally believing themselves to be living in a modern version of an Orwell/Huxley/Zamyatin totalitarian paradigm. *Brazil, Dr. Strangelove, Starship Troopers,* and especially *The Matrix* (Truthers often talk about the moment of conversion, when you see the truth about the towers, as being like "taking the red pill") are often unironically recommended as "research material" in Truther gatherings.

The weird moment of *Everybody's Gotta Learn Sometime* came when a lengthy segment of the movie *Network* came on the screen. This was the scene in which the secular ex-anchorman prophet Howard Beale, by now given his own show by the evil networks, implores his audience to abandon TV and get back to reality. "We deal in illusions, man, none of it is true!" he shouts. "But . . . you're beginning to believe the illusions we're spinning here!"

In the scene, Beale is shouting against a background of phony stained glass in the fake studio "temple" that the networks had designed as a set for his *Mad Prophet of the Airwaves* show.

The stained glass in the movie was a kind of visual joke—a symptom of the TV falseness that had already crept into Beale's act, a symbol of how TV conquers the genuine dissident by assimilating him. Even as Howard Beale denounced television, he was, simply by virtue of being a staged act on television, part of the problem. "Turn off your television sets . . . !" Beale shouts. "Turn them off right in the middle of the sentence I'm speaking right now! Turn them off!" Then Beale collapses, apparently dead, and the studio audience cheers as the show's directors urge them on.

No one, of course, has turned his TV set off. This was supposed to be a very darkly ironic moment in the movie, but here it was, twenty years later, repackaged in a homemade Truther movie and shown in an actual church in southern Texas—the cinema stained glass appearing right in front of an actual dais—as unvarnished, earnest reality.

The irony of the moment was overwhelming. Seeing these people consume this commercial entertainment as a canonical revolutionary tract to me underscored everything the Truther Movement was about. The 9/11 Truth Movement, no matter what its leaders claim, isn't a grassroots phenomenon. It didn't grow out of a local dispute at a factory or in the fields of an avocado plantation. It wasn't a reaction to an injustice suffered by a specific person in some specific place. Instead it was something that a group of people constructed by assembling bits and pieces plucked surgically from the mass-media landscape—TV news reports, newspaper articles, Internet sites. The conspiracy is not something anyone in the movement even claims to have seen with his own eyes. It is something deduced from the very sources the movement is telling its followers to reject.

This has always been one of the key features of the 9/11 Truth Movement. When the left finally found something to revolt over, it turned out to be something entirely fictional, something that not a single person had seen with his own eyes, or felt directly in his bank account, in his workplace, in his home. No one here was revolting over the corrupt medical insurance system, the disappearance of the manufacturing economy, the exploding prison population, the predatory credit industry, the takeover of electoral politics by financial interests. None of the people in this room were bound together by a common problem. What they had in common was a similar response to a national media phenomenon. At some level, this wasn't even a movement—it was a demographic.

Anyway, the meeting continued. Although the point of the Q&A session was supposed to be a discussion of the movie, the movie had seemingly been forgotten minutes after it ended, and the activity we were now engaging in involved circling the room and giving each individual a chance to vent his or her own personal insane theory of reality. On the side of the hall opposite me was a young man with a shaved head. Angry Bald Guy's theory was that the Bush family had been involved in these kinds of world domination plots for centuries. He seemed to be frustrated that no one was focusing on this.

"This Bush crime family, they're hardcore gangsters!" he said.

"Mmm, yes," said Geoff, nodding.

I could see that this est-style nodding of Geoff's was only making Angry Bald Guy angrier. His eyes screamed, Stop nodding, you dick! "I just think," he said, "I just think we have to do something!"

"Well," said Geoff, "that's what we're doing. We're educating people."

"No, I mean besides that!" snapped Angry Bald Guy.

Geoff nodded. "Well, I hear you," he said. "But at this stage, I think that we're best served by just getting the message out. Making sure people see these DVDs. I think that we're really accomplishing something here."

I sighed. If there's one thing you can always count on, it's that a lefty political activist will find a way to convince himself that he's changing the world by watching a movie.

Some weeks later I went with a friend to a meeting of the Houston chapter of the same Meetup group, at a Churchill-themed bar called the Black Lab. My friend "Frank" was actually a reclusive, salt-and-pepper-haired musician who by a factor of at least twenty was a more dedicated neurotic/misanthrope than even I was. I'd convinced him to help me try to make a 9/11-themed dramatic movie, recruiting the local Truthers to take part. The idea there would ostensibly have been to harvest on film the comedy of Truthers trying to think up a 9/11-themed movie plot, which with any luck would have been pretentious and fantastical; there was always the danger that their creative ideas would have turned out to be brilliant and witty, but I thought it was worth the risk.

"It'll be like *Spinal Tap,* except no one will be acting," I said. He shrugged. Frank had suffered greatly at the hand of hare-brained, poorly thought-out projects of mine in the past—I still owe him money for work he and his girlfriend did on my now-defunct Buffalo newspaper—but he was bored and decided to give it a shot. Our movie project was stillborn, though; just as in Austin, none of the Houston Truthers wanted to do much more than sit around and talk about their plight.

At the Meetup, led by a laboriously, ponderously slow talker named Mark, the group was on its third monthly meeting and was still trying to decide how often to meet and where. A pale white guy in his late twenties or early thirties who I suspected would end up as the much-hated manager of a chain copy shop someday, Mark had strict rules about who could talk and when, and participants had to follow the rules to a tee or he would cut them off. It was decided at one point that we should list the group's goals; Mark had us go around in a circle and offer our ideas for a statement of the group's purpose.

"Let me just say at the outset," he said, "that those of us who have the views that we do . . . Well, it can be very lonely, difficult socially, that is, to be a dissident in this day and age. So one of the goals of this group, I would say, is that it will provide all of us with a safe place where we can feel at home, comfortable being ourselves."

He looked around the room. I couldn't tell if everyone was embarrassed or whether they agreed with him.

"So I'm just going to write that here on the paper—safe place," he continued.

Frank glared nervously at me. He had a bit of a panic-attack problem and I could tell this scene was moving him in that direction.

Meanwhile Mark motioned for the next person in line, a

quietish student from the University of Houston, to offer his idea.

"Well, I think we have to create an entirely new system of media, completely reforming the existing system," he said. "Because the current system isn't telling us the truth, that's for sure."

"Damn right," said someone else at the table.

"Okay, good," said Mark. He spoke as he wrote: "Create new system of media."

Frank glared accusingly at me. I smiled.

"Sure, let's create a new system of media," I said, out loud. "Might as well start small, right?"

Everyone looked up at me; nobody laughed.

The group ended up split down the middle on the issue of whether or not to schedule an informal "hangout night." We did agree loosely to try to schedule a movie showing, though settling on an actual date proved too difficult. But the real thrust of the meeting seemed to be a battle for control of the group. Right from the start, Frank and I could see that Mark had a rival in John, an older fellow with a balding head and glasses. John seemed more knowledgeable about 9/11 issues than Mark and also ideologically purer—Mark, heretically, had even expressed doubts about the controlled demolition thesis at the beginning of the Meetup. And the two seemed to disagree about everything, how often to meet, what activities to plan, everything. I personally could feel the energy in the room drifting toward John, and maybe he could feel it, too, because at the end of the meeting he boldly came out with his strategy for the group.

"I think we should post on the message board more," he said, lightly tapping the table. "Have more discussions!"

Murmuring all around. The group liked that idea. Mark swallowed hard and wrote the idea down on his sheet of paper. Above him, a portrait of Churchill frowned blankly off into space.

Some days later we looked on the Meetup Web site. John

had, indeed, been posting more, and so had some other members, including a mysterious new person named "Mauricio," who was posting quite a lot in semigrammatical English. Mauricio's posts had titles like "Passport Cards to Go Hi-Tech In the United States" and "Official 9/11 Story on Life Support: The Truth is Taking Over." Inside the actual posts, Mauricio would simply retype in some piece of text from another site and then add a link to the rest of the story. None of his posts had any replies. This was certainly "more posting," and it obviously irked the territorial Mark, who quickly rattled off a lengthy text about posting etiquette.

The letter included six general guidelines about posting, guidelines that included "Take some time putting your message together" and "Try to watch the grammar and spelling" and even "Communication is a 2-way street. If you want folks to read and respond to your messages, you should read and respond to other people's messages too." Frank found the post and read the guidelines to me out loud—we almost fell over laughing at number three:

"'Three. If you make more than 2 or 3 posts in a day, you are posting way above average,'" Frank read. He went on: "'You'd better have something extraordinarily important or people will just start ignoring you.'"

"Way above average?" I laughed. "There are only like six people on the board as it is!"

"No, it gets better," Frank said. "Listen to this: 'I think it will benefit YOU as a message poster if you more-or-less follow these suggestions, because people will take you more seriously and are more likely to read what you post.'" He laughed. "And here's how he ends it: 'Again, just suggestions. Other folks might have different visions of how this message board should function. Take care. Have fun. Keep up the good work. Mark.' Have fun? Fun? What the fuck is wrong with these people? Do other people know about this?"

"Dude, this is like 36 percent of America, according to recent polls," I said.

"Bullshit." He frowned nervously. "That can't be true. You're lying again."

I said I wasn't, but he refused to listen. He kept staring at the screen, muttering to himself. "Fun," he said. "Have fun. Jesus."

Back to the site: almost immediately, Mark's rival, John, posted a soothing letter to Mauricio, but it was too late. That was the end of Mauricio on that board. So much for a "safe place."

Soon after, Mark dropped out of the group and John took over. In a letter to me, Mark explained that he had become disillusioned with the movement. "My initial beliefs about conspiracy came from a general understanding of how our government operates and what kind of agenda it follows," he wrote. "And I believe strongly that these are the questions the 9/11 Truth Movement should focus on. We can argue for the rest of our lives about all the different theories about the towers' collapse, and the 'shocking proof' in the form of highly speculative interpretations of photos and videos, and while we struggle with that argument, the noose draws steadily tighter around the neck of American democracy."

So there! Mark didn't even sign his name—it was like he wasn't even talking to me, but to God, to the Fates. And with that, dramatically, this would-be leader was out of the movement. But there were more to take his place; the Meetup kept growing and growing. Months later, the numbers had doubled—but the group was still stuck trying to set up a movie night.

IN THE SPRING a friend of mine named Joel Barkin called and invited me to lunch. Joel is the executive director of the Progressive States Network, a group dedicated to passing progressive laws in America's state legislatures. He's a young guy, very ideal-istic, who grew disillusioned with certain aspects of the system while working as a congressional aide years ago. Whenever the Democrats sell out their electorate somehow, I can count on getting a call from him. And now he was calling me on the heels of the Democrats' latest failed attempt to stop the war.

He was fuming. He said that since the Democrats won the Congress in the midterm election, an entire peace-movement bureaucracy had magically appeared in Washington, a bureau-cracy staffed not by grassroots peace activists but, by and large, by the same hacks who were manning the Democratic ship when the Democrats supported the war.

"It's the same groups meeting with Pelosi and Reid all the time," he said. "It's groups like Americans United for Change, Americans Against Escalation in Iraq, MoveOn, and so on. But here, take a look at this."

He handed me a piece of paper.

"These are quotes by a guy named Brad Woodhouse," he said. "Brad Woodhouse is the head of Americans United for Change. He's one of the leaders of the so-called peace move-ment in America right now. But check out what he was saying a few years ago, when he worked for [North Carolina Senate candidate] Erskine Bowles."

There were two Woodhouse quotes on the page:

"No one has been stronger in this race [than Bowles] in supporting President Bush in the war on terror and his efforts to effect a regime change in Iraq," said Bowles's spokesman, Brad Woodhouse.
—*Charlotte Observer*, 9/20/02

"The fact of the matter is, as Defense Secretary Donald Rumsfeld said, we still have a long, hard slog to finish

this job in Iraq," said Brad Woodhouse, spokesman for
the Democratic Senatorial Campaign Committee.

—*Detroit Free Press*, 12/15/03

"A few weeks ago, I was in a meeting with Harry Reid's
people and the peace activism community," Joel said. "And they
were discussing how they were going to pitch the news to the
public that the Democrats had decided to pass the war supplemental. And I'm thinking to myself, Why is the activist community working with the Democrats to figure out how to deal
with the people? It should be the other way around."

What Joel was talking about made perfect sense. All along,
the thrust of the Democrats' strategy with regard to the war
had been to find a way to take political advantage of antiwar
sentiment without hurting themselves electorally. Momentum
seemed to have gathered around a strategy of taking a superficial stand against the war while also allowing it to continue long
enough to be useful to the Democrats in the '08 presidential
race. Which meant no cutting off the war money, no risking
being accused of taking guns out of the troops' hands during
an election season, even if it meant unnecessarily prolonging a
deadly conflict. For the activist community to sign off on such
a baldly political strategy was monstrous; it was the rankest sort
of Washingtonian incest.

And yet, sure enough, after the Democrats buckled that
spring and voted to give Bush his money for the war, the
spokespeople for the peace activism community could be seen
everywhere giving excuses for the Democrats. Woodhouse
himself was outspoken in that regard. "We're disappointed that
the war drags on with no end in sight," he told Reuters, "but
realize Democratic leaders can only accomplish what they have
the votes for."

Joel went on to tell me a story about having seen a notice
that Barack Obama had been invited to speak at a conference

for the American Legislative Exchange Council (ALEC), a notorious conservative action group dedicated to passing conservative laws in the state legislatures. Joel and his group quickly issued a press release calling for Obama to denounce ALEC, one of the most regressive organizations in the country. Instead, they got a slew of e-mails from the Obama campaign.

"They were all asking me, 'Hey, why didn't you just call us first, before you went to the press? We could have cleared this up.' And my answer was, one, I don't work for you. That's not how this works. Two, if you don't like ALEC, take advantage of the situation. Use this as an opportunity to tell people about ALEC, denounce them. But the point is, we see this all the time. Everybody acts like they're on the same team. Nobody is really advocating. And worse, there's this pervasive sense that if you challenge power, you'll lose your ability to get hired by the right people down the road. Like me, I'll never get hired by Obama now, but so what? But that's why their people were so surprised that we blindsided them. They're not used to it. That's the attitude within the Democratic Party. There's no ideology at all. It's all about power—nothing more."

The Democrats' error was in believing that people wouldn't notice this basic truth about their priorities. They were wrong on that score. In fact, a Quinnipiac poll taken around that time found the approval rating of Congress had fallen to 23 percent. Other polls saw the number plummet to the teens. The rating of the Democratic Congress was even lower than Bush's, and it was not hard to see why. Bush was wrong and insane, but he stood for something. It was a fucked-up something, but it was something. The Democrats stood for nothing; they viewed their own constituents as problems to be handled, and even casual voters were beginning to see this.

Around that same time, there was a surprising piece of news from noted peace activism icon Cindy Sheehan, the so-called war mom who'd gained notoriety by holding a sit-in against the war at Bush's ranch in Crawford, Texas. Sheehan announced that she was leaving the organized peace movement, among other things because she was frustrated by the attacks she'd received from the left once she began criticizing the Democratic Party for its ineffectual opposition to the war.

"Blind party loyalty is dangerous whatever side it occurs on," she said. She went on:

> People of the world look on us Americans as jokes because we allow our political leaders so much murderous latitude, and if we don't find alternatives to this corrupt "two" party system our representative republic will die and be replaced with what we are rapidly descending into with nary a check or balance: a fascist corporate wasteland.

And right at the time Sheehan left the orbit of the Democratic Party, she made another announcement: she was supporting the 9/11 Truth Movement. "It does look to me like a controlled demolition," she said. "I do see some very high-profile people saying it was an inside job."

After Sheehan made her announcement, you started to see a change in the 9/11 Truther rhetoric. Suddenly they were selling themselves as the true peace movement. Now we were being told that understanding the truth about 9/11 was the key to righting all the wrongs of American politics, including the war. An end-the-war conference, "in honor of" Cindy Sheehan, was scheduled for the Fourth of July at Independence Hall in Philly.

I went to the conference feeling glum. The whole situation made me uncomfortable. I was raised in the cradle of American liberalism, in the touchy-feely schools of Massachusetts and New York, and for better or worse my whole view of humanity has been colored by twenty years of the politics of the liberal arts world, pseudo-Marxian indoctrination with a touch of noblesse oblige. Hard as I try to get these concepts out of my head, terms like "the people" and "the ruling class" are always in my thinking, and in the case of 9/11 Truth and the peace movement, it was now very hard for me to avoid the simplistic notion of a voiceless subject population abandoned by its political parent class, i.e., "the people" cut loose by the Democratic Party.

All along I couldn't help but see the Truther movement as a symptom of a society whose political institutions had simply stopped addressing the needs of its citizens. When people can't trust the media, and don't have real political choices, and are denied access to the decision-making process, and can't even be sure that their votes are being counted—when even their activist advocates are lunching with the Man in fancy restaurants in Georgetown—they will eventually act out on their own. And when they do, who can blame them if the cause they choose to pursue is a little bit crazy?

That was what I was thinking as I headed down to Philly for the peace conference. Against the backdrop of the continued carnage in Iraq and the Democrats' cynical maneuverings vis-à-vis the war, I felt embarrassed to be attending in the guise of a defender of the "official story." I decided to lay low, stay out of their way—I kept reminding myself that these people were victims of a broken culture, that it wasn't their fault, there was nothing to be done about it. It was sad, but it wasn't evil.

Then the conference began.

It was held in a meeting room on the second floor of the Independence Visitor Center downtown. It was a biggish hall, and within a short time after the conference began it was packed to the gills with activists, bloggers, and panelists. The sheer numbers alone testified to what everyone already knew, which is that the movement was rapidly growing and becoming more mainstream. Every day there were new celebrity converts. Rosie O'Donnell. Charlie Sheen (who was said to be in negotiations with Mark Cuban to distribute *Loose Change*). Even blink-182 rock star Tom DeLonge had signed on lately. Minnesota's Keith Ellison, America's only Muslim congressman, was comparing 9/11 to the Reichstag fire, and Bush to Hitler. There was even a video showing Michael Moore wondering aloud about the "strange explosions" in the towers on the morning of 9/11 circulating of late on YouTube. Moore in that video had also asked why the government hadn't released more videos of the attack on the Pentagon, endearing himself to the movement.* And the most recent news was that Cindy Sheehan was even considering running against Nancy Pelosi in Pelosi's district. Sheehan and Michael Moore were a powerful duo; 9/11 Truth was on the verge of becoming synonymous with mainstream liberalism.

The conference ended up being a succession of speakers culled from the upper ranks of the movement—speakers who included Dr. Bob Bowman, a former Florida congressional candidate, impeachment expert Dave Lindorff, the one-man conspiracy clearinghouse Webster Tarpley, journalist Barbara Honegger, and one of the loudest people I've ever seen, a heavyset, bespectacled "new media" wunderkind named Samuel Ettaro. One by one they got up there, and though some were more subdued than others, the whole scene quickly devolved into something far different from a conference on how best to end the war. It instead resembled a blogospheric version of the Westminster Kennel Club Show, in which each dog took the floor, ran in a circle, and showed off his credentials as a member of a triumphant new class of True Patriots.

The tone of the conference was strange. There was anger

---

*I took Moore's participation to be evidence not so much that the filmmaker bought the Truther theory, but that he had recognized the strength of its demographic. Five years ago a Michael Moore might have been able to afford being labeled a left gatekeeper, but not now. In any case, Moore has always surfed financially on the momentum of the movement; after all, while it may not have blamed the attacks on Bush explicitly, *Fahrenheit 9/11* sure didn't spend a lot of time blaming bin Laden for the disaster.

there, but more real than the anger was a kind of joyful celebration of their collective status as subjects of the evil corporate-Bushite-royalist-Illuminati-Amerikan-military-industrial paradigm. Everything about America—fat, lazy, embarrassingly opulent America, the country of too much stuff, the country where life isn't quite real enough for most of the people who live in it, and certainly not for these people—that America was depicted as a cruel, repressive Reich, an unceasing misery of crushed liberties for its aggrieved citizens, morally trailing far behind even such paradises as Iran. As such, every mention of any representative of the "system" drew riotous whoops and catcalls, like for instance when Ettaro held up a copy of his home-published magazine, *Republic,* a "resource for the modern patriot."

"So take that *Time* magazine and that scumbag Rupert Murdoch and throw them in the garbage!" he shouted.

Cheers all around. Ettaro went on:

"We have the distribution that we need to beat the mainstream media," he shouted. "And nothing short of someone taking me out is going to stop that from happening!"

Jesus Christ, I thought. Who would bother to take this guy out?

Later in the day Bowman took the stage for the second time—some of the "stars" of the event got tedious second and even third go-arounds at the lectern—and offered his take on what his inauguration speech would be like if he were elected president. He assumed an air of almost inexpressible solemnity as he promised to deliver an America in which "policemen, nurses, and poets can afford a decent house . . . an America free of terrorism because it is no longer feared and hated."

I thought making sure poets could afford houses was a strange cause to be fighting for, but whatever. Bowman put his hand over his breast. "Like Brother Malcolm," he said, "I have been to the mountaintop."

Bowman was white and looked like an insurance salesman, but it is a distinguishing feature of the 9/11 Truth crowd that everyone gets to act like a repressed minority of sorts, so the Brother Malcolm thing passed without comment. Later, he indulged in a lot of syrupy imagery:

"So keep the dream alive," he said. "Drop your own pebbles in the pond, and make your own waves . . ."

The day was filled with metaphorical pebbles and waves and trees and towers and bonds that tie and dogs that bark and other such flowery images. One speaker commented that "for every thousand people hacking at the branches, there's one hacking at the root," before pausing to try to figure out which one he was supposed to be. A second said that "we've started to put another crack in the Liberty Bell, because it needs ringing." That one had me puzzled for almost ten minutes. And still another noted that "we don't wanna fight the machine, we wanna go around front and see who's driving the machine."

"And then fight him," called out someone from the crowd.

"Right," he said. "Right, right."

Later on in the day the meeting spilled out onto the streets, where groups of protesters held up signs and chanted "9/11 was an inside job! 9/11 was an inside job!" at passersby on their way to Philly's Independence Day parade. Then more chanters appeared on the balcony of the visitor center, which prompted security officers to show up and ask them to stop. Some time later, a woman ascended to the lectern and asked the people on the balcony to come inside, noting that they had promised the landlord of the property that they wouldn't be hanging signs outside the building.

"Screw them!" someone in the crowd shouted. "They can't keep us silent forever! We have our rights!"

"Well, actually, these aren't the authorities," the woman said. "They just own the building."

"Well, still!" came the shout back.

As the day went on I sank deeper and deeper into my chair. Suddenly I understood. The People aren't always victims in the historical narrative. Sometimes the People are preening, chest-puffing, ignorant assholes, too. And maybe the polls are right, and these people aren't the minority—maybe, I thought as I looked around the packed room, I'm the minority. Maybe this is just how Americans like to roll. You can cut them out of the political deal, lie to them, exile them to some barren cultural landscape of shopping and TV and perpetual powerlessness, sell them a cheap dog-and-pony show for an election, and their way of fighting back will be to parade around like strippers in some amateur lunatic forum, dressing up in the garbs of Martin Luther King, Jr., and Thomas Jefferson and César Chávez as they bang their silly heads against the wall, screaming about the Illuminati and holographic airplanes and the free-floating currency exchange

Or they'll pray for Israel and the speedy arrival of the battle of Armageddon, when those lunatics on the opposite side will be cast into the fires of Hell.

THIRTEEN

THE END

★ ★ ★ ★ ★ ★ ★ ★ ★ ★ ★ ★ ★

SATURDAY, APRIL 28, Radio City Music Hall, New York City. I'm at the NFL draft, slouching in a chair in the press section, trying to sleep off a headache. Unfortunately the media affairs people have dicked me around and left me without an assigned space, so I have no desk and no place to put my computer. Which is only fair, I guess, since I'm not really covering this thing—I just decided to come out of sheer boredom. But the NFL press office doesn't know that, so I'm feeling kind of shafted.

I may not have a desk, but at least I have a good seat near the front. A nice comfortable place to sleep. But as I close my eyes, I feel a finger tap me on the shoulder.

"Excuse me," a voice says. "Can we get through?"

I look up. A pale, thin-shouldered bald man with a tawny mustache, a dead ringer for eighties pseudo-icon Gerald McRaney of the old *Simon and Simon* series, is trying to step past me and sneak through my row of seats with his preteen son. I frown. Fans and their goddamn kids, violating the sanctity of the press section—this country really is going to hell!

"Well?" the guy says.

Simon is glaring at me. His kid is bouncing up and down, like he has to pee. Sighing, I raise my hands in surrender.

"Right. Sorry," I say, getting up and letting them through.

The kid, as he walks past, steps on a corner of my computer bag. I hear an ugly crunching sound as he walks away.

A few minutes later I'm booting up my computer to make sure it isn't ruined. The Windows screen pops on, and everything seems fine, but I'm still pissed.

"Don't they have security at this place?" I mumble to a writer for NFL.com who's been sitting behind me with his girlfriend.

"What, what do you mean?" he says.

"That asshole fan who just walked past," I said. "His kid just stepped on my computer. Didn't even turn around."

"Dude, that was Brad Childress," the writer says. "Coach of the Vikings."

I pause in my seat.

"No shit," I say finally.

"Yeah, no shit," he says. "You sure you're a sportswriter?"

"Of course," I say. "And I knew that was Brad Childress. I was just fucking with you."

"Whatever."

The NFL.com guy goes back to talking to his girlfriend. Stealthily, I get up and sneak down to the buffet. The spread is deli sandwiches, warm tortellini salad, ricotta-filled mini cannolis, macadamia white-chocolate cookies, Krispy Kremes, mineral water, and coffee. A pair of ESPN cameramen are ahead of me in line. One grabs a cannoli, holds it up, and motions to the other:

"Dude, if it's not catered—it's not journalism!"

"Right-on to that!" the other guy says, stuffing his face.

I dump a pile of cookies and donuts into a napkin, fold it up, and sneak back up to the press section. By now they've found me a desk next to a tired-looking young guy who works for the Giants Web site. I plug in, cue up the Red Sox–Yankees game on the Internet, and start stuffing cookies into my face.

A few hours later I'm still glued to the same spot, covered in crumbs and in full bloat, an off-duty media pig in a state of unabashed psychic regression, watching grimly as a parade of no-necked, clumsily tailored 250-pound black jocks get auctioned off to their new corporate masters. A mechanized boom cam swings across the Radio City floor and stops queerly in front of my seat; I bat the crumbs off my face and give a lazy wave at it. It occurs to me to wonder if anyone back in Texas is watching. What would they think? What possible sense could they make of their quiet fellow Christian Matt Collins sitting behind Mel Kiper, Jr., at the NFL draft in New York, a big brown press badge around his neck and cookie bits all over his face? It was an ugly thought and I tried to put it out of my mind.

"Hey," a voice next to me asks. "Who was that who just went?"

It's the Giants guy, back from the bathroom.

"Anderson," I say. "Jamaal Anderson. A defensive end."

"Where out of?"

"Arkansas, I think," I say.

"An-der-son," he mumbles, typing the name in. "Okay, Miami on the clock . . ."

I frown, pick up my cell phone, and start dialing, feeling guilty all of a sudden. After a few rings, a voice answers.

"Thank you for calling John Hagee Ministries," the voice says. "All of our prayer partners are currently assisting others. You may have called at a peak period. However, your call will be answered in the order it was received . . ."

"So, who do the Fins take?" Giants guy asks, interrupting.

"It's gotta be Quinn," I say, my ear still pressed to the phone.

"They need a quarterback. Shit, they had Joey Harrington start-ing games for them last year. You've got to at least try to win, you know?"

"Yeah," he says. "But the thing about Miami is, when ev-erything's on the line, you can always count on them to fuck things up."

"Yeah, I—hello?"

A chirpy female voice crackles over the phone.

"God bless, welcome to John Hagee Ministries prayer line, this is Carol!"

"Yes, hi, how are you?"

"I'm fine, thank you."

"Yes," I say, "my name is Matt. I'm a member of the church. I went away to the Encounter Weekend, and I recently went through the Discover the Difference program. And I'm very happy, I feel blessed and all that, but I'm having trouble praying in tongues. You know, they tried to teach us that, but when I try to pray in tongues, it comes out sounding like a squirrel!"

"Gosh! Mmm-hmm," comes the response.

"When I'm praying, you know, it just doesn't sound natu-ral," I go on. "I just don't know what's wrong. I guess I'm just looking for some advice on what to do."

"Okay," the woman says. "Hold on one second, would you?"

"Yes," I say.

Weirdly, abruptly, she puts me on hold. The Giants guy, totally oblivious, is typing away next to me. Suddenly we hear the announcement over the loudspeaker; Miami has picked, Houston is on the clock. NFL chief Roger Goodell trots up to the lectern.

"Here it comes," says Giants Guy.

"With the ninth pick in the 2007 NFL draft," the com-missioner says, "the Miami Dolphins select Ted Ginn, wide re-ceiver, Ohio State University."

Pandemonium!

"Noooo!" come the shouts from the crowd.

"Booo!"

"Dolphins suck! Dolphins suck!"

Giants Guy shakes his head. "Didn't see that coming," he says.

"Neither did I," I say. "Shit, Quinn could fall all the way to the second round now. He's fucked."

"Look, they've got a camera on him!"

We look up at the monitor; close-up on jilted Notre Dame quarterback Brady Quinn's harried face. With his curly Laguna Beach locks and his square jaw, Quinn is supposed to be some kind of sports sex symbol, the Hunkback of Notre Dame, but to me he looks like every smug public school bully who ever dumped my books in junior high. Now he doesn't look so tough, though; in fact he looks like he could burst out crying any minute, and ESPN, it goes without saying, wouldn't miss that for anything. Extreme close-up now, the whole hall staring at him. Meanwhile, on the phone, the woman's voice returns.

"Okay, I'm back, I'm sorry about that," she says. "For your problem, I can give you some scriptures."

"Okay," I say.

"Like, Ephesians chapter six, verse eighteen. 'And pray in the spirit on all occasions with all kinds of prayers and requests.' "

"Okay. Ephesians six-eighteen."

"Okay?" she says. "And Acts chapter one, verse eight. 'Ye shall receive power, when the Holy Ghost will come unto you,' and then it goes on and on . . ."

"You see, that's what I mean," I say. "I feel like I'm not receiving power."

"Well," the lady says, "sometimes you have to do it on faith."

"Right, on faith," I say. Whatever that means.

"And eventually it comes," she says.

"Right," I say, still watching the screen. Quinn not crying yet.

"And then there's Acts chapter one, verse five," she says.

"Okay."

"And, um . . . Acts chapter two, verse four."

"Okay."

"That's a real good one," she says, brightening. "Acts two-four is a real good scripture."

"What does that one say?"

"It says, um, 'And they were all filled with the Holy Ghost and began to speak with other tongues as the spirit gave them other utterance.'"

"Hmm."

"You know, the only thing I can say is, you have to do it by faith."

"Right," I say.

"It's just like salvation. When you gave your heart to God and accepted Jesus Christ as your personal savior. You had to do it on faith."

I look around at the crowd, then down a few rows ahead of me. Adrian Peterson, the star Oklahoma running back just picked by Minnesota, is making his way through the press section with his entourage. A spindly-legged, middle-aged white fan with his pimply kid staggers forward and hounds Peterson to take a picture. The old creep puts his arm around the poor tie-clad new black millionaire, smiles, and, amazingly, gets his little son to take the picture. Peterson, too late, realizes he's not stopping for the sake of the kid, but for this creepy grownup suburban white clown in a Packers jersey. What the hell, you can see him thinking, I guess this is what I'm going to get all that money for. He smiles weakly as the little boy snaps the flash photos. I lean into the phone.

"Look," I say, "I feel like I'm trying as hard as I can to pray in tongues, but you know there are other people in my family, it just seems to pour right out of them—blada bladada bladada, you know—but I'm just standing there watching out of the corner of my eye like a jerk. And then I just make these squirrel sounds. And they all seem to be so filled with the spirit, and here I am with these little squeaky sounds. It's embarrassing, you know what I mean?"

Silence on the other end of the line. Houston was on the clock. Giants Guy gives me a look, as if to say, Who do you like? I cup my hand over the phone and whisper, Okoye.

"Well," the woman on the phone says finally, after a pause, "maybe on a one-to-one basis with a minister, you could work this all out."

"Yeah," I say. "That's what I'll do. I'll meet with a minister."

"Okay," she says. "Well, good luck and God bless."

"God bless you, too."

I put the phone down, feeling dirty. For a moment I was almost overcome by a powerful sensation of living in a sick world. I wasn't sure whose fault that feeling was—mine at least in part to be sure, but there is also this crowd, this scene, that bored volunteer housewife on the phone hawking cheap dial-a-scriptures to crazed strangers in the void. Here, take this fucked-up prerecorded advice, just don't get too close . . . Wait, you're with Adrian Peterson? For real? Can you get me his autograph?

I'm still thinking about all of this when I get a nudge from Giants Guy. I look up. Goodell is walking to the lectern. "With the tenth pick in the 2007 NFL draft," he says, "the Houston Texans select Amobi Okoye, defensive tackle, Louisville."

"Nice call," says Giants Guy.

"It had to be him," I say. "Peterson was gone already. The only other option was a corner."

"Yeah," he says. "You're right."

I reach down and grab another cookie.

EPILOGUE

★ ★ ★ ★ ★ ★ ★ ★ ★ ★ ★

Winter Park, Florida, early afternoon, August 2007

MITT ROMNEY is in town making a campaign appearance, and I'm stuck out here covering him. As it is for all campaign reporters, this early stage of the election process is the hardest for me—you sit there at these dreary events in half-filled halls all over the country, listening to computerized speeches and doing the awful math. We all have such a limited time on earth, and here I am, spending another year in places like this, listening to the same drivel, day after miserable day. No matter which candidate you cover, it's almost always the same flag-and-slogan backdrop behind the lectern, the same canned question-and-answer exchanges, the same pundit-generated opinions bouncing back at you in the "man-on-the-street" interviews on the way out.

In this case, the Mormon ex-governor's "Ask Mitt Anything" town halls are not, of course, designed to allow people to Ask Mitt Anything; like all such meetings, the potential questioners are at least semi-screened, in this case by a trio of breasty young things the candidate has cleverly sent weaving through the crowd in search of folks with "good" questions. I've been to a million of these events, and it's always the same; the Democratic screeners always manage to find people desperate to know how we're going to stop that awful George Bush, while at Republican events like this one, the questions always seem to end up being about how we're going to keep Hillary out of the White House. Batting practice for candidates, basically.

But in this case one of the Romney spokesmodels screwed up and picked out a portly gentleman in a T-shirt in the back row who had a question about Canadian prescription medication. As "John Originally from New York" rambled through his inquiry, it became clear to all the good Republican central Floridians in the crowd that John was mentally disabled—I mean clinically so; he could barely get his question out, and, at the end, no one really knew what he was asking. You could feel the impatience in this stern conservative audience—like they were all thinking, "Who let the retard get the mic?" Romney, unnerved for just a second by his questioner's stammering, recovered quickly and spouted out some bullshit response about safety concerns. Meanwhile, the crowd glared angrily at the spokeschick for puncturing the veneer of Romney's would-be Stepford audience. At that moment I decided that John Originally from New York was the only person in the room worth interviewing. Maybe this was a way to do the whole campaign, I thought.

The meeting broke up, and I went outside the building to wait for the crowd to file out. While waiting, I glanced at a Romney poster. It read:

ROMNEY
The Strength for America's Future

I tried to imagine what it would be like to have the balls to put the phrase "The Strength for America's Future" under ten million posters with my name on it. Who are these guys who run for president in this country? These constantly lying, blow-dried egomaniacs must all come from a common source somewhere. But where?

Just then John Originally from New York lumbered outside. He was huge and round and grimacing; he looked like a bouncer at a minor-league hockey event. I introduced myself and asked him what he thought of the governor.

He looked into my camera as if something were hidden in there. Satisfied finally that nothing was, he spoke.

"The thing, the thing, the thing about medicine from Canada is, it's okay, but the American guv'ment can't be responsible for it," he said. "If something goes wrong with it, you've got to go to Canada to fight it out. You can't do it over here, you know."

Made cense. But what about the governor?

"I don't think Canada will do anything to poison the American, though," he answered. "Because they need the business."

True again.

And what did he think of the slogan "The Strength for America's Future"? What did he think that meant?

"That just means about the Space Center, you know. When we have the Space Center, it makes the United States a superpower, and—"

"Uh," I said, trying to follow him.

"And that just means that with the benefits, we don't need to have the draft anymore."

I nodded. "That's what that slogan means to you, that we don't need to have a draft anymore?" I asked.

"Yes," he said.

"Okay, great, thanks a lot," I said, giving him my card. He took it and walked away, cradling the card in his hand.

* * *

A FEW MINUTES LATER I broke down and interviewed some ostensibly mentally healthy Republicans. One couple was very pleased with Romney's performance. Hubby was almost beaming.

"I had been considering Giuliani," he said, "but now I have to say that I'm going with Romney."

"Yes, me too," said Wife.

I wrote that down. "I see," I said. "And what is it about Romney that is different from Giuliani?"

Hubby's smile vanished.

"I don't know," he said.

"He just is," added Wife.

"He talks good," chimed in Hubby.

"Okay," I said, writing. " 'Talks good,' got it. Thanks a lot, folks."

They stood there, still staring at me.

"Okay," I said, repeating myself. "Thanks a lot!" *Dismissed!*

Slowly, they walked away.

THE KIND OF PEOPLE who come out to support a carefully scripted corporate frontman like Mitt Romney or even Hillary Clinton are either outright cynics—and I've met some of those, grinning upper-class folk who see through the candidates' spiels, but vote for them anyway because they want their taxes slashed or less regulation of their Wall Street businesses—or actual believers in the dreck the candidates are selling. And if they believe, it's usually because they tune in to political shows on TV or radio and believe everything they hear, right down to the commercials. So when election season comes around, they choose their candidates on the basis of what appears to be an almost completely random neurological process—all of those mainstream media opinions bounce around in their heads for a while, and then when the merry-go-round stops on Election

Day, they look to see which ones stuck and vote accordingly. When your voter-on-the-street is a John Originally from New York, you get a vivid picture of that Random Opinion Generator at work. But sometimes it's just as obvious with your run-of-the-mill, ostensibly freethinking Republican or Democrat. Why do you like this candidate? *I just do.* No, seriously, why? *Uh, I don't know. Because he's tough on terrorism? And he's for "change"!* And so on.

Mitt Romney is your prototypical full-of-shit presidential candidate. He represents nothing so much as the system itself, which builds up politicians who look the part, frown with import at the appropriate cues, heave with concern about Our Children ("There are twenty-nine thousand registered sex offenders on MySpace!" Romney crowed at today's event), and have a stern word or two or ten for the Terrorists who want to wreck Our Way of Life, whatever the hell that is.

This system used to work just fine. The Republicans were once masters at appropriating public unhappiness for their own ends, telling people who'd been put out of jobs by the exported manufacturing economy that their lives now sucked not because they were unemployed, but because Sean Penn was a little communist weasel who didn't believe in God besides. And because people now went mostly to movies instead of union meetings, they ate it up. The image of the spoiled, traitorous rich most people saw on television was not a CEO who played golf in Scotland with congressmen while slaves in the Marianas replaced his American workers. It was a Hollywood actor with a half-assed liberal arts education who wrecked Porsches, snorted coke off the asses of strippers, and visited Hugo Chavez in between movie shoots.

It was a nice little setup for bullshit artists like Romney, who could then go into sad little towns like this one and blast Hollywood values, saying, as he did today, "We have to clean up the water our kids are swimming in." Not the *actual* water, of course, which might be polluted (or disappearing, as it is here in Orlando, where homeowning decent folk like those in Romney's audience use 75 percent of their water irrigating high-maintenance St. Augustine lawn grass; experts expect a crisis by 2013), but the cultural water, the water where actors who don't even believe in Jesus aren't satisfied with the money they make, and then speak out of turn. And if not actors, gays or professors or someone else with too many ideas. For a long time, those monsters were villain enough to keep the conservative vote captive.

On the other side, voter manipulation turned into a similarly easy proposition. Vilified unfairly for the wrongs of the nation, wounded and defensive American liberals focused exclusively on unseating the horned Republican beast. They gave Democratic candidates their vote almost without a thought, supporting "winners" over candidates with something to say. A burgeoning third-party movement spearheaded by Ralph Nader disappeared into almost total irrelevance after Nader's 2000 run ended up being perceived as the crucial factor in electing George Bush. Things got so bad that for a brief time former General Wesley Clark, a man who in the 1960s and 1970s traveled the world giving speeches in support of the Vietnam War effort, became the darling of American liberalism, a segment of society whose modern roots lay in the development of a movement to oppose that same Vietnam War.

The next little thing about this vote-for-the-lesser-evil trick, of course—and this is no secret to anyone anymore—is that it drives all the "serious" candidates toward what is commonly referred to as the "moderate center," even if these serious candidates aren't, in fact, moderate or centrist in any meaningful sense and the so-called center moves further to the right with each election cycle. For nearly two decades now this process has been steadily advancing on the Democratic side, as liberals are trained to accept the idea that the national majority will never accept a true labor party, or any candidate perceived as "soft" on defense.

In *What's the Matter with Kansas?* Tom Frank wrote mostly about conservatives when he described a process by which Middle America was trained to vote on social issues while ignoring its own economic situation. But, in fact, the same exact thing happened to liberals.

At the tail end of the Reagan years the Democratic Party, with the aid of Clinton/Gore–led groups like the Democratic Leadership Council, presented us with a new kind of "business-friendly" Democrat, one who voted the right way on choice and minority rights but was "willing to work with business" on such matters as free trade, deregulation, privatization, government spending, and personal debt. Such a Democrat, we were told, could win: we'd be giving up a thing or two in terms of workers' rights and other matters, but at least *Roe v. Wade* would be safe for now.

That led to the absurdity of the late 1990s and the early years of this century, a time when a massive empire that dominated the world economy chose its leaders almost exclusively according to their stances on such matters as abortion rights and gay marriage. On the substantive economic issues the main candidates were very nearly identical, resulting in the outrageous comedy of 2000, an election in a 250-million-plus population that ended in an exact statistical tie. This was a situation so absurd that it even made a comedian out of reviled lefty oracle/MIT professor Noam Chomsky, who remarked that this was the result you would expect if Americans were asked to choose the president not of their own country, but of Mars.

But the joke passed almost unnoticed among most of the population and the commercial media, setting up a near-repeat of the same situation in 2004. The key battleground state this time around was not Florida but Ohio, and once again almost no one noticed that neither of the main candidates was interested in discussing his stance on the key issues that actually affected voters in that state.

Ohio's economy had been cardinally affected by NAFTA. A onetime manufacturing powerhouse, Ohio now suffered through mass layoffs and crushing economic uncertainty. But when the election rolled around, and both John Kerry and George Bush flocked to the state in search of its up-for-grabs twenty electoral votes, neither candidate mentioned free trade at all. In the national political media, pundits wondered what the "liberal" Kerry (who had voted for NAFTA) would have to do to win votes in a tough Middle America state like Ohio. Chris Matthews suggested on MSNBC's *Hardball!* that Kerry might need to save a baby from a burning building; his middlebrow cohort Howard Fineman agreed. "He's got to do something like that," he frowned. Unsurprisingly, General Electric, the parent company to MSNBC, had laid off thousands of workers in Ohio in the years prior to the election.

But with the grotesque failure of the Iraq war and with some of the other foibles of the Bush administration came a late change in Republican strategy. Rather than their usual tactic of redefining the center further rightward, by 2008 the Republicans, just like Democrats, were offering to their base a spate of "moderate" candidates whose chief virtue to the party was their potential for a general-election victory against a Democrat like Hillary Clinton. Candidates like Rudy Giuliani, John McCain, and even Romney fell short according to the usual social orthodoxies, with none of them being born-again Christians or staunchly anti-abortion. Just as the Democrats had done for years, the Republicans were now asking their voters to sacrifice their own interests in favor of a candidate who would be viable to "swing" voters.

As a result, the 2008 presidential race going into the primaries looks like a perfect storm of electoral cross-purposes. With the exception of Barack Obama, all of the major candidates the predominantly antiwar Democratic base will be asked to choose from were originally pro-war. On the other side, fundamentalist Christians may be forced to vote for a cross-dressing pro-choice New Yorker like Rudolph Giuliani. When once again asked to vote against the candidate they dislike, voters on both sides will now have real trouble figuring out which party's offering they're supposed to hate more.

But out there, on the campaign trail, you can already feel the vibe changing. Particularly on the Republican side, you can see that the paranoia conjured by all those years of right-wing oracles telling people that they've been lied to by the "liberal media" is blowing up in some prominent faces. This is the problem with training people to believe they're being lied to; after seven years of Bush, some Republicans raised on that kind of education are beginning to wonder just who else exactly has been lying to them.

OUTSIDE THE ROMNEY EVENT in Florida there was a protest of about thirty people, all supporters of antiwar libertarian Ron Paul who came to shout at the cars on their way in and out of the civic center parking lot. When I went over to visit with them, I found that almost all of them told the same story. Excepting a few cases here and there, they were all former dyed-in-the-wool Rush Limbaugh Republicans who had experienced holy conversions. Many talked about being reunited with liberal family members with whom they had argued for years.

"I'm a conservative, I used to be a neocon even, I used to think Cindy Sheehan was . . . I mean, I ended up going out and buying a Dixie Chicks album, just because I feel bad, you know?" said J. C. Braithwaite, a thirty-something ex-Ohioan who was emerging from a Sleeping Beauty-esque sojourn in the Limbaugh woods. J.C. would later tell me that she once won the Daughters of the American Revolution's Citizen Bee

Award and had the Statue of Liberty on her class ring in school. "I get misty-eyed at the 'Star-Spangled Banner,'" she told me. "I called Mike Eruzione's answering machine when the U.S. beat Russia. I want to fall in love with my country again."

J.C. is at this protest with her mother and her brother, Aaron. Her brother used to be the reviled family liberal, a "conspiracy theorist" who had a lot of ideas about 9/11 his family didn't even want to listen to. Now Mom, Sis, and Brother are all together under one banner, campaigning for Ron Paul. And while all the protesters here seem genuinely smitten with their candidate, I get the feeling that it's more what Paul represents that turns them on. The vibe here is very science fiction, very *Invasion of the Body Snatchers;* Romney, an insectoid big shot among the pod people, is to be protested, while the unpodded, still-human Paul crowd holds its banners and tries to stay awake.

"It kinda felt like in *The Matrix,* where it's like, 'Take the red pill,' you know?" she said. "They make it sound like if you support Ron Paul you're some crazy 9/11 conspiracy wacko. But we've just been lied to so many times, you feel like you've just been chumped, you know what I mean?"

"Well, yeah . . ." I said.

"And I'm ready to blow up my TV!" J.C.'s kindly bespectacled mom shouted. "Ready to blow it up and watch YouTube!"

"Yeah," said J.C. "I used to watch all that stuff . . . O'Reilly . . . Fox . . ."

"I used to think everything on TV was true," chimed in Mom.

"Now we know," said J.C. "And the worst thing, we used to be so hard on Aaron," she said, referring to her brother, who was holding a banner across the street.

"We thought he was paranoid," agreed Mom.

"Now we all get along again," said J.C.

I asked what family gatherings used to be like.

"We didn't even talk at Thanksgiving," said J.C. "About politics we couldn't talk at all. I mean, he was the tree-hugging Democrat, while I was the conservative, married to a Republican doctor . . ."

"Didn't talk much," agreed Mom.

Just then, while I was talking to J.C. and her mother, a reporter for the local Orlando TV station, Channel 6, swooped in to shoot some protester footage. The reporter had a perfect helmet of wavy anchorman hair. One of the Paul supporters leaned over and whispered to me. "Check it out, it's Mitt Romney," he said.

"You mean the hair?" I asked.

"Not just the hair," he quipped.

AMERICAN POLITICAL MOVEMENTS always seem to have an *us* and a *them*, and the *them* is often more important than the *us*. With plenty of justice the Ron Paul movement identifies the *them* as an incestuous oligarchy of insider assholes: congressmen and businessmen and TV reporters who show up once every four years dressed in nearly identical Halloween-like costumes—ties, sculpted hair, high-production values. Canny campaign strategists have always keenly understood the depth of popular distrust of those types, which is why you'll seldom see a mainstream campaign event without a candidate taking a shot here and there at the superficial trappings of his own political class. Even Romney lately has been making haircut jokes—not at his own expense, of course, but at the expense of John Edwards, whose plan for a federal savings program that would save $250 a year for most Americans seemed ripe for ridicule to Romney's handlers. "That wouldn't buy John Edwards a haircut," cracked Romney today, eliciting a half-fart of muted laughs from the crowd.

But not many people are buying this bullshit anymore, and

that may mark the beginning of something genuinely new in the American political system. The Derangement that I describe in this book kicked off when Americans finally figured out that they'd been betrayed by their mainstream political system, but still failed to abandon that old paradigm completely. The 9/11 "Truth" and Christian End Timer phenomena are both basically crude parodies of the same old left/right canned media Holy War. Adherents abandoned their former champions in the Republican and Democratic parties not because they realized they'd been conned into hating each other, but because they felt those champions of theirs had failed to act on that hate aggressively enough. So instead of having a political awakening, they just went further down the rabbit hole of geeked-up patriotic paranoia, into a place where the other side isn't merely wrong, but made up actually of conspirator-killers or terrorists or agents of Satan, not even really human beings. They reached out to or built movements whose object was not defeat of the Other Side, but its utter destruction (as in the case of the End Timers) or its overthrow (the Truthers).

From that point of view the Derangement was a grotesque black comedy. It was Monty Python's Crack Suicide Squad brought to life; screwed by a corrupt ruling class, the Population at Large rebelled by ramming itself into twin brick walls of pure idiocy. It was hard to say what was more absurd, the preposterous corruption of our politicians or the utterly irrational response of the people they betrayed. For most of the time that I worked on this book, it looked like an utterly hopeless situation, the kind of maelstrom of pointlessly destructive behavior and willful misunderstanding that could leave us all fucked for a generation, with nothing left to do but laugh.

But who knows, maybe things aren't so bleak. At the extremities of the Derangement there are signs now that the mainstream attempt to freeze-dry the debate in a permanent predictable struggle over the same old symbolic issues, voiced by the same media-political complex, has failed. And maybe the Paul campaign, as marginal as it seems, offers a glimpse at the new fault line. It's not blue and red so much anymore. It's on the farm and off the farm. And the numbers off the farm are growing.

And sure, some of those people off the farm are Truthers and End Timers and other members of the Crack Suicide Squad rebellion. But increasingly some are people who have their eyes wide open, who are seeing the Big Con for what it really is.

"Yeah, I've never contributed to a campaign before, but that's because I couldn't afford it," said Terence Reilly, one of the Paul protesters. Terence does geek-squad-type computer maintenance for a central Florida company; he's got a wife and a newborn child, and he's getting by. He came to the Ron Paul campaign via the usual route; disillusioned with mainstream politics and the Washington media, he surfed and he read and he decided that this little-known politician was the man who stood for his values.

"There are people out there who don't have the time, or the energy, or the . . . the Internet to find things out for themselves," he said. "They don't take that time."

And it isn't just on the Republican side, in the Paul campaign, that I saw this kind of thing. On the Democratic side, the John Edwards campaign seemed, to me, to have been crafted specifically to appeal to those voters who felt they'd been left behind by their party. Edwards not only promised to eschew lobbyist donations and corporate bundlers but went out of his way to shed light on the kinds of manipulations that ran the Senate he served in. In fact, part of the Edwards stump speech in the fall of 2007 was an exposé of exactly the kind of behavior described in the congressional portions of this book—in particular, he talked about a slowdown of legislation that would have eased the way for more production of cheap generic pharmaceuticals, a slowdown effected by key members of his own Democratic Party who had accepted massive donations from the pharmaceutical industry. This was heretical behavior for a formerly "mainstream" Democrat, and Edwards's admonition to audiences not to "replace corporate Republicans with corporate Democrats" led to standing ovations when I saw him in Iowa and New Hampshire that fall. Even longtime Democrats like Harold and Patricia White, an elderly couple from a small Iowan town called Monticello, nodded immediately when I asked if they agreed with Edwards's statement that there was "no difference" between the two parties.

"He's telling it like it is," said Harold, who incidentally was also a devout Christian—as much as he liked Edwards's views on Washington corruption, he disliked his use of the phrase "give 'em Hell." The evangelical Christian who turned up at speeches of reformist Democrats like Edwards and Dennis Kucinich was another phenomenon I would see a lot that fall. This was something I certainly did *not* see in 2004, when the makeup of Republican and Democratic crowds was far more predictable.

Beyond Edwards, you found some off-the-farmers at the speeches of Barack Obama as well. While Obama almost certainly represented the same kind of obscenely funded insider Democrat who'd let down generations of party members over the years—he raised almost $100 million before the Iowa caucus alone, with heavy support from Wall Street and the other usual corporate villains—it was the *tone* of his campaign that was different. Maybe it was because Obama, with his natural charisma, felt he didn't need it, or maybe that's just the way he is, but the Buck Fush/ unseat-the-Republican-devil stridency was completely absent from his whole approach. "I'm so tired of Democrats waving Bush in front of me and thinking I owe them my vote," one woman in Nashua, New Hampshire, told me. "Just tell me

who you are and let me think about it, okay? I don't need to be
hating someone else. I'm really tired of all that. It's tiring, you
know? Why do I need to hate some dolt in Alabama? I don't
even know those people."

At the peak of its intensity, in 2004, the blue-state/red-state
split represented, in a way, an enormous triumph for mainstream politics. It was a time when huge masses of the population could be organized into two rival groups, each trained
to hate the other intensely. But what's happening now is that
many people are beginning to resent being lumped simplisti-
cally into shallow, media-created *Crossfire*-style categories of
"left" and "right"; on the one hand they distrust the very media
that celebrates those simplistic distinctions, and on the other
they see that the elected politicians who ostensibly represent
those would-be opposing ideologies actually do no such thing.

So now they are not only seeking their own far more in-
dividualized identities, they're actually demanding that those
identities be recognized. And some of these new politicians are
responding—by running against the economic betrayal, like
Paul and Edwards, or by rejecting the left-right partisan hatred
deal, à la Obama. It's not much, but it's at least providing a
few more choices. And the more things move in that direction,
the more the original problem of a monolithic, corrupt political
orthodoxy withers away. Because a mass Balkanization of the
political landscape in this country would, of course, be enor-
mously dangerous to that kind of dug-in, corrupt elite. When
the country is split not into two neat sides but in a million little
pieces, how do you tie up the population with hatred for the
"other half" while you burgle the national treasure and run
Congress like a medieval Khannate? How do you get families
hating each other at Thanksgiving over trifles while you cook
up phony wars and pad the Pentagon budget with billions in
political kickbacks? The answer is, you can't. When the *Crossfire*
paradigm loses its force, all that's left is a bunch of people with

different views all sitting together in a room, wondering why they're all paying three bucks a gallon for gas, why they have no health insurance, why their tax rates are higher than Warren Buffett's. If we're all equally a bunch of suckers, how could any of us be worth hating? Only a madman wastes his time hating a sucker. And increasingly, the J.C.s and the Terences are realizing that we all of us have been suckers all these years.

MAYBE THAT SIMPLE OBSERVATION is our path back to reality, if it's not too late.

AFTERWORD
TO THE PAPERBACK EDITION

★ ★ ★ ★ ★ ★ ★ ★ ★ ★ ★ ★

Thursday, September 11, 2008

I'm sitting here in my home in Jersey City, staring out my window at the Hudson River. Seven years ago I might have had a pretty good view of a pair of super-advanced holograms as they made their way south over Manhattan, crashing finally, and with awesome fictitious effect, into the surreptitiously mined Twin Towers.

But alas I wasn't here seven years ago. I was in Moscow, spending most of my time shuttling back and forth on subway rides to pharmaceutical kiosks in the Tekstillshiki region known for their liberal attitudes toward prescriptions. I was so tuned out to America that my initial response to hearing about 9/11 was to make a joke about it—a bad one, not worth mentioning here.

I wasn't much of an American back then. As a longtime resident of the Russian capital, where terrorist bombings were commonplace and no one worried much when the 1890-foot Ostankino television tower spontaneously burst into flames,

I mostly had trouble grasping the mentality that had folks at home so freaked out.

You would never catch a Russian needing to go into therapy over, say, the massacre at Budennovsk, or the bombing of the Pushkinskaya train station (which missed killing me by a few hundred yards, by the way). Russia is a country where people are born expecting to have their heads crushed in totally avoidable industrial accidents, or to be mistakenly shot by mob assassins who've read an address upside-down, or to die on an operating table when a doctor slips on a patch of wet floor.

These are people who haven't been raised on five decades of TV commercials teaching them to expect a pain-and-death-free existence. In America people can't handle ring around the collar, or crow's feet around the eyes—of course we were going to have problems dealing with something whose meaning was as heavy as 9/11's.

And what was that meaning? I'm asking myself that right now. I've just returned from Minneapolis/St. Paul, where I watched a junior-league dimwit named Sarah Palin become a political superstar overnight. "Al Qaeda terrorists still plot to inflict catastrophic harm on America," she railed. "And [Obama's] worried that someone won't read them their rights?"

Palin's speech described an America infected at every level with queers, liberals, and other such traitor-types, a country teetering on a precipice of European defeatism and no longer willing or able to defend its children's suburban soccer games from the International Terrorist Menace that so jealously yearns for their destruction. It was the kind of speech that only made sense if you had spent the last half-decade waiting—almost hoping—for your local Best Buy to be RPG'ed by a Hamas terrorist led to the spot by a Columbia University professor of French literature.

Wherever bin Laden plunged the knife back in 2001, it's pretty clear the wound hasn't healed yet, at least not in crowds like the one in St. Paul. And to see citizens of a country that once worshipped strong, silent types like Lincoln, Teddy Roosevelt, and Ike reduced to yelping, flag-waving, paranoid hysterics over a single lucky shot dealt by a bunch of old-world cave-dwellers seven full years ago is enough to drive any American with any pride left at all to complete and total distraction.

In Russia I saw, with the crystal clarity only available to a foreigner, that the people who were the biggest "patriots"—the defiant old bats who marched down Tverskaya Street every V-E Day carrying Stalin posters, or the fortysomething male loners who stank of beer and dried fish and passed out raggedy copies of anti-Semitic scandal-sheets like *Zaftra* and *Russky Poryadok* outside the subway stations—were the very people who were the most embarrassed and the most ashamed of their poverty and backwardness, who felt the most intimidated by the outside world and scared of the future.

I remember once sharing a sleeper car in a train with some old Russian patriot who was enraged to the point of not being able to sleep a wink, by the sight of a hundred-buck Swiss watch on the wrist of a younger Russian man in our car. Seeing that ostentatious display of foreign wealth on the wrist of some city slicker from Petersburg drove this old nutter into a torrential diatribe against Jews, America, and the loss of the "good old days" of collective farms, snitching, and "Doktorskaya" sausage. I had these conversations a million times over there and they always ended the same way: with me, the abashed representative of modern civilization, having to reassure the poor old provincial that the Hoover Dam really isn't that tall and that both the M.R.I. machine and the motion picture were indeed, as he claimed, invented by Sikorsky.

So you wonder what causes these huge crowds of pale-faced Midwesterners to feel the need to wave flags and spittle-scream "U-S-A!" in the faces of total strangers. It can't be because they're feeling good.

From my point of view 9/11 and all the subsequent disasters/humiliations of the Bush years—from Katrina, which made parts of America look like Bangladesh, to the constant battering of the dollar against the Euro, to the Wal-Martization of the once-proud industrial landscape and the commensurate rise of China, to the collapsed real estate market that led to waves of Brits and Germans buying up chunks of Brooklyn and lower Manhattan out of sheer boredom, hell, even to losing to Argentina in basketball—all this has Americans aching for some way to feel good again, to flex their muscles.

The only problem is that the only thing Americans really know how to do anymore is eat huge quantities of Doritos and buy shit on the Internet.

WHEN I first started writing *The Great Derangement*, my read of what was happening in America was that the system had broken down, that the distance between what our politicians said they were doing and what they were actually delivering had become so great that even in a vast empire full of people as gullible and mostly unthinking as Americans, large percentages of the population were finding themselves unable to swallow what they were being told, and searching for new explanations for their political disappointment.

I specifically talked about two of those explanations—the End Timers' and Truthers. Finally prodded to think about their problems, followers of both these groups devoted themselves to political movements that were even dumber and more fake than the ones that had already failed them. It was like losing six grand to a direct-mail scammer offering a phony Royal Carribean Cruise and trying to recover the money by helping Prince Aluisi Ilassis reclaim his fortune from the Nigerian Petroleum Company. These were just lateral moves.

Once *The Great Derangement* came out, though, and I

started touring the country and giving speeches and interviews on the subject, I quickly realized that I'd failed to spell out my argument clearly enough. I noticed that when media figures and interviewers tried to describe the book, they often presented it as a story about how collective disappointment with the political system had caused Americans to radicalize and become extremists. And in one of the more embarrassing psychological developments of my life, I actually heard this description often enough that I began repeating it myself.

But *The Great Derangement* is not really about a movement toward "radicalism" or "extremism." The phenomenon the book describes is not nearly so novel, I'm afraid. In truth both of these movements are mostly evolutionary side-mutations of the same idiotic red-state/blue-state culture war horseshit that's been raining down from the airwaves for what seems like forever, sold to us in the hope that we'll be mesmerized long enough to ignore what actually goes on in Washington.

And what is going on in Washington? What I tried to show in the congressional chapters of this book is that the rhetoric of both political parties is mostly a fraud, and that the true business of both is to hand out favors in the form of policies and contracts to their campaign contributors, who happen to be substantially the same people on both sides.

In our recent history, they've been able get away with this largely because the public is so overwhelmingly focused on the daily exchange of insults tossed back and forth on television according to the old *Crossfire* paradigm, which broke the electorate into nice, clean halves: your politically liberal college student learned to blame George Bush for all the world's evils, while your churchgoing Rush Limbaugh listener came to blame liberals for all of society's wrongs.

The innovation of the Derangement is not that it has lit a radical's torch to the old dynamic, or fractured the old politics. Instead, the Derangement takes the old dynamic, amps it up a level, and transforms it into a dark parody of itself. It isn't a fracturing of mainstream politics, but an intensification of them. The result is that the psychological distance between all of these supposed enemies has widened to an unbridgeable chasm. To find any common cause with a Bush voter, a Truther wouldn't just have to ignore the usual differences of culture and politics, he'd also have to allow himself to become complicit in a wild homicidal plot. And for an End Timer to vote for a Democrat, say, because she wanted better healthcare, she'd have to first overlook the Democratic Party's binding fealty to Satan. People are not only still steeped in the same old deceptions, they're more steeped in them than ever. More than ever, they're hating instead of seeing the big picture. I wouldn't call this a popular movement toward radicalism or extremism. I would call it a strengthening of the ruling party's position over the actual voters, who are in fact more divided and lost and fucked than ever.

At the beginning of the 2008 campaign season I thought I saw some signs of things getting better. Among other things, the campaigns of some of the entrants, in particular Barack Obama (who in a somewhat syrupy, non-ideological fashion refused to play the hate game at all), Ron Paul (who tried to unite voters on both sides against the aggrandizement of federal power), and John Edwards (who tried to focus public anger in the general direction of its proper target, the conspiracy of business interests in Washington) all attempted to capitalize to some degree on the exhaustion the public must be feeling at being asked all the time to hate other ordinary Americans.

Edwards was out relatively early, but Paul's candidacy was stubborn and more intense—no Republican I saw had even close to the number of active volunteers besieging debates, town halls, and other campaign hot spots. Obama's campaign, meanwhile, took off like a rocket, and I'm not going to pretend it had everything to do with appealing to the better angels of America's nature; a lot of his success was clearly due to the appeal of Obama's personality, his RFK-resurrected heartthrob act. Still, after Obama triumphed in Iowa, it looked like we might make it at least to the nominating conventions without the usual rancor. And then the Hillary campaign fought back.

Facing defeat, Hillary Clinton reached deep down and tried every trick in the book to rally the troops using all the old methods. She assailed Obama's patriotism. There were subtle hints about his religion, Internet campaigns in which pictures of Obama in ceremonial Muslim garb were circulated, surrogates dispatched to make disparaging remarks about Obama's supposed "sexism," the evidence for which chiefly involved Obama putting a hand on Hillary's shoulder and calling her "likeable enough." As a last ditch, Clinton questioned the very validity of the primary process. By the end there were ferocious contests for votes involving masses of lawyers on both sides.

Once Hillary launched her ferocious attacks on Obama, Obama's supporters also became "radicalized." The talk at Obama's rallies was increasingly focused on the iniquity of the Hillary people—and suddenly the campaign that in the beginning had been all about chumminess and inclusiveness saw its followers ranting about Vince Foster and Whitewater and other Clinton scandals in a desperate attempt to silver-stake the Clinton vampire by any means necessary.

It was far worse, however, in the Clinton camp. I even saw materials circulated at one Hillary rally which suggested that Obama's mother had gone to a high school whose teachers had been dragged before the House Un-American Affairs Committee back in McCarthy's day. I asked the person circulating these fliers if she remembered that until 2008, it was Hillary who had often unfairly been accused of being a communist, that right-wingers constantly circulated materials highlighting her relationship with the "socialist" Bella Abzug, claiming also that Hillary had praised Mao in college papers, and so on.

"That's a lie!" the woman shouted. This was in Pennsylvania, on primary night.

"Well, yeah, exactly," I said. "It's a lie and it's stupid. You really think Barack Obama is a Marxist?"

She shrugged and took off. Four legs good, two legs bad. That was the intellectual level of this kind of behavior.

It's important to remember that this hate-fest was absolutely, utterly divorced from any policy meaning. The biggest political difference between the two candidates was a small loophole in Barack Obama's health care program that did not make it mandatory for all citizens to buy in (as opposed to Hillary's program, which ostensibly would force everyone to join).

Watching the fundamentalist rage that surrounded the debate between Democrats over this one tiny difference in two largely identical health care proposals was awe-inspiring. Hillary supporters raged against Obama's plan as though he had proposed paying premiums with the blood of Christian children; the "missing 15 million" (Clinton supporters claimed Obama's plan would leave 15 million people uninsured) became a Clinton war cry. A petition even began circulating that attempted to raise $1 for every one of the 15 million Americans who would be left out under Obama's plan.

When eighty leading physicians started circulating a statement to the effect that this was all stupid, that the Clinton and Obama plans were essentially identical, that non-compliance with mandates in states like Massachusetts was demonstrably a serious enough problem that it was really impossible to say whose plan would actually leave more people uninsured, that the real problem was that no one was trying to expand coverage and make it cheaper, and that on the whole either plan was, one might say in a spirit of goodwill and generosity, a step in the right direction—when that statement came out, it was largely blasted by Hillary supporters as the covert work of the Obama campaign, horseshit, without evidence and not to be trusted. What do a bunch of doctors know anyway?

From my point of view the whole thing was stupid for another reason, namely: When did any politician, Democrat or Republican, ever deliver a real health care plan in this country? But this was never really an argument about health care. This was about Hillary supporters hating Obama supporters, and vice versa. The politics, as always, were incidental.

Internet wars between the "Obamiots" and the "Clintonistas" raged with white-hot intensity, with both sides accusing the other of the worst intrigues. By mid-April the Obama-Hillary race had, itself, turned into a microcosm of the Derangement. The rift between the followers of these two candidates—whose policies, remember, were virtually identical—was violent, profound, and irreparable.

Things got so bad that as late as the beginning of the Democratic convention, polls showed that less than half of all Hillary voters said they definitely planned to vote for Obama, an astonishingly low figure. More shocking was the sudden appearance of groups like PUMA (Party Unity My Ass), who aimed to unite shunned Hillary supporters against Barack Obama in the general election, apparently for the crime of beating Hillary in the primary season.

By the general election season, some Hillary voters were still backing John McCain and Sarah Palin despite their opposing positions on traditional hot-button women's issues like abortion, child care, equal pay for equal work, and health care for children. Never in our history has there been a clearer case of hatred and yahooism overwhelming issue politics.

Compounding all of this was the re-emergence of Karl Rove and his protégés (Rove charge Steve Schmidt is running McCain's campaign), who rallied the so-called "Republican base"—in fact a repeatedly fucked-over segment of lower-to-middle-class white America that has seen most of its jobs and its savings pissed away in the last eight years of Republican rule—against Obama with their canny choice of Palin and their nut-cutting makeover of John McCain. With their wild charges of sexism and media conspiracy and their accusations of various shocking crimes on the part of Obama (running an ad accusing Obama of favoring explicit sex ed for kindergarteners, when in fact the program was designed to help children recognize and avoid child molesters), the McCain strategists finally turned the campaign of two traditionally middle-of-the-road, milquetoast politicians into an all-out Holy War of cross-cultural idiocies.

At this writing the whole country is abuzz over Obama's decision to describe McCain's policies as "lipstick on a pig," one of the dumbest political controversies I have ever seen. Actual policy has been completely removed from the equation. It's all about who hates more now. You either hate Barack Obama for calling Sarah Palin a pig, or else you hate John McCain and his advisors—as even I do—for clouding the real issue with such an absurd and baseless insinuation.

As a man I interviewed at a McCain rally in New Orleans earlier this year put it, speaking of Obama: "You either are or you aren't. And he aren't."

Choose one side or another. There is really no middle ground. And therein lies the trick. For in reality—and this was supposed to be the point of this book—we're all on the same middle ground. And that middle ground is being fucked. While we're wasting our time steaming and stewing over the other side's latest atrocity, the nineteen people who actually run this country are quietly siphoning off $200 billion of our tax money from the Treasury to bail out their most recent string of bad investments.

Those people are not circulating petitions about Barack Obama's missing 15 million. They could give a fuck about the missing 15 million. They don't care who called whom a pig, or a pig with lipstick, or whatever. They don't care which reporter is being sexist by asking Palin to explain her nutty beliefs, and they certainly aren't feeling anything except amusement about John McCain accusing Barack Obama of teaching sodomy to six-year-olds.

No, they only care about one thing: money. In the end politics is not about pigs or lipstick or middle fingers surreptitiously raised during debates or whose Mom once shook hands with a Logical Positivist in the fifties or who waves his flag the hardest or puts his "Country First" or any of that. Politics is about who gets what. And that's something we don't talk about that much anymore, busy as we are shouting at each other and screaming at the TV and generally being fat, stupid suckers while the thieves in D.C. rob the store.

I'd like to be able to say that I feel better now about things than I did when I finished this book, but I don't. I thought it would be at least a step forward if we could get through an election season without the usual partisan bloodlust and hatred, or less of it at least—that a season of red-blue madness dialed down would lead to people getting a better glimpse of the reality. But instead we got more, and more varieties of hatred. Instead of just red and blue, there's now a full spectrum of hatreds to choose from. You can hate the other party or the other guy within your own party; you can hate as a woman, you can hate women; you can hate as a bitter member of the working class, you can hate the media; you can hate Chris Matthews, you can hate the guys who want him out of a job. And so on and so on.

I'm afraid that the binary, red-blue dynamic of hatred is analogous to the early days of cable. Once there were only a few channels. Now there are forty, and soon there will be six hundred. But in the end, it's all still watching the same TV. It's still the same crap. There's just more.

ACKNOWLEDGMENTS

THANKS TO S&G editor Chris Jackson for his superhuman patience throughout the embarrassingly long ordeal that was this book. Without his stoic bravery in the face of my general assholeness, this book would never have been published. Thanks also to his assistant, Mya Spalter, who spent countless hours trying to find me when I was hiding from Chris, and also to the many members of Spiegel & Grau's publicity and marketing team—and also, of course, to Celina Spiegel and Julie Grau themselves, who showed tremendous confidence in the project throughout.

I would also like to thank my editors at *Rolling Stone*, Will Dana, Eric Bates, and Jann Wenner, for having patience with me while I wrote this book. Naturally, thanks should also be extended to my agent, Lydia Wills at Paradigm, who has frequently had to hold both of my hands during this process.

Thanks also to my friends and family for their continued encouragement and support, in particular my mother, Veronica Whelan, who nearly went off the road many times talking to me on the phone throughout this period.

ABOUT THE AUTHOR

Matt Taibbi is a contributing editor for *Rolling Stone* and a columnist for RollingStone.com. He's the author of two essay collections, *Spanking the Donkey* and *Smells Like Dead Elephants*. He lives in New York City.